AN END TO ARMS

BOOKS BY

WALTER MILLIS

WALTER MILLIS

AN END TO ARMS

A CENTER FOR THE STUDY OF DEMOCRATIC
INSTITUTIONS BOOK

ATHENEUM   NEW YORK

1965

This book is a product of the
Study of War and Democratic Institutions
by the
Center for the Study of Democratic Institutions

FOREWORD

THERE IS ALREADY SO LARGE A LITERATURE ON disarmament and the limitation of arms that a word of explanation may be required of anyone who offers another book in this field. Actually, this is not another technical study of disarmament, of which there are many available; rather, it is an examination into the possibility of a demilitarized international society. Obviously, a demilitarized world must also be a disarmed world; but it is a major contention of this book that disarmament and demilitarization are not synonymous. Before there can be any real hope for the reduction and elimination of the massive modern armaments, the way must be clearly seen toward a demilitarized system of international politics to which the armaments will be superfluous. Only when it is realized that our huge modern armaments are as unnecessary as they are already both dangerous and useless will disarmament conferences yield any significant results and the armaments themselves begin to disappear.

This book is, consequently, an inquiry into possible demilitarization of the international politics system, rather than merely into its disarmament. For almost three quarters of a century—since the first Hague Conference in 1899—the goal of disarmament has been assiduously pursued, by able and dedicated men, with almost no significant result. The long history of disarmament conferences can record but two very partial successes: the Washington treaty on naval limitation in 1922, which survived for barely ten years, and the test ban agreement of 1963, much more far-reaching in its implications but more limited in its actual scope. The test ban agreement is, however, of overwhelming importance as a first faint recognition of the fact that brute military power is no longer the *ultima ratio* in international politics. The question to which this book is addressed is the question of whether this dawning realization can be carried onward into the acceptance of a demilitarized world.

What follows is not a technical study dealing with the issues of matching force reductions, of inspection and control, of reconversion of arms industries. It is not, in short, about disarmament. It attempts to assess the factors that have stultified all disarmament conferences for the past sixty or seventy years; to take a fresh look at the basic problems of power, of law and order, of our ideas about international politics, which have blocked almost all advance through the disarmament approach, and to ask whether these problems and these ideas are not undergoing changes that will make a demilitarized (and therefore a disarmed) system of international politics an actual possibility for the first time in the history of mankind. It may propound more questions than it answers. But the questions are, I believe, fundamental to our modern problem; and they are asked in a hopeful spirit.

CONTENTS

AN END TO ARMS

THE PROBLEM OF WAR

T̲O MANY THOUGHTFUL PERSONS TODAY THE ONE most serious problem confronting, not only democratic institutions, but all present institutions of human order and governance is the problem of war and armaments. This is a problem which has only been apprehended as a specific problem in quite recent times. Men have always been preoccupied by the scourge of war as they have been by the scourge of poverty and hunger; they have dreamed of the achievement of lasting peace as they have dreamed of the achievement of plenty. But until our own day they have not often been inclined to examine armaments and war as an inherent but hopefully remediable consequence of the total social-political system within which we all live.

Until the development of socialist, and particularly of Marxist, economics there was little notion that the observed extremes of hunger, poverty and deprivation in the world might be the systemic consequences of prevailing economic ideas and organization, potentially remediable through the modification of the system. Until lately there has been little notion that the agonies, the devastations, the senseless costs of organized war might similarly be the inherent results of our system of international politics and might be similarly remediable through a modification of the total system. The transformation of the problem from one of particular wars, of particular causes of war, or of specific "disputes" or imbalances into the problem of war and arms in general is recent; it is still, judging by much in the current discourse, only partial.

The world's first general disarmament conference, which was also the first formal recognition by serious statesmanship that a war problem as such existed, took place, after all, less than three quarters of a century ago. It was on August 24, 1898, that Nicholas II, newly acceded as Czar of All the Russias, circularized the Great Powers, inviting them to a general peace conference. The head of the largest, as it was also the most backward, of the great military states pointed out that something was seriously wrong, not with specific power relations among particular states, but with the whole international situation of the time. The Imperial Rescript read:

In the course of the last twenty years the longings for a general appeasement have been especially pronounced in the consciousness of civilized nations. The preservation of peace has been put forward as the object of international policy; in its name, great States have concluded between themselves powerful alliances; it is the better to guarantee peace that they have developed, in proportions hitherto unprecedented, their military forces and still continue to increase them without shrinking from any sacrifice.

All these efforts, nevertheless, have not been able

to bring about the beneficent results of the desired pacification. . . . The armaments less and less fulfill the objects which the Governments have set themselves. The economic crises, due in great part to the system of armaments *à l'outrance,* and the continued danger which lies in this massing of war material, are transforming the armed peace of our days into a crushing burden. . . . It appears evident, then, that if this state of things were prolonged, it would inevitably lead to the very cataclysm which it is desired to avert, and the horrors of which make every thinking man shudder in advance.

The result was the first Hague Conference of 1899, which not only initiated the modern history of disarmament but represents the first, primitive attempt at an attack upon the war problem as such. Before it met, the Czar's ministers prepared and circulated a series of specific proposals embodying almost all the leading ideas that have been brought to this problem ever since. They included an initial "freeze" on then existing military force levels and appropriations; a ban on aggressive weapons; a prohibition on new, "destabilizing" weaponry (intended to halt what we would now call the technological arms race); together with proposals looking toward the peaceful settlement of international disputes. The conference, of course, achieved virtually nothing. By the time it met, the foreign offices and the publicists in all the powers had developed all the arguments which made acceptance of any proposals such as these impossible at the time and which have insured the rejection of almost all similar proposals ever since.

The first Hague Conference took some rather innocuous steps toward the peaceful settlement of disputes; it could do nothing about the perils of the "armed peace" in which all the participants were involved. The alarming "state of things" noted by the Czar's ministers was in fact "prolonged." It did lead "inevitably to the very cataclysm" which all proclaimed themselves desirous of averting. Its horrors, when it came, were more dreadful by far than those at which every thinking man in 1898 had shuddered in anticipation. The actual roll of devastation and of death—it included even the Czar himself and his family, assassinated in 1918—was beyond anything then imaginable. Nor could even this enormous disaster bring the "general appeasement" for which the peoples had longed. The new order erected shakily upon the ruins was to perish in turn; tens of millions more were to die painfully and uselessly; still a third world order was attempted, yet the desired "pacification" continues to elude us. Nearly three quarters of a century after the circularization of the Imperial Rescript, the world is left in a "situation" more or less indistinguishable from that which it described in 1898, except that the putative horrors at which thinking men shudder today are incomparably more horrible than anything then envisaged —more horrible, indeed, than anything in even the worst, the most atrocious, of human experience.

This is the somber history that is forcing us all to reconsider, as analytically and dispassionately as we can, the nature, the foundations, the possible and probable future, the viability of the existing international order. It is compelling us to take a new look at the processes of an international politics which appears to be working, not toward the freedom of man, the enrichment of his economy and the realization of his potentials, but toward the ultimate destruction of his civilization if not of man himself. The war problem, to be sure, is not the only one which raises such possibilities. That unbounded confidence in "progress" which illuminated the Western world in the decades before World War I has faded in more than one direction under corrosive doubts as to the workability of our world culture. The very power of modern intellectual and moral development, the very success and subtlety of the economic, technological and social institutions that we have evolved, often seem to us to be trending, not toward progress, but toward impasse—toward the creation of demands which can neither be denied on the one hand nor fulfilled on the other, toward the establishment of goals which are inherently unrealizable yet cannot be relinquished, toward deadlocks between means and ends which, since they cannot be resolved, can lead only to destructive breakdown. Can modern knowledge, on which all our triumphs depend, even keep up with its own proliferation? Is modern democracy, with its just checks, balances and protections, a practicable method in the long run for organizing the affairs of great peoples? Can even modern technology cope with a "revolution of expectations," which defeats itself as it advances through multiplying numbers more rapidly than they can be satisfied? We are confronted by many such ominous questions. But none is more ominous, in none does the possibility of deadlock seem more immediate nor the resultant disaster more extreme, than the field of international politics and of war.

The population problem may contain the seeds of our

destruction. The war problem does contain more than
the seeds; it has brought into existence the actual physical instruments of a destruction which could, if these
weapons were so employed, be very nearly total. It is
believed that the world's military arsenals today contain
nuclear explosives equivalent to about seventy tons of
TNT for every living human being; these explosives,
moreover, are usable *only* for the destruction of human
life and its ecology.[1] It is unnecessary to repeat the
many available estimates of the "megadeaths" (millions
of deaths) and the environmental megadevastations
which the actual employment of these weapons would
probably produce. More shocking than the statistics—
too huge in themselves to be comprehensible—is the
simple fact that in the United States, the Soviet Union
and other advanced states a large number of the best and
most highly trained brains that the community can produce are almost wholly devoted to the design and production of amazingly sophisticated and costly instruments which can be put to no actual use except the
mass torture and destruction of man and the probable extinction of his culture. It is a fact so inhuman, so patently immoral and so pointless as to stagger the intelligence. The scientists, however, as well as the weapons
technicians and the bureaucrats who direct their efforts
are all upright, humane men—good fathers and hus-
bands, as a rule, with a strong moral sense, with a belief
in man's future and with first-rate minds. They understand what they are doing and realize, when they permit

[1] Some of the weapons stocks may, no doubt, be ultimately converti-
ble into nonmilitary power sources or usable in peaceful earth moving.
Such applications could at present account for only a trivial fraction of
the total existing supply.

themselves to think about it, the horrible absurdity of their endeavors. Yet they are as powerless to escape their situation as a man trapped in a quicksand. And all the rest of us seem equally powerless to escape the probably disastrous consequences.

The multimegaton thermonuclear weapons and their incredibly ingenious missile carriers are the existing, entirely tangible demonstrations of the appalling contradictions into which our system of international politics has already led us. The Communists have long cheered themselves by contemplating the allegedly fatal contradictions within capitalism; the West has taken encouragement from the quite obvious contradictions within Communism. But here are grand contradictions peculiar to neither system. They are inherent in the present structure of international politics itself; they weigh as heavily upon statesmanship on one side of the iron curtain as upon that on the other. Here is the grisly impasse to which international politics is leading us—more immediate, far more ominous and seemingly more inevitable than other problems—and in which all, Communist and non-Communist, democracies and dictatorships, new states and old, haves and have-nots, are alike entangled.

The thermonuclear weapons have powerfully demonstrated the unworkability of the present international order, but they can hardly be regarded as the cause of contradictions which were beginning to be apparent to Nicholas II and many others half a century before the detonation of the first atomic bomb. It is true that in 1898 they were only beginning to appear. The imperial Russian initiative advanced at most an hypothesis, and one which obviously carried little general conviction since it was of so little operative effect. The arguments on which it rested—that war "did not pay," that major war was economically and tactically "impossible," that it was strategically and politically self-defeating—were all being developed at the turn of the century, but to most practical politicians and soldiers they seemed too fantastic for serious consideration, and to most publics too strange even to grasp. The military and sovereign nation-state stood at the time at the height of its power and prestige; and the militarized international politics to which its development had given rise seemed to most not so much an acceptable and successful international order as the only possible or conceivable one.

As one looks back upon it now, the international politics of 1898 possessed an almost idyllic simplicity—easily recaptured in the writings of the younger nationalist politicians, the theoreticians and militarists of the time. The globe was then populated by little more than 1.5 billion human beings—only about half the total now alive. The overwhelming majority of them got their living through hard physical labor, not greatly mitigated in even the wealthiest states by such automation as was possible in a still predominantly steam-powered age. The discrepancy between conditions in such populous and underdeveloped areas as China and India and those surrounding most inhabitants of even the advanced states was less extreme than it has since become, and many of the issues which now concern the political and social scientist on the international stage had not then arisen.

These 1.5 billion human beings were organized in an

international political-military system which seemed to the confident generation coming to power around 1900 to be admirably balanced, stable and enduring. Its basic constituent elements were the independent, armed and sovereign nation-states, each (very generally speaking) corresponding to an ethnically and linguistically separate and identifiable "people." There were many hundreds of such different peoples in the world, each theoretically entitled to independent armed sovereignty; but the anarchy to which this might have led was in fact tempered by a considerable measure of higher organization. The great Continental empires—Russia, Austria-Hungary and, to a lesser extent, the German and the Turkish empires—brought many peoples and former nation-states together under unified policy direction. The "sun never set" on the British Empire and the many peoples whose affairs it controlled from London. The other colonial empires, either relics of great pasts (the Dutch and the Portuguese) or bids for great futures (the French, the Italian and the American), brought the larger part of the world's population (in Africa, Asia and the East and West Indies) under the governance of a small number of Euro-American great powers. These claimed in varying degree the right to direct the internal affairs of their subject peoples but always asserted a final authority over their military and foreign relations. There were numbers of smaller independent states, notably in Latin America, involved among themselves in local issues outside the immediate purview of the great-power system; but in effect the international order, various and anarchic as it might seem, was actually operated by a few, primarily European, imperial states, which actually kept the great majority of the world's peoples in a high state of peace and order.

The great powers were rivals for power and prestige, but in fact they competed for little else. The territorial settlements established by the nineteenth-century wars of unification were in the main acceptable; and even where they had left much bitterness behind—as, for example, in the case of the German appropriation of Alsace-Lorraine[2]—they were at least quite tolerable. Theoreticians of the time may have talked much about the possibility of war for such economic objectives as markets, raw materials or even money tribute, but it was not over such prizes that threats of war actually arose. Even the competition over the imperial partitions of Africa and Asia was motivated only in small degree by the economic rewards of colonial exploitation (it was to prove, in the end, that there were almost none); it was mainly a competition for military position and power. Economically and ideologically as well, the international order at the turn of the century had all the appearances of stability. It may not have presented an epitome of justice, but it seemed—as, for instance, did the European political world around 1750, on the eve of the age of revolution —to have all the attributes of permanence.

In this generally prosperous and well-ordered world, universally assumed to be in "progress" toward consistently better things, the struggle for power remained. It presented serious and difficult problems to statesman-

[2] Alsace-Lorraine assumed far greater importance *after* World War I as a justification for it than the provinces ever had before the war as a potential cause. The French passion for *revanche* and for the recovery of the lost provinces would never in itself have precipitated another Franco-German struggle.

ship, but none which seemed insoluble. The international system was a military-political one, and the military arm was always available to meet issues impossible of political (or diplomatic) resolution. The statesman, whether he served a small, independent state or a great empire, was faced with two tasks: he had to provide for the country's military security against territorial aggression or external dictation of its policies; and he had to maintain its power position, from which he could, if need be, threaten others and render nugatory the threats which others might launch against him. For both purposes the national armaments were available and usable. To go to war was unpleasant, economically expensive and costly in terms of life and suffering. But it was always possible. Whether in defense against a patent "aggression" or in offense against international developments that threatened to undermine the nation's power position, it afforded a seemingly practicable exit from any difficulties raised by the power struggle.

Europe had known no really great war since Napoleon's time; the United States none since 1865. To many, the technological developments in the latter half of the nineteenth century seemed to be making war less, rather than more, destructive. The calculus of war could seem simple. At the time of the Venezuela crisis (1895) young Mr. Theodore Roosevelt was quite willing to have a war with Great Britain; he did not care "whether our seacoast cities are bombarded or not; we would take Canada." The British went into the Boer War with a similarly reckless undervaluation of its probable costs and overvaluation of the political consequences to be achieved by military action. War and armaments seemed

entirely practicable—and, indeed, obviously indispensable—instrumentalities for securing both the safety of
the state and the integrity of its power position in the
world, and when the Czar's ministers suggested that they
might in fact end by securing neither, the answer of the
great powers was, in effect, that it was obviously impossible to do without them.

The total international system at the turn of the century seemed balanced, stable and enduring. It had many
problems in both the domestic and the international
areas; but these represented at worst only passing storm
waves on the surface of a great sea of lasting order, in
which the underlying tides were working ever toward
"progress" in the direction of peace and freedom. The
storms might cause much trouble, but none that could
not ultimately be taken care of by the operation of the
gold standard, the market system, private enterprise, the
military defenses and the basic politics of representative
government, only modified by the hierarchies of birth,
education and acquired or inherited wealth that governed in most of the great state organizations. Even in
the great autocracies the future seemed clearly to belong
to liberal parliamentary institutions; ultimately to self-
government and to that reign of substantial peace which
all governments professed to desire and on which, it
was erroneously supposed, all peoples would insist once
they achieved the power to direct their own affairs.

The reasons why these confident expectations were
overthrown, the ways in which these hopes were so
disastrously defeated, constitute one major theme of this
book; the possibility of so modifying our established
system of international politics that it will not continue

inevitably to give rise to disasters now become intolerable constitutes the other. Pursuit of the first theme may seem a somewhat tiresome introduction to the second; yet it is believed that it is indispensable. Only in the measure in which one can understand a political, cultural or historical process can one usefully discuss its possible modification to yield other than the currently predictable results. A real understanding of the international politics of the past half-century is undoubtedly developing in many quarters, but it is still heavily overlaid by the mold of ancient concepts. One still hears serious (and high-minded) students of war and armaments advancing ideas that were perhaps appropriate in 1898, but that are as useless today as they were then to meet the issues of a viable international politics. Many notions, demonstrably erroneous, still load the discourse, just as if almost seventy years of bloody history had not irrefutably disproved them. One must look at those seventy years to see, if possible, what were the ideas that they have refuted, what went wrong, what in them may today be remediable. And from such a re-examination one may derive a clearer idea of what may be requisite to develop the new international politics that most responsible statesmen and students recognize to be necessary, although few see how it may be attained.

Politics may be defined, among other ways, as the organization of power. Broadly, what went wrong with the seemingly stable and successful international political system ruling in the world around 1900 was that it proved increasingly defective as a mode of organizing power in the increasingly populous and complex world of the twentieth century. The international political system, or organization of power, failed in 1914 to produce any of the results confidently expected of it. It destroyed three of the great empires that had pinned their hopes of survival upon it; it undermined the British Empire; it put an end to the safety and security of many states (the United States was one) that had confidently relied upon the system to conserve these values. The world after 1918 was more perilous for all the great social-political groupings than the world before 1914 had been; an international politics based on military force was considerably less viable than before, and when the relatively weaker or defeated states—Japan, Italy, Germany and the Soviet Union—revived war as an instrument of power politics, the results for all concerned were even more disastrous than those that had followed upon the catastrophe of 1914.

It is true that two imperial powers—the United States and the Soviet Union—emerged, at relatively colossal costs in life and productive wealth, in commanding power positions. But both faced an ironic situation. Each very nearly all-powerful, each equipped with supergiant weapons of military destruction, both were at the same time very nearly powerless to control the development of world politics. Each has been compelled substantially to accept the power organization and the frontiers delimiting it as they were established at the end of World War II in 1945. The most salient fact of the post-1945 international political system has been the "revolution of expectations" in the former colonial areas of Asia and Africa and in Latin America. Neither of the superpowers has been able to control this development, to appropriate it (though both have tried) to its own purposes, to establish its own mastery of the world or to create an adequately nonviolent system of global law and order. Relying, as both still do, upon an essentially military system of international politics, they have between them set up an arms race leading logically to vastly more calamitous consequences than those of the similar race set up before 1914, but in itself equally incapable of resolving any of the social-political issues with which serious statesmanship, in Moscow no less than in Washington, must deal.

This is the dilemma that the Russians, somewhat vaguely, perceived in 1898; it is the dilemma that has come home to almost all thinking men with crushing force in the seventh decade of the century. There is one obvious resolution—the demilitarization of international politics. Though force is an apparently indispensable basis of law, and violence, or the "credible" threat of violence, is perhaps the basis of all politics, it is nevertheless the function of politics (regarded as an organization of power) to minimize violence in the power struggle, if not to eliminate it. This is what our existing system of militarized international politics has notably failed to do: it has maximized rather than minimized the violent death and destruction consequent upon the conduct of the power struggle in the international world. The struggle for power appears to be an inherent characteristic of human society that cannot be eliminated, but it can be conducted with less or greater savagery. Riot, murder, political assassination are recognized instrumentalities of social change, but in well-ordered societies they are reduced to a minimum. That the colossal mass murders entailed by modern organized war both should and can be reduced or eliminated from the processes of international politics is now widely recognized. The world's two most powerful military states are now in theory agreed upon the necessity for ending the organized war system; both have accepted the goal of "general and complete disarmament," which, if ever achieved, can only mean the demilitarization of international politics.

Unfortunately, while both have announced themselves as looking toward an eventually demilitarized world society, neither has produced any plausible picture of what such a world would look like, and even less has either proposed any program for attaining it. It is with these difficult problems that the present book is concerned.

THE HISTORY

THE MILITARY NATION-STATE AS IT FLOURISHED around the turn of the century was a comparatively recent phenomenon in human affairs. The soldiers, publicists and politicians of the time (including those who participated in the first Hague Conference) saw in it and in the international politics which had developed around it only the "natural" and immutable order in human affairs. They were suffering from an illusion— the very common illusion that whatever is is both right and eternal. The modern, military nation-state had in fact been born out of the decay of European feudalism hardly more than four centuries before; it had not begun to come of age, so to speak, until around 1600, and it was not for another century that the system of international politics based upon it was shaped into the mold to which international affairs have since substantially conformed. Even as late as 1900 the modern nation-state had not yet (as it has since done) extended its dominance as a mode of human power organization from the European culture out of which it arose to the rest of the globe. Hundreds of millions in China, India,

Southeast Asia and Africa were still living without benefit of its fundamental concepts of independence, state-
hood and armed sovereignty.

The international system that seemed to statesmen at
the turn of the century to reflect the eternal, unalterable
verities of the human power struggle was actually hardly
two centuries old at the time; and in more ways than one
it represented a peculiar, if not a unique, mode in the
organization of power. It is perhaps illegitimate to specu-
late on the possibility of history taking different courses
than it has done; but it would seem that rather minor
changes in the chains of causation could well have led to
different modes of international political organization—
of which, after all, we have many past examples.

The concept of "one world" as we describe it today is
actually a very old one. Perhaps every one of the great
empires of antiquity expressed, not merely the ambitions
of conquerors, but a basic human need for a universal
order, a warless system of world politics providing substantial equality of justice for all under a universal rule
of law. The Romans in fact achieved such a universal
system, embracing the whole of the civilized world as
they knew it. Theirs was a working concept of what
would today be called world government through world
law, exhibiting many analogues to the institutional arrangements imagined by modern advocates of "one
world." [1] In 27 B.C. Augustus, consolidating the im-

---

[1] Augustus put an end to the field armies that had torn each other to
pieces in the civil wars, much as the various European national armies
tore themselves to pieces in the great, essentially internecine, wars of our
times. The Roman legions were distributed as frontier garrison forces,
which, with the local auxiliaries in the various provinces, provided the
equivalent of an international police force. The extension of Roman cit-
izenship to leading provincials created a body of "citizens of the world"

perial power, closed the gates of the Temple of Janus (for the first time, it is said, in 200 years) upon the incessant wars of the ancient world; and for some two and a half centuries thereafter the Pax Romana successfully organized the power struggles of the most diverse peoples, the most diverse ethnic and linguistic groups, without serious resort to organized war. When the system finally began to break down (primarily under external influences beyond its power to control), it left behind it a concept of universality, conserved in the Roman Catholic Church, which was powerfully to affect the minds of men and the actions of government for 2000 years thereafter. To an objective observer the universal and internally peaceful empire of Rome might seem as valid a model for the international organization of power as, for example, the anarchic and suicidal Greek city-state system, which modern international politics has largely imitated.

The idea, or theory, of a universal system in fact never died. When, around 400 A.D., the imperial throne was divided between East and West, the Empire itself, in men's minds, was not; although there might be two emperors for political and administrative purposes, there remained but one Empire. And through all the political fragmentation of the feudal era there survived this notion of "one world," Christendom, unified in a common faith or "ideology," whatever local political arrangements might be necessary. It survived to challenge the

from whom the legions were recruited; they were, as well, the core of the powerful bureaucratic system which administered the empire with centralized effectiveness but with a considerable measure of local autonomy—suggestive at least of the global bureaucracy which is tending to develop out of the United Nations economic and technical agencies.

new, particularist nation-state organization as it arose from the decay of feudalism; European politics through some three centuries can, indeed, be regarded as primarily a struggle between the particularist or national and the universal or catholic principles in the organization of power, and it was not until 1806, in the final triumph under Napoleon of military nationalism, that the Holy Roman Empire was formally dissolved. As a mode of political organization it may have enjoyed little substance since the Carlovingian empire of a thousand years before; but as a concept of order among men it had existed and had lent continuity to political thought over a span of two millennia.

The feudal wars of the Middle Ages were unceasing, but they were not particularly damaging to the fabric of the societies in which they occurred. Of the four dread horsemen—War, Famine, Pestilence and the Death which in the most stable times stood always at the elbow of medieval men—the last three probably claimed far more victims than War ever did. The organization of power was reasonably economical and adequate to the needs of the time; it was not the hypertrophy of war that brought the feudal power system to an end, but changing times, to which it was no longer sufficient. The feudal order could no longer meet the developing social, political, economic and technological imperatives of European society. While adequate to deal with the organization of power in a society based upon the self-contained village community—largely isolated groups of peasants huddled around a baronial or monastic keep for security and economic production—it could not handle the problems of an advancing technology, introducing an increasing division of labor, specialization, exchange and the consequent necessity for order and organization. The feudal system could not fulfill the new requirements; it could not adequately police the roads or protect the sea routes; it could not provide the minimum of order necessary to the new methods of industrial production; it could not provide the fiscal instruments required by the expansion of trade—banking systems, sound coinage, adequate tax structures—nor the efficient bureaucracies required to administer the ever more complicated affairs of the new age.

The military nation-state developed as an organizational form capable of meeting these new requirements. It was in its origins and growth a military system, based upon military concepts and institutionalizing politics by institutionalizing war. "The necessary concomitant," says Wolf, "to the rise of great military powers was the development of standing armies and fleets." [2] It might better, perhaps, be put the other way: the necessary concomitant to the development of standing armies and fleets was the rise of the great military powers. The first, most basic, task of the emerging nation-state was to establish police systems adequate to the needs of an integrating, increasingly complex European society. The first business of the absolutist national kings was to suppress the chaotic feudal military institutions—the uncontrollable warrior class of armored knights, the rag-tag peasant levies, the mercenary bands and their *condottiere* captains—that were impeding the development of ordered trade, production and politics. The primary

[2] John B. Wolf, *The Emergence of the Great Powers* (Harper & Row, 1962 ed.), p. 8.

function of the new standing armies was not so much to fight each other as to impose internal order and co-herence upon the nascent national societies. They may be regarded as police forces first of all; and while they continued, like the feudal military systems out of which they grew, to fight foreign wars, it was only through the internal logic of their own development that they finally imposed on Europe and on the globe the lethal system of militarized international politics which obtains today. Wolf puts it well:

> The standing armies were at once the expres-sion of the authority of the central government and the instruments for increasing its power. The civil disorders, characteristic of the dualism that had disturbed all Europe from the sixteenth to the last quarter of the seventeenth century, came to an end with the rise of strong military forces. . . . At the same time, the necessity to feed, clothe, equip and pay an army obliged the king to create bureaucratic machinery to collect taxes and admin-ister revenues. This in turn facilitated the develop-ment of the bureaucratic police state characteristic of the eighteenth century. When great political up-heavals led to war on a scale never heretofore seen on the continent, these armies became the instru-ments of the power that shaped the Europe of the next two centuries.[3]

This overlooks the extent to which the standing armies themselves led to war on the new scale of violence, and the nation-state organization created the "great

[3] *Op. cit.*, pp. 8-9.

political upheavals," but it seems to describe the essentials of the process. But the nations and the armies developed slowly, of course, preserving many medieval institutions, both military and political, over the next two centuries. If the first function of the new national armies was to police the internal order, it was not as easy then as it is now to draw the line between what was internal and what external. The infant nations did not have the sharply defined characters they now possess; they were entangled in the universals of the Christian faith and the surviving remnants of the imperial idea. The famous Spanish infantry, trampling the Netherlands in the interests both of Hapsburg empire and of the universal religion in the sixteenth century, were by no means the obvious interlopers, aggressors and "foreign" oppressors that were, for example, the German tank crews and paratroopers who overwhelmed the same Low Countries in 1940. At Lepanto, in 1571, the Turkish infidel was turned back by a supranational coalition of Christendom; and a century later Pope Innocent XI could organize and foment the War of the Holy League (for the rescue of Vienna from the same infidel) as a kind of last crusade, in which all Christendom, Protestant as well as Catholic, could combine.

But that was about the last occasion of its kind. The Reformation—the great schism of the European culture in the sixteenth century—had many causes and implied many things. One of its most basic implications was that the military nation-state, growing out of the feudal institutions to meet new social needs, could not live with the universal concepts that had underlain the power organization of the Middle Ages. The state could not adjust either the temporal or the spiritual claims of the popes to its own ideological requirements. As it had evoked the centrally controlled, disciplined and bureaucratically administered standing army to its support, so it was obliged to evoke the emotional, ideological and political sanctions of nationalism to sustain the army, together with the developing bureaucracy, technology, supply and fiscal systems which it demanded. A national standing army was impossible without a unifying nationalist ideology; a nationalist ideology, at the same time, was the virtually inevitable consequence of the standing army and the military social organization that it implied. Such necessities of the nation-state made it increasingly unable, as it grew, to tolerate the universal claims of the Church. The great schism of the sixteenth century announced the fact. Since then the Church (and not only the Church of Rome, but also the nationally oriented Protestant sects derived from it) has made innumerable compromises with military and militant nationalism. In doing so, the Church may have preserved its identity and some of its social-political functions; but it has never regained its authority as a unifying and pacifying force in human affairs.

The military nation-state was to prove as inimical to the tradition of universal empire as to the tradition of a universal religion. The notion of empire was still real in the sixteenth and seventeenth centuries. The wars of Philip II, the Austrian Hapsburgs and Louis XIV for the "mastery" of Europe were quite consciously wars for the imperial idea, for the unitary organization of power. At the height of the Sun King's power a "French Europe," comparable to the Roman West of 2000 years before, was a theoretic possibility, defeated only by the very nation-state on which Louis had risen to his eminence. While the state gave France the organization that made her powerful, it was promoting everywhere else the same particularist nationalism that rendered universal empire—whether fostered by France or Spain or Austria—impossible. The members of the coalitions that arose against every attempt at imperial "mastery" were no longer the barbarian tribes subdued by the Roman legions nor the quarreling and amorphous feudalisms whose dynastic and marital relations were of little consequence to the underlying structure of European life. They were themselves military nation-states, growing to great power and authority—essential devices in the social, technical and political organization of the new age, but impossible to constrain (as were Charlemagne's loosely organized tribes) within the confines of medieval empire.

With the end of the War of the Spanish Succession, early in the eighteenth century, the pattern of international politics that has since endured (first in Europe, now throughout the globe) was substantially established. Dreams of universal empire had faded, and even the more modest notion of "hegemony" was to be seldom realizable for long. International politics was confined to a "balance" of military power among the great states. The *dramatis personae* assumed a measure of permanence. States might rise or fall in the scales of "power"; enlarged states might be formed through consolidations (Austria-Hungary, Italy, Germany, the modern federal United States) but these were without universalist pretensions. They might claim the name of "empire," but they remained nation-states among other nation-states, relying for their unity upon the militant emotions of nationalism and for their security and power on their national standing armies.

Throughout the eighteenth century this system of military international politics worked at least reasonably well in organizing power in Europe and in the spreading European colonial possessions. The wars that were thus made inevitable were not intolerably divisive or destructive; while the system cradled a tremendous development in the arts, in the sciences, in technology and economic production and in political and social advance. It was not, however, without its defects, of which the most obvious lay in the fact that organized war tended to grow by what it fed on, to impose its own necessities and its own goals regardless of the real political aims of the warring peoples. Even in the War of the Spanish Succession (as in all subsequent major conflicts) armies grew bigger, better equipped, much better organized and consequently more deadly. They were no longer confined, perforce, to the leisurely and economical warfare of maneuver and siege that had characterized the seventeenth century, or to the moderate political results to which it led; they imposed grimmer imperatives upon the societies that created them. With new tools in their hands, generals of the new school, such as Marlborough and Eugene of Savoy, decided (as have later generals) that "the object of war is victory"—not checkmate in a military chess game, but a crushing destruction of the enemy's total power and force. Marlborough aimed for decisive battlefield victories; and to get them he began to spend life with the prodigality of a Napoleon or a World War I strategist of trench warfare. Like them, he was called "the Butcher" for it. But if he accepted, and demanded, heavier battle casualties than before, it was not because he was unusually bloodthirsty by temperament, but because the new conditions of war made butchery on this new scale a seeming strategic necessity. He was in the position of the modern air generals and missile strategists who accept and calculate upon the possible slaughter of men, women and babies by the scores of millions, not because these generally admirable men regard the prospect with any relish, but simply because the advance of war has made such action possible and they are unable to see how it can be reliably prevented.

Actually the new strategic ideas were neither as valid nor as forward-looking as they have sometimes seemed. The Butcher's bill at Malplaquet (1709) was not equaled until Borodino, a century later; but even this slaughter tended to bring, not "victory," but stalemate. The general wars of the early eighteenth century ended, fortunately, in something very like that "peace without victory" that by the early nineteenth and in the midtwentieth century has become impossible. Again to quote Wolf, "After 1710 the armies could do no better than the diplomats. Prospects of decisive victory had vanished." [4] It was all wrapped up in a series of treaties beginning with the Treaty of Utrecht in 1713, in which the diplomats repaired the follies of the soldiers and got a viable European system in operation again. It is perhaps significant that a century elapsed before there was another Malplaquet. As a means to the organization of

4 *Op. cit.*, p. 86.

power, as an instrument of international politics, the chess game had advantages over the savagery of all-out war, and these the generally temperate and urbane spirit of the eighteenth century was capable of appreciating. And in spite of Frederick the Great and other disciples of the new order in warfare, the eighteenth century, repelled by the useless slaughters it was bringing, tended to go back, on the whole, to the chess game. The economical and, it must be argued, politically more useful forms of siege, "position" and "geometrical" war remained prominent throughout the eighteenth century, until the American and the French Revolutions and the career of Napoleon swept them away in new extremes of inhumanity and savagery.

How far the French Revolution represented a messianic movement, an effort to recapture a universal system under the rubric of *liberté, égalité, fraternité,* remains a matter of debate. The Napoleonic empire may have been erected in the name of libertarian and equalitarian principles; but in fact it represented almost purely a drive for military power—a drive generated by the great armies now technically possible and fueled, not by any yearning for individual liberty, but by the passionate nationalism out of which those regimented fleets and armies sprang. Napoleon was a clear forerunner of Hitler in that he set out upon the conquest, first of France, and then of Europe, not in pursuit of any clearly perceived goal, but simply because the military instruments that made conquest possible, together with the skill to use them, were available to him. And the opposition he raised was a blind defensive reaction on the part of established military power systems that knew no more than did Napoleon how to use the military power for which they contended to construct the new order that the great wars made inevitable. It was not the great wars themselves which established the new order, nor the "settlements" at the Congress of Vienna. That task remained to the subsequent fluid, complex and creative history of the nineteenth century.

What did emerge from the Napoleonic era was the unified, technologically advanced, industrialized and populistic military nation-state as a power organization of tremendous strength and capacity. Consolidated, rather than disrupted, by the revolutionary movements of 1830 and 1848 and by the wars of national unification (which, except in the United States, were relatively not very costly), it had established itself by the end of the century as the "natural," indeed the inevitable, mode in the organization of power. It had brilliantly accomplished what was, as has here been argued, its primary task when it first emerged around 1500 from the chaotic decay of feudalism. It had adequately policed the European and an increasingly large area of the non-European world, giving to world society as a whole a degree of law and order probably greater than it had ever known before. Without the state's performance of this function, the modern age could never have come about. Over vast areas it had made politics possible—a politics, that is to say, of minimal violence. With the development of a considerable body of international law and the subtle negotiatory techniques of diplomacy, a large measure of order has been brought to the international world as well. But what the state, by its origin and nature, could not do was to establish a workable and tolerable inter-

national political system. It had sufficed to regulate and
tame the power struggle on most of its many levels: the
struggles of individuals, groups, communities, rival
economic interests and political ambitions; but mankind
had become organized into a system of armed and sovereign nation-states, offering no basis for a workable
and acceptably nonviolent structure of international
politics. The militarized international political system
to which the nation-state mode of power organization
gave rise could no more meet the coming needs of the
new world order than could the feudal system out of
which the nation-state had developed.

None of this, of course, was apparent in the bright
dawn of the twentieth century. A few, like Nicholas II
and his advisers, might entertain their reservations, but to
most, "peace" seemed as possible as progress and prosperity. The world might still be strewn with the detritus
of various small wars, but these were, surely, phenomena
of diminishing significance in the integrating order of
international law, finance and production. There was
nothing atypical in the celebrated proviso which An-
drew Carnegie attached to his grant creating the Endow-
ment for International Peace, that when the object had
been attained, the revenue was to be devoted to other
causes for the betterment of man. As has been said, the
nation-state then stood at the height of its prestige. Its
magnificent armaments would defend its people and
secure their "vital" interests in the larger world, while
behind these military shields it would promote their
liberties and procure the economic and social satisfac-
tions on which the sense of liberty depends. The protective armaments obviously had to be maintained at

"adequate" levels; and while the possibility of conflicts or "disputes" among the great power systems remained, the possibility that the armaments would be used had to be accepted. No doubt war might at any time demand the ultimate sacrifice from some individual citizens of the state—especially young male individuals without "business or family responsibilities" who were, in reasonable numbers, expendable—but the state and the community that it organized would remain unimpaired in power and permanence. And there seemed no intrinsic reason why this system of militarized international politics should not, as had the national systems, develop in the direction of stability, pacification and the increasingly nonviolent resolution of such "disputes" as might continue to arise on the international level.

In fact, the system was doomed. Politics is the working organization of the power struggle in such a way as to reduce the violence attendant upon it to tolerable minimums while maximizing the achievement of the goals of the political society. The militarized international politics, framed around the armed, sovereign and populistic nation-state, was bound to defeat itself in both respects. Inevitably, it operated to maximize the violence in international relations while minimizing the possibility of the peoples' attaining those goals of peace and prosperity which they (quite rightfully) hoped to secure from the integrating global system.

Thirty years before, as a matter of fact, the Franco-Prussian War had provided an object lesson—which might have been better heeded—in the way in which the new militarized international politics, framed around the new technologized and populistic states, was bound to operate. The war really had no cause other than the massive new armaments which had appeared and the massive military power structures which they represented. Between the French and Prussian peoples there was no significant clash of economic, commercial or territorial interest; there was no ideological chasm to divide them; the particular "dispute" which provided the igniting spark was of no intrinsic importance to either people and had, indeed, been settled by diplomacy before war was declared. Yet this war for which there was no "cause" had been generally accepted in Europe for some years as probably inevitable. Both sides had been assiduously preparing for it; they had been competitively reweaponing their armies with the new, more deadly products that an expanding military technology was providing them and competitively enlarging their military structures upon the emotions generated by the new populistic nationalism. This naked clash of military power in the abstract could be resolved only by war under the ruling international political system; this war was without reason to begin with and, as it was to turn out, had no decisive result in the end.

Michael Howard, the most recent student of the conflict, puts it clearly:

After 1866 the French were in that most dangerous of all moods; that of a great power which sees itself declining to the second rank. In all ranks of French society war with Prussia was considered inevitable. It required little insight to see that a French foreign policy based on prestige was incompatible with those swelling forces of German nationalism to which Bismarck had so skillfully harnessed the Hohenzollern monarchy. . . . In Germany war also was recognized as being sooner or later inevitable; and a war with France was bound to be popular. . . . France with her record of past aggression and repeated revolution was the disturber *par excellence* of European peace. . . . To render her impotent, and at the same time to reclaim the German lands of Alsace, would be to satisfy the demands both of practical policy and of the nationalist ideal.

No one held this view with greater conviction than did Moltke [the Prussian chief of staff] himself. For him France was the hereditary foe. . . . The safety of Prussia over which he watched could never, in his view, be guaranteed until France was deprived of all power to do harm.[5]

This is the way in which men in command of the huge military power organizations represented by the modern state not only do but must think; it is, unfortunately, the way in which the lesser politicians, publicists, demagogues, run-of-the-mill nationalists and ordinary people —all so important in modern decision making—also think. What is striking about such a mode of thought is its almost complete irrelevance to any concrete needs or ends of the great communities for whom these people speak and whose fate they determine. Here was the power struggle in almost its pure form—a struggle basically irrational because it deals, not in present actualities, but

[5] Michael Howard, *The Franco-Prussian War* (Macmillan, 1962), pp. 40-41.

in future dreams. The power struggle, on whatever level it occurs, is not a "dispute" over spoils, or territory, or markets, or how to cut up any actual piece of pie. Such arguments, because they involve finite and factual situations, are usually manageable. The power struggle is a contention over who will have the power to decide any and all such disputes as may practically arise in the future, which is limitless in its possibilities and unmanageable by men. It is a contention over ideal and essentially unrealizable future goals, not over the facts that determine the present. Moltke could no more guarantee the "safety" of Prussia by rendering France militarily impotent than the Second Empire could guarantee a power position, already slipping under its feet, by launching a preventive war on Prussia. The only real issues involved were such as could not be decided or determined by war; yet the militarized nation-state system had rendered war the only possible exit from the situation that had developed.

Power issues of this kind recur constantly in the struggles of individual men, groups, communities, corporations and nations. It is, as has been said, the business of politics—of any political system—to insure that the inevitable shifts in the power structure within the community take place, are recognized and are, so to speak, recorded in new institutional arrangements with a minimum of violence, bloodshed and disruption. On the international no less than on national levels vast power shifts have on occasion occurred and have been accepted with, on the whole, surprisingly little violence. The modern, integrated and controlled nation-state organization has played a prominent role in such shifts. But

it did so at the cost of creating a militarized international political system which, as it rendered massive
international wars the more senseless and unnecessary,
at the same time rendered them the more impossible of
avoidance.

The fact that a war between France and Prussia was
generally accepted as inevitable for some years before
it occurred means that it was recognized, perhaps un-
consciously, as simply the systemic result of the international political order developing in the mid-nine-
teenth century. Because it was that kind of system, it
had to eventuate in that kind of war. It is immaterial
which side one chooses to regard as the "guilty" party;
in point of fact, it was the French who actually declared
the war and moved out aggressively with the intention
of invading and crushing the upstart Prussians. "Whatever
may be the road we take beyond our frontiers," Napoleon III told his soldiery, "we shall come across the glo-
rious tracks of our fathers. . . . On our success hangs
the fate of liberty and civilization." [6] This perennial
illusion has accompanied every descent into military
savagery in modern times; it was as unfounded in this
case as in all the others. Both liberty and civilization
were to survive the soldiers' disastrous failure. They
were not even to get beyond their frontiers; it was the
competent Germans who did all the invading.

The two armies were mobilized in unprecedented
numbers, they were deployed with unprecedented speed
and clashed in battles much bloodier and more savage
than had been anticipated—all this the gift of the new
technology combined with the new politics of populist

[6] Cited in Howard, *op. cit.*, p. 78.

nationalism; but the Germans were much superior as technicians, and in six weeks it was all over: the French armies had been destroyed or immobilized, the French emperor was a captive and a uniting Germany was the "dominant" power on the Continent. The power issue —the only issue out of which the war had arisen—was decided. A century or so earlier, the matter would have ended there. With the war "won" and the king a prisoner, nothing would have remained except for the diplomats to pick up the pieces. Even if the king were required to ransom himself with a couple of provinces, such as Alsace-Lorraine, no one would have seen anything remarkable in the occasion, not even the inhabitants of the provinces themselves. Now, unfortunately, things were not so simple. With their resort to war, the Germans had not merely established their "dominance" over the Second Empire; they had, to their own embarrassment, destroyed it. The capture of the emperor put an end to the empire, and neither was thereafter available to the victors as a symbol around which to frame a working recognition of the new power relationship. Instead of a respectable monarchical government with which to make a respectable peace, the Germans found themselves facing a republican chaos, a "nation in arms," a republican Paris defiant behind its fortress walls, scratch reserve armies equipped from the bulging imperial arsenals and the *franc tireurs*—the guerillas who had no regard for the rules of civilized war. And nowhere was there any firm authority with which peace could be made. The Germans, having neatly won their war in six weeks, were left to worry through another messy and ultimately disastrous six months before achieving their victory—a victory which in itself was to fulfill few of the expectations of those who had contended for it with so much blood and bitterness.

The war imposed its own imperatives, neither intended by its authors nor controllable by those who waged it. At the beginning, the Prussians had been in a basically defensive mood, and the reannexation of Alsace and Lorraine had been no part of their settled policy. But as the blood costs of the organized fighting mounted—even more, as the passions engendered by the inevitable reciprocal brutalities of *franc-tireur* warfare were inflamed—there arose the old and ever-illusory cry: "This kind of thing must never happen again"; France "must be rendered impotent to wage war again on Europe"; *"Cartago delenda est."* The peoples, incited by nationalist passions and propagandas to support a war in the settlement of a somewhat abstract power issue, were reduced by the war itself to a state of fear and hatred that rendered rational solutions unattainable. To write a peace that did not include the German appropriation of the frontier provinces and their covering fortresses was now out of the question; it had become politically impossible. Bismarck strove against Moltke and the soldiers for a peace of moderation—a peace that, while adequately recording the real shift in power that had taken place between France and Germany, would establish a stable European international system. By comparison with later efforts of the kind, he succeeded remarkably well, and Bismarck's peace of 1871 was in fact to endure in Europe for another forty years. But moderation, it turned out, was not enough. The war itself had taught each nation to believe, as neither had believed before, that "it alone was upholding civilization against a race of barbarians which could only be bullied into submission by brute force. Forty-four years later that belief was to be even more disastrously revived." [7]

In a way the Franco-Prussian War—short, not too bloody or destructive and in its own terms decisive—was a great success. In another way it was a great failure, in that the power issue which it apparently decided in fact was not settled. The victory recognized and recorded the new German Empire as "dominant" on the European continent; but this kind of dominance gave the Germans hardly more actual power than they had possessed before to control the processes of European history or bend them to the attainment of German hopes and aims. Bismarck was to spend the rest of his career trying to convert the great victory of 1871 into the basis for a peaceful and stable system of European politics. He was a statesman of high stature; but he was defeated in his attempt by the nature of the militarized nation-state system with which he had to work. It was certainly rash of the young Kaiser, Wilhelm II, to dismiss him. But the fact of the dismissal represented the intractable character of the political stuff with which he was forced to deal. His successors were to do no better than he. One may well ask whether he could have done any better than his successors.

The darker implications of the Franco-Prussian War were not clearly perceived in the bright dawn of the new century—nor, it would seem, are they clearly perceived by many even now. The comparative efficiency and economy of the Prussian operation were the impressive

[7] Howard, op. cit., p. 381.

elements. In the result, the Prussians were everywhere imitated, with their general staff organization, their advanced military techniques, their mass conscript armies. The Japanese—the one Asian people successfully forcing their way into the European military-political-economic system—may have bought their battleship designs in England, but they took over from the Germans the essentials of their military policy and organization, lock, stock and barrel, down to the peculiar institutional requirement under which the war and naval ministers, responsible only to the emperor, had to be serving generals and admirals. The Germans had shown the world how "security" and "power" could be achieved by all. Overlooked was the fact that what worked so brilliantly for one could not possibly work for all when all attempted it. It seemed that while small wars would of course continue, statesmanship and diplomacy, now fortified by the German methods, could manage the great power balances to reasonably tolerable results. The statesmen and diplomats were to spend the forty-odd years between 1871 and 1914 trying to do so, only to find in the end that it was impossible. As a means of dealing with the power struggle on the international plane, the modern form of militarized international politics as the Germans had perfected it was as unworkable as it was grotesque.

There is a significant difference between the years that preceded World War I and those preceding World War II. The earlier period was filled with wars of increasing scope and savagery and with international crises of greater and greater difficulty. But the wars, even when they reached the scale of the Russo-Japanese struggle in 1904-1905, seemed peripheral and secondary; the crises seemed essentially manageable. The shadow of a great European war was darkening over the Continent, but it was still entirely possible to believe that it would dissipate. One could expect that diplomacy, which had handled so many crises with success, would continue to do so. On June 28, 1914, when the fatal shot was fired at Sarajevo, Europe—despite its drilling armies, its furious naval competition, its suspicious general staffs and savage publicists—was profoundly at peace. There were no insoluble, or even very complex, political or economic issues. Many of the responsible leaders were enjoying holidays, without any expectation of being disturbed. Even after the Sarajevo assassination, the tiresome Austro-Serbian problem seemed for some time to imply no unusual perils with which the diplomats could not deal. When the extremity of the crisis was at last realized, the great war was barely three weeks away. In 1914 the diplomats and statesmen were afforded something like three weeks in which to resolve all the basic issues that had been implicit in the European political system since the Franco-Prussian War— issues which had been smoothed over and compromised again and again but which had never been fairly faced.

Suddenly the issues were all there, impossible any longer to evade. The problems created by the overgrown militarisms, the split-second military mobilization tables, the power policies that had produced the war plans and the war plans that made any rational resolution of the power problem impracticable, the fiercely nationalistic propagandas, the unstable defensive alliance systems, the popular emotions cultivated to support national power and which now forbade the leaders of the populistic state to retreat to workable positions—all these converged in the giant crisis that was, in an exact sense of the word, insoluble. It could not, certainly, be resolved in three weeks. The shock of this discovery was extreme. It led to the floods of self-exculpation and denunciation immediately poured out by every warring power. It led to the search, which went on for years thereafter, for the "guilty" men or wicked nations that had produced the enormous catastrophe. High-minded statesmen in most countries were to go to their graves convinced, like Sir Edward Grey, that if only this or that "reasonable" proposal they had advanced had been accepted by the other side, the disaster might have been averted. They could not see that the fairest and most reasonable proposals were not acceptable because they were advanced in the contexts of a power struggle in which there was no reason or justice. The catastrophe was in fact the product, not of evil men, but of a system —a system of ideas, political-military relationships and behavioral norms shared by all, which could ultimately lead to no other result.

Twenty years later the situation was quite a different one. Europe in 1939 was not at peace and had not really been so since 1918; the summer of 1939 was filled with fears and tensions totally foreign to the atmosphere of 1914. No one now doubted the extremity of the peril or supposed that diplomatic negotiation or the tenuous development of international law could be relied upon to exorcise it. The terrible instability of the post-1918 order had long been plain to all. The statesmen had been given a decade or more in which to struggle with what were

essentially the same basic problems that had overwhelmed
their 1914 predecessors in a space of three weeks. With
time in which to work, with a wealth of grim experience
not available to the men of 1914, they were to be no
more successful. The goal of all—the most brutal and
aggressive as well as the most pacific and conservative—
was in concept the same: to establish a working and
peaceful international political organization in which
every great power system would be "secure," not only in
its territory and economic opportunity, but in its "just"
power position. That this was the goal of the Western
democracies it is hardly necessary to point out. But in a
real sense it was also the goal of all the others. The Russians' declared aim was to communize the world and so
set up a reign of perpetual peace. Hitler promised a
"new order" so justly proportioned that it would endure
(as did the Romans') for "a thousand years." The Japanese militarists set out, not to conquer Asia, but to
establish an "East-Asian Co-Prosperity Sphere," in which
all members would prosper equally. All announced the
same underlying goal of peace and reason. It was inherently unattainable by any with the instrumentalities
available to them. They might just as well have set out to
square the circle with ruler and compass, a problem that
is genuinely and demonstrably insoluble—and therefore
meaningless in the terms stated. That the world problem,
in the terms in which it was stated through the late 1920's
and 1930's, was not only insoluble but therefore meaningless as well did not occur to the men who wrestled so
desperately with it.

The political and diplomatic history of the interwar
years was bitter to those who lived through it and can

bring only bitterness to all who read about it now. The search after World War I was for those men or nations who by their guilt precipitated the catastrophe; the search after World War II is for those who by their folly allowed it to happen. With the lions of wickedness disposed of by the various war trials, we are now after the rabbits of weakness. It is a more ignoble and more painful pursuit, but perhaps it reflects a better understanding of the fact that rabbits and lions are all of the same species and that the species is our own. Folly and weakness are no better as explanations for what happened than are brutality and evil. The truth is that the materials out of which to build the new order of general pacification, to which all were in one way or another committed in accordance with their lights, simply did not exist.

The building blocks of armaments, threats, military politics, nationalistic passions, populist pressures and ideological conflict, which were all that any of the statesmen had to work with, were too refractory to be fitted into any workable international structure. The whole period is studded with what seem lost possibilities. If only France and Britain had combined to stop Hitler at the Rhineland; if only the West had rearmed sooner; if only the West had joined hands with the Communists to crush Fascism or with the Fascists to crush Communism . . . One could go on indefinitely with the tale of missed chances, of opportunities muffed because any logical course of policy was repeatedly paralyzed by its opposite. It would be idle to do so; and most of the "great mistakes" alleged against policy in the interwar and war periods are really beside the point. The mistakes were not in the courses adopted, but in the inability to follow any course consistently. History happened as it did because the forces and factors available to the men who were trying to shape it were such that it probably could not have happened otherwise. It is true that the rise of Russian Communism introduced a peculiar difficulty. The post-1918 world was divided in three ways, not in two; and in one crisis after another this split produced an ambivalance in all policies that helped to defeat any rational policy whatever. But the bipolar organization before 1914 (represented by the Triple Alliance and the Triple Entente) had worked no better; nor has the bipolar organization since 1945 (represented by the Communist world led by the Soviet Union and the non-Communist world led by the United States) brought any marked improvement. It seems reasonable to conclude that if Russian Communism had not existed, the statesmanship of the interwar years would still have had no better success in constructing a viable international politics out of the military, political and psychological factors with which it had to work.

Through the interwar and war years the great democratic states no doubt suffered more than did the totalitarian ones from conflicts and confusions of policy. Their almost continuous paralyses of policy—between the "nationalists" and the "internationalists," between the "appeasers" and the "resisters," between the Communist sympathizers and the Nazi-Fascist sympathizers, between the rearmers and the pacifists—have been fully recorded and frequently castigated. The similarly paralyzing conflicts within the great totalitarian systems have not been so fully reported and are often overlooked. That they existed is, however, quite clear; and that the dictators, commanding their monolithic states, were no more successful in the end than were the democratic statesmen in shaping the world to their desires seems obvious from the results. Mussolini was dethroned and murdered; Hitler committed suicide; the Japanese militarists involved their country in total defeat, and many of them were hanged in the result. Stalin survived; but he made colossal miscalculations and his countrymen themselves have covered him with obloquy. It is at least symbolic, if not particularly significant, that the one figure who was to outlive them all was Churchill, the aristocratic leader of a democracy.

We are only too familiar with the follies of the West. The feebleness of the Franco-British response to Hitler's reoccupation of the Rhineland—which in retrospect seems to have been the crucial moment in modern history —is often adduced now as one of the basic causes of World War II. There are many similar instances. The inability of the Western democracies to deal, either within the League of Nations or outside it, with the Japanese attack on Manchuria in 1931, with Mussolini's histrionic antics in Ethiopia, with the Spanish civil war in 1936-1939, may all be symptomatic of the disease that was rotting the policies of the West. In the final crises of 1938 and 1939 it is only too clear how the Western appeasers vitiated the policy of resistance and how the resisters vitiated any results which might have been gained through appeasement. All this makes up a tale which has been told many times. What is less often remembered is the extent to which the totalitarian systems suffered under the same disease and in the result dug even deeper graves for themselves.

A. J. P. Taylor's view that Hitler never really intended

a war—not a big war, at any rate—but expected to
sweep the board of power politics by threat and intimida-
tion alone is a persuasive one. If it is correct, the outcome
shows how badly Hitler miscalculated the real forces at
his disposal. Stalin's quite similar miscalculation in the
summer of 1941 seems in retrospect to have been as great
a folly as anything of which the democratic statesmen
were guilty. Though warned through many channels of
Hitler's plans, the Russian took none of the steps that
might have diverted them. Stalin wanted, plainly, to escape any involvement in the war in Western Europe, but
at the same time to garner all the rewards of power
that would fall to him through the West's self-destruction.
The two aims were essentially incompatible, and he
could never bring himself to sacrifice one for the other.
His complete cynicism succeeded no better than did
Franklin Roosevelt's perhaps less earthy approach—in
the period of "all aid short of war"—when the American
likewise hoped to gain the rewards of victory without
being compelled to condemn the American people to
fighting for them.

Mussolini's descent upon Ethiopia not only failed to
gain for him any of those rewards of wealth, power and
security which he may have anticipated, but it even
helped powerfully to dig the grave into which he and his
tawdry corporate state were ultimately to fall. His "stab
in the back" of France in 1941 turned out to be a gigantic
miscalculation that was to prove disastrous to him personally and very nearly so to his country. Acceptance of
a dictator is no guarantee to any people against the evils
of what Harvey Wheeler has called "simulopt"—the si-
multaneous pursuit of mutually contradictory policies.

We know less about the development of policy in the other totalitarian states. We do know something, however, about the tortures the Japanese went through in trying to adjust national policy to the world problem as they saw it. Should they go north against the Russians or south against the Anglo-Americans and the Dutch? Should they pin their future on Hitler, as Mussolini had so rashly done, or should they maneuver for somewhat greater freedom of action? Like everyone else at the time, they were working with blunt, brutal, unhandy instruments, ill-adapted to securing any of the rational goals of the Japanese state or the Japanese people. Like the democracies, they made what seemed the momentarily expedient response to crises as they arose—usually only after agonizing and paralyzing arguments among themselves as to what was the expedient course—rather than following any broadly conceived policy design. And consistently they failed to achieve the results for which they hoped.

Their war itself represented as pure a power issue as did the wars of 1870 or 1914. However one chooses to apportion the blame, the fact is that by mid-summer of 1941 a situation had been created from which neither the Japanese nor the American statesmen dared retreat, not because any particularly vital *immediate* interests of either side were at stake, but because each believed that the consequence of any retreat, even a partial retreat toward possible compromise, would be to deprive each side of all power to control the future. Subsequent to the American (and Allied) oil embargo of July, 1941, the Japanese could only calculate that the longer the embargo lasted, the less would become their ability to wage any war at all. The United States, on the other hand, could not raise the embargo on the kind of terms which the Japanese leadership felt it must have without losing its alliances with the Chinese, Dutch, French and British in the Far East, thereby undermining and probably destroying the power position that was its only hope of influencing events on the larger European stage.

For both sides there existed one of those situations, so grimly familiar in the modern international power struggle, of "now or never": fight now or lose all hope of ever being able to fight again. From this kind of situation, inherent in the working of our militarized international political system, there has seldom been any exit except in war, no matter how little either side "wanted" one. The Japanese civilians certainly did not "want" to initiate a great war in the Pacific, in which success was at best doubtful; insofar as the military men insisted upon it, it was because the only alternative visible to them spelled defeat for their nation (incidentally involving the defeat and probable destruction of the military caste). The Japanese navy "wanted" war much less than did the army, and we have Admiral Yamamoto's celebrated warning (tragically misunderstood in the United States) that the Japanese could not succeed unless they could "make peace in the White House."

No one between Washington and Tokyo knew how to handle the factors and forces available in such a way as to secure the ends that all in a real sense desired. Ironically, Yamamoto himself, probably Japan's most able military leader, was to provide the classic case, with the attack upon Pearl Harbor. In devising the plan, in forcing it on the military staffs and thereby on the civil government as representing the only way in which their war, if they were going to have one, could be won, Yamamoto unwittingly insured the total defeat of his country.

The brilliant victory of December 7, 1941, turned out to be the greatest defeat Japan had ever suffered in her long military career. As so often happens in war, the victory was less complete than had been anticipated, and its results were incommensurate with the expectations pinned upon it. Nagumo's bombers either missed or neglected the really important targets, which were the American aircraft carriers and the Pearl Harbor docks, shops and oil-tank farms. The battleships they sank and the planes they destroyed were really of no great importance in themselves; the fact that they sank them and killed over 2000 of their crews in a "treacherous" surprise was to be decisive in world history. After Pearl Harbor, Japan never really had a chance—as she might have had if Yamamoto and his military and civilian colleagues had possessed a better grasp of the basic realities in world politics. A couple of years later the Americans went to great risk and trouble to shoot the admiral down in flames when the opportunity offered. For the moral or ethical values involved in the whole Yamamoto story one would have to go, it would seem, to Greek tragedy.

As with the Greek protagonists, Yamamoto's tragedy was both personal and universal. If Japan never had a chance after Pearl Harbor, it might be said that in the post-1918 world—the world "settled" by Versailles and the accompanying treaties—nobody really had a chance. The 1918 settlement recorded the fact that Germany had been drastically defeated, that Austria-Hungary had fallen apart, that Russia had been removed, or had removed herself, from the international concert of power, that Japan was in great-power status. All this represented tremendous changes in the international power structure. But it was never possible to create the new institutional system capable of recognizing these changes and incorporating them without undue stress or violence in a working organization of international politics. With the signing of the Locarno Treaty, the elements of such a system seemed to have appeared. A temporary stabilization had been achieved in the Pacific with the Naval Limitation and Nine-Power treaties of 1922. The Dawes Plan of 1924 had introduced at least some sanity into the grotesque fantasies of "reparations." The Locarno Conference of the following year provided a four-power guarantee of Germany's western frontier, returned Germany as a voluntary and independent member of the new concert of Europe and admitted her to membership in the League of Nations. This all seemed hopeful; on such foundations it should, surely, be possible to put together a comparatively nonviolent international political system. The hope was to be disappointed.

It is curious to reflect that the international organization of power, based on the militarized nation-state as it existed in 1925, was destroyed by the domestic rather than the international power struggle. Generally speaking, the great national entities were able to accommodate each other in their external relations. The Washington treaties, the Dawes Plan, Locarno—these measures of pacification were possible and were effective in their time. The militarized nation-state was an organization conceivably capable of adequately regulating international affairs. What it could not do was to control the internal power struggles to which its own militarization and military foundations offered invitation and opportunity. There was really nothing in their external relations to have prevented the great powers, as they existed in 1925, from working out among themselves a viable system of international politics. What did prevent such accommodation was the internal rise of military-populistic dictatorship, transforming the powers as they existed in 1925, yet born out of the military factors, military principles and military organizations that underlay the organization of all of them.

Mussolini was the first of the great military-populist dictators of modern times. Beginning as a revolutionary socialist publicist and politico—he was hailed in his early days as "the Lenin of Italy"—he imitated the Russian revolutionaries. But he saw that the military and political power of the nation-state organization could be more easily seized and converted to the ends of personal power and ambition than destroyed in the interests of a new ideology. The Russian imperial state had been in dissolution when the Bolsheviks completed its destruction and rebuilt upon its ruins. The Italian monarchy was, certainly, in trouble in the early 1920's, but it was not in dissolution; Mussolini, having (with others) done much to create its troubles, used the opportunity to capture rather than to destroy it. In their "seizure of power" in Russia, the Communist ideologues had made a clean sweep of everything—the government bureaucracy, the army, the police, the owning classes, the economy, finance. To the new exponents of populist dictatorship it was easier simply to appropriate the existing power structure; and Fascist theoreticians were to develop a whole doctrine of the "seizure of power," in which the seizure, rather than the subsequent uses which would be made of the power, seemed the only element that really mattered. The revolutionary destruction of the old power structure had become unnecessary. The disruptive appeals to class, sectional or economic interest could be replaced by appeals to abstract national power, national glory, a "place in the sun" or "the nation is in danger." Such were the powerful weapons that the military-populist state had placed in the hands of personal ambition. Mussolini did not need an ideology because he had discovered a technique.[8]

The new techniques in the conduct of the internal power struggle were not initially inspired by any particular concern for the nation's international power position; and international politics—which had always, wisely, sought to avoid the power struggles within the nations—might well have lived with them. In many cases it was able to do so. As military-populist dictatorship spread through the Western world (Primo de Rivera in Spain, Salazar in Portugal, Mustafa Kemal in Turkey, Pilsudski in Poland, Horthy in Hungary and so on) it was not always disruptive of the international order. But because it was based on armed and militant nationalism, because it really had no goals to proclaim except those of military threat and power, its perils were always present,

[8] One is tempted to point to the much more trivial but parallel case of Joseph McCarthy in the United States. McCarthy had no ideology, but he developed a technique through which he attained, for a time, a tremendous personal power in the United States. It was based on the same underlying factors: a superheated nationalism, the defense of the state against the foreign enemy, "the Republic is in danger." And its effect, insofar as it had any, was to make the foreign relations of the United States more difficult, irrational and perilous than they would otherwise have been.

and when it appeared in the great states, these were soon to become acute.

The Japanese military cliques found their paths to power within the state along the ways Mussolini had indicated; and they were soon embarked upon their military adventures in Manchuria and China—adventures that had little more relevance to the real needs or interests of their people than did Mussolini's brutal and outrageous assault on Ethiopia, but that were similarly essential to the maintenance of domestic power. Hitler was Mussolini's avowed admirer and imitator, and with a firmer base on which to operate, he was soon terribly to improve upon his master. In 1919 the world had been thoroughly sick of the whole war system as the basis of international politics; everywhere the overwhelming mood was "never again," and by 1925 some slight steps had been taken in the direction of the war system's abolition.[9] The military-populist dictatorships, by reviving the war system, primarily in the interest of their own grasp of domestic power, made inevitable World War II—much greater than the first, far more destructive of human life, less manageable toward any ends of justice, politics or interest, and less necessary.

The process was repeated in many states on many levels. It was most clearly apparent in Germany, where its consequences were, of course, the most disastrous. Hitler "seized power" in Germany—which is to say that he resolved the whole complex of the internal power struggle

[9] I distinguish here between measures, such as the Briand-Kellogg pact or "collective security" under the League Covenant, that were showy but ineffective, and such steps as the Locarno pact or the large measure of disarmament that in fact took place between 1918 and 1930, which seem really to have pointed, however feebly, toward an ultimate demilitarization of international politics.

in his own favor; he made himself the final arbiter of its complex courses, the ultimate law, the ultimate judge and the ultimate policeman. He did so basically by detecting and exploiting an enemy and promising to protect the state against him with military threat and violence. This was simply technique, not state policy. Any enemy would do, provided he could be made to seem sufficiently menacing; such a circumstance was to lead to much of the inconsistency and ambivalence of *Mein Kampf* when taken as a guide to the actual policies later to be followed. In accordance with the tactical situation, Hitler could, for example, be friendly with the British and probably convince even himself that what he really wanted was a partnership with the British Empire, or he could denounce Great Britain as an "aging whore" [10] responsible for leading more innocent nations into a life of prostitution, whose evil influence would have to be utterly destroyed.

The point in the rise to power was to have an enemy. Initially the Communists and the Jews sufficed. The first were an alien influence; the second could be made to seem to be, and neither had command of the organized quasi-military violence necessary to meet the Nazi bravos and storm troopers. But as power approached, the enemy remained no less necessary than before; and he had to be raised to new levels of menace to justify the savior of the state in his role. With all the tremendous resources of the German nation-state in his hands, how could Hitler sustain himself as protector against such relatively feeble menaces as the Jews and the Communists—both of whom

[10] I once heard Ribbentrop, in a great public gathering, employ this inelegant metaphor.

he had already triumphantly overthrown? The process is wearisomely familiar in power politics. We have seen Fidel Castro driven to substitute the United States for the discredited Batista as the enemy worthy of his mettle (and warranting a continuation of his invaluable services as protector of the Cuban people). We have seen the way in which the American Federal Bureau of Investigation, grown to power and greatness on the Communist menace, has continued to exaggerate the menace since no practicable substitute seems available with which to replace it. With domestic power complete in his hands, Hitler—like so many, many others—had to have an enemy. Without an ideology, the menace was even more essential than before and could now be found only on the stage of international politics.

During the rise to power, the "Diktat of Versailles" had served very well as an adjunct to the Communists and the Jews. It now moved into the center of the scene. To overthrow it became not only the major but almost the sole object of policy. Just as in contemporary Cuba the United States is the one cause of almost any and every ill from which the Cuban people are suffering, so in the Germany of the 1930's the "Diktat"—which was hardly any longer a dictate, which had been frequently revised, which was in no important sense controlling in German history—was the one great source of every German discontent. The "Diktat" became the convenient enemy. To destroy it, Germany had to rearm; to retake the Rhineland province; to re-establish "defensible" borders; to restore Austria to the German community and recapture the other "out-German" racial brothers. In advancing such policies, Hitler was not so much expressing German

wants and needs as inventing them. Like any advertising
genius from Madison Avenue, Hitler was "educating" the
Germans to want what they had not known that they
had wanted before, to make demands that only he could
satisfy and that must therefore redound to his own power
as he proceeded to satisfy them with his great new armaments, military threats and military postures. With all
this, he successfully destroyed the "Diktat." At the same
time he also destroyed whatever possibilities the Versailles
agreement might have had as an at least potential
foundation for a workable world order. He transferred
what had begun as a domestic power struggle to an international plane, thereby rendering it unresolvable by any
means at his own or anyone else's command. From the
situation thus created, neither he nor anyone else could
find an exit except through still another world war.

Hitler, as has been suggested, was but one among
many. They existed in the democratic states, where they
influenced policy even though never achieving command
of it, as well as in the totalitarian systems. Except in the
sense that Hitler was more reckless, more brutal, more of
an ignorant gangster than the others, it is hard to say
that he was any more immoral or fundamentally to be
held any more "responsible" for the collapse of a system
of international politics of which he, like the others, was
a systemic product. Through the agonies of 1938 and
1939 the high-minded, generally public-spirited, statesmen of the West simply could not deal with the situation
Hitler had powerfully helped to create. But neither could
the Russians; and neither, in the last analysis, could
Hitler. The situation was too big, too difficult, too unmanageable by all the military-political instrumentalities

of nation-state power available to them. Nothing in fact turned out as anyone had hoped or as most, on all sides, had expected. World War II duly ensued. Six years and some forty million dead later on, it was possible to conclude that international politics was not structured around "aggressive" and "peace-loving" nations or around "good" and "evil" men. Such concepts had all been tried and had all failed over and over again to control the workings of a system that apparently led ineluctably to these bloody and unnecessary results. Hitler saved himself from the hangmen only by committing suicide. But it was not Hitler who was basically at fault. It was the system that had made him possible, that had produced him and that had no answer—no more than it had in the days of the first Napoleon, no more than it has today for a problem like that of Castro—to the conundrums that he embodied.

THREE

THE COLD WAR

ORLD WAR II ENDED IN SEPTEMBER, 1945, to the crashing echoes of the two atomic bombs that had been released in the final hours upon the Japanese. The long, ghastly horror was over. Again there was complete "victory"; once more the righteous had triumphed and the wicked had been confounded. Again it seemed to millions that a world order of substantial peace and justice was attainable; and again the statesmen—though probably wiser and certainly more sophisticated than their predecessors of a quarter of a century before—found themselves without either the intellectual or the material tools with which to bring such an order to realization. Peace was now possible. But in none of the great centers of power, East or West, had leadership been able to discern any way of constructing it. Throughout the war years minds had been molded to the conviction that the end of this great power struggle would be simply the prelude for another; and to none had it occurred that the new struggle could be waged, in the last analysis, by any other means than the immemorial instruments of blood and arms.

The now victorious coalition of East and West had, from its origins, been one only of uneasy convenience. Winston Churchill had once remarked that if the devil himself should take up arms against Hitler, Mr. Churchill would "be prepared to make a favorable reference to him in the House of Commons." After the Germans booted the Russians into the war in July, 1941, the favorable references were many; but for most Western statesmen the Russians remained the devil. That the Western capitalist democracies continued to play the devil in the eyes of Stalin's Russia was made plain on numerous occasions. At Yalta in February, 1945, a really earnest effort was made to close the fissure and reach agreement upon the terms of the peace the now imminent victory would give Russia and the West the power to impose. The effort failed. With the intellectual, emotional and military instruments available to them the statesmen could not accomplish even this elementary task of peace making. The hollowness of the published agreements was apparent even to some of the participants in the Yalta Conference and was soon to become plain to all. The "cold war" was already well developed months before the hot one had been concluded, and it was not long thereafter that it received a quasi-formal declaration.

On February 9, 1946, Stalin, in a so-called election speech, committed Russia to a massive five-year plan of industrial and military reconstruction, explicitly based on the assumptions that a peaceful international order was "impossible under the present capitalist development of world economy" and that this defensive effort was required "to guarantee our country against any eventuality." To many Western decision makers it came as a declaration of war; and in the following month Mr. Churchill made the answering declaration in a speech delivered improbably, but no less impressively, in the small college town of Fulton, Missouri.

"An iron curtain," he said, "has descended across the Continent. . . . This is certainly not the liberated Europe we sought to build up. Nor is it one which contains the essentials of permanent peace. . . . The Communist parties or fifth columns [outside of Russia] constitute a growing challenge and peril to Christian civilization. . . . I do not believe that Soviet Russia desires war. What the Russians desire is the fruits of war and the indefinite expansion of their power and doctrine." Churchill summoned the Western democracies to a united front in defense of Christian civilization—a summons to which the ruling groups in the West were quick to respond. It was just a year later, in March, 1947, that the enunciation of the "Truman Doctrine" made the cold war both explicit and official.

The immediate crisis arose from Soviet pressure on Turkey and a Communist guerilla war against the Greek government. President Truman saw the situation in what may seem rather simplistic terms: "Greece and Turkey were still free countries being challenged by Communist threats both from within and without. These free peoples were now engaged in a valiant struggle to preserve their liberties and their independence. America could not, and should not, let these free countries stand unaided." [1] Asking Congress for a $400 million appropriation in aid of Greece and Turkey, the

[1] Harry S Truman, *Memoirs*, Vol. II (Doubleday & Co., 1956), p. 101.

President declared that "it must be the policy of the United States to support free peoples who are resisting attempted subjugation by armed minorities or by outside pressures. . . . We must assist free peoples to work out their own destinies in their own way." Specifically, the message referred only to Greece and Turkey; but it announced a broad policy. As Truman was afterward to say, it marked a "turning point in America's foreign policy, which now declared that wherever aggression, direct or indirect, threatened the peace, the security of the United States was involved." [2]

Like Stalin's quite similar, if opposite, view of the world problem, Truman's was an apperception of world politics—a way of looking at the international power problem—which made war ultimately unavoidable. One hardly needs to waste time on the question of "responsibility." Like Hitler before him, Stalin was a brutal, shrewd and fundamentally ignorant individual, far less attractive than the better-educated but possibly less able Western statesmen; and if it satisfies one's moral sense to attach the chief blame to him, it is difficult to raise any objection. But the ethics seem hardly relevant. Truman, in his own way, was at least as ignorant as Stalin. Truman's simple concepts—"aggression," "free peoples," "liberties," "independence"—scarcely fitted the complex facts of a situation such as the one created by the guerilla war in Greece any better than did Stalin's worn-out Marxist tags about "capitalism" and "imperialism." Neither set of concepts offered any remotely adequate description of the intricate power struggles of individuals, parties, groups and nations to which they were

2 *Op. cit.*, p. 106.

applied. But the Truman message of March, 1947, fixed the pattern of all these power struggles as they reached the international level. The pattern was one of "cold war." For the West cold war meant containment, rearmament (which was soon to come) and military threat, in order to retain those power positions that appeared to give the West the ability to control the future. For the East it involved expansion into threatened or weak positions, rearmament and military threat, in order to retain those positions (as often political or psychological as they were crassly military) that would enable the Soviet Union to control the future.

The pattern was gruesomely familiar in the long tale of history. Again and again, in great affairs as in lesser ones, coalitions have arisen to sustain a power conflict and then, once the victory was won, have fallen apart in a struggle for power among the victors. Many of the great coalition victories in history have simply left the victors committed to another war with each other. The great victory of 1918 so fractured the coalition that won it as to create the conditions that, within a bare twenty years, precipitated the next war. The great victory of 1945 established a cold war, for which the only logical outcome seemed to be a third gigantic bloodletting. Yet after the lapse of nearly another two decades there is no third world war; there is no really acute fear of one, and nowhere is there any important body of opinion or significant element in the governmental bureaucracies that appears to be calculating on one. There is only the "cold" war, fearfully dangerous in its potentialities but in actual fact rather remarkably successful over the past fifteen or twenty years as a system for regulating the international power struggle without precipitating total disaster.[3]

There has never been a good definition of cold war. The common definition—a state "that is neither war nor peace"—defines nothing. A situation that is "neither war nor peace" may be, and commonly is, regarded as nothing more than a war from which bloodshed is temporarily absent; but it can equally be regarded as a peace from which pacification is temporarily absent. Conflict, on any level from the family quarrel to international war, is always, as H. L. Nieberg has observed, a "means of discovering consensus," and any conflict can be viewed from either aspect. Normally one tends to see the cold war in terms of competition and the family quarrel in terms of achieving adjustment and consensus.

> [But] one can reverse these conceptual fields. The cold war can be viewed in terms of the large areas of consensus that exist between two power blocs, for example, the wish to prevent the spread of

[3] The time scale is of interest, particularly in an era in which the tremendous acceleration of all media of communication and response is supposed to have lent an equivalent acceleration to the military-political processes. World War II ended formally on September 2, 1945, which, when these lines were being written in the summer of 1963, was eighteen years past. World War I ended on November 11, 1918. Another eighteen years brought the world to the lamentable year 1936. The second war was by that time only three years away. Europe was full of the tramping battalions and the superheated oratory preparing it. Mussolini's adventure in Ethiopia; the Japanese in Manchuria and China; Hitler, Mussolini and Stalin in Spain; German rearmament and German reoccupation of the Rhineland, all were tearing the world of 1918 to shreds. Most thoughtful persons felt themselves already deep in the shadow of the impending Armageddon. The summer of 1963 may have been heavy with distant menace, but it bore almost no resemblance to the tottering summer of 1936—strangely, frivolously but perhaps no less appositely symbolized for millions in the West by the conversion of Britain's Edward VIII into the Duke of Windsor.

nuclear weapons to each other's allies; the wish to avoid giving each other's allies the power of general war and peace between the main antagonists; the common interest in reducing accidental provocation . . . etc. Conflict can be considered merely as the means of perfecting these areas of consensus. In the same way one can view the family situation negatively in terms of competition and hostility.[4]

The cold war is usually seen as no more than a prelude to a hot one. It may be more accurate to look at it as a substitute, as a means of "discovering consensus" without the necessity of first slaughtering millions of men and wrecking the existing world order. Commonly considered as no more than a specialized form of war, it has actually operated over the past twenty years or so as a peculiar, but oddly effective, form of peace. It has at the very least introduced a system of international order differing drastically in its policies, its diplomacy, its military planning and its structural relationships from the the system that obtained between 1871 and 1914 and almost as sharply from that obtaining between 1918 and 1939.

It is hard to deny that the primary factor in the creation of this novel system in international politics was the appearance of the atomic bombs. One may well hesitate to assign to this one technological development the sole credit for results already implicit in the general hypertrophy of war and military technology. If the embattled scientists had failed with the atom, they would

[4] H. L. Nieberg, "The Uses of Violence," *The Journal of Conflict/ Resolution*, March, 1963, p. 45.

undoubtedly have succeeded—as indeed they were suc-
ceeding—with other methods of mass extermination:
biological warfare, for example, or improvements upon
the gruesome incendiary raids that at Hamburg and
Tokyo had produced agonies and slaughters rivaling
those achieved by the "military application of atomic
energy" itself. The Hiroshima bomb was not so much the
crux of the technological disaster as the unanswerable,
inescapable symbol of it. At least since the Hague Conference of 1899 military technology had been seen as
fearsome, but one could (and most did) overlook its
probable consequences. The mushroom cloud over Hiroshima and the tortured victims of the city were something that could not be overlooked or denied. Science,
married to war in rites of impeccable legality under all
the accepted mores, had finally produced a monster too
hideous and too huge to be disregarded. Something
would have to be done.

This was instantly apparent to almost everyone. In
the West, at any rate, the triumphant ending of World
War II was almost lost in the excitement over this other
triumph of a more dubious kind. From the first hours
there was more intense and impassioned debate over
what should be done with the atom than over what
should be done with the victory. Should America give
this tremendous "secret" that her scientists and engineers had unraveled to the collective wisdom of the world?
Should she keep its immense potentials under her sole
control? America alone possessed what appeared to be,
at long last, the "absolute" weapon. What could she do
with it? What could she not do with it, even up to dic-
tating an American peace (one of justice, of course, by

definition) to the war-wearied globe?

On September 11, with Hiroshima barely a month old and only nine days after the surrender ceremonies in Tokyo Bay, Henry L. Stimson, the then American Secretary of War, wrote a long letter to the President in which he sought to bring some sense and perspective to the argument. Even at this early date, Stimson saw some matters quite clearly. The "secret" could not be kept forever; the American monopoly was bound to be transitory. While it lasted, the destructive, military power of the bombs would be less important than the political effects that would flow from their existence. The politics of the postwar world would revolve, overwhelmingly, around the relations between the United States and the Soviet Union; and these relations would be "not merely connected with but virtually dominated by" the problem of the control of the bomb. Stimson punctured the notion, then held "in many quarters," that the bomb could be used in a vague and general way as "a substantial offset to the growth of Russian influence on the Continent." He looked at the matter more precisely, rather like the skilled chess player who knows exactly not only the threat value of his own pieces but of those in the hands of his opponent. There were really only three choices offered by the chessboard as history had set it up. The first (which Stimson did not even mention) was to employ the atomic monopoly at once to crush Soviet military power in a third great war, before Russia could achieve a nuclear capability of its own. The second, which Stimson favored, was to "approach" the Soviet Union immediately and directly to get an agreement that would "limit the use of the atomic bomb as an instrument of war" as well as "encourage the development of

atomic power for peaceful and humanitarian purposes."
The implication was that America would throw all her
existing bombs, together with the information as to how to
make them, on the international table, in return for a
Soviet undertaking not to develop bombs of her own
and to confine all future nuclear development to peaceful uses.

The third, which was the course finally adopted, was
simply to "negotiate" with the Russians through some
"general international scheme" involving all the small
nations; such a course would not "be taken seriously by
the Soviets." The result, Stimson quite accurately prophesied, would be merely to drive the Soviet leadership "to
acquire this weapon in the shortest possible time," leading to a "secret armament race of a rather desperate
character." If, he added, America would "merely continue to negotiate with them, having this weapon rather
ostentatiously on our hip, their suspicions . . . will increase." The Russians would simply be inspired to an
"all-out effort" to solve the problem the United States
would be forcing upon them, and if the solution were
achieved in that spirit, it would be unlikely "that we
will ever get the kind of covenant that we may desperately need." [5]

The situation boiled down to this: America had only
a limited number of years in which to enjoy the atomic
monopoly. Short of employing the weapon in an immediate and colossal preventive war (from which even
the most chauvinistic were inclined to shrink), there
were but two ways in which the country could use it. One

[5] Text in Henry L. Stimson and McGeorge Bundy, *On Active Service
in Peace and War* (Harper & Row, 1948), p. 643.

was to trade it, so to speak, for the complete abolition of the whole nuclear-weapons system she had created; the other was to conserve it as an arm of purely national policy. Hugging the "secret," America would carry the weapon "ostentatiously on our hip," expecting thereby to negotiate a better and more stable answer to the global problem. Whether the first course would have offered any chance of success is perhaps debatable; it was inevitable, in any event, that the nation would opt for the second and that the consequences Stimson had foreseen would ensue. On September 21 President Truman held a long Cabinet meeting. The exact record of what was said is obscure and controversial, but the upshot was plain. America would hug the secret and try to use it while it lasted as a lever with which to pry open a better world. Politically, it was the only possible decision; that it would not work with the Russians, Stimson had already foretold.

It was soon realized that the "absolute" weapon was not as absolute as had been supposed. When the British and Canadian prime ministers arrived in Washington in November, 1945, the President agreed with them that "the only complete protection for the civilized world from the destructive use of scientific knowledge lies in the prevention of war." This was a more shattering observation than even its authors may have realized. Many had been looking to the bomb to abolish war. Here it was said, in effect, that the world would now have to abolish war in order to get rid of the bomb. The full import of this idea was not grasped at the time, but, like the Hound of Heaven, it has been dogging international history from that time on. The giant feet have been padding after us ever since, down to the moment when President Kennedy agreed in 1962 with Premier Khrushchev that general and complete disarmament—the demilitarization of the world—was the only rational answer to the world problem.

The idea was again prominent in an influential report produced early in 1946 by Senator Brien McMahon of Connecticut, after he held committee hearings that amounted to a kind of high-level seminar of scientists, soldiers and administrators. The monopoly would be short-lived; not much could be hoped from international agreements, and the only "real protection against the atomic bomb lies in the prevention of war." But no one saw any way of achieving such an end; and policy followed the predictable line. The domestic Atomic Energy Act put the whole development under rigorous governmental (though civilian) control, with savage provisions for complete secrecy. The Acheson-Lilienthal report, as elaborated in the Baruch Plan, was laid before the United Nations. Under it, America would retain the secret monopoly and the supposed power it gave her until an ironclad international control system, in a form that seemed just and safe to the United States, had been established. With the hands of the Soviet Union and its scientists thus firmly tied, America would then turn over bombs and secrets alike to the international authority. America was astonished by her own generosity and statesmanship in making this offer—so much so that many doubted whether the Senate would ever accept the proposal even if the Russians did. It is now easy to see in retrospect that of the latter there was no chance. Kremlin policy also followed the predictable line.

The Baruch Plan failed in more ways than one. Its authors were unable to see the problem from the Kremlin's viewpoint. It overvalued the effective political power of the military monopoly. And it was an attempt to buy from the Russians a tremendous advantage—their assent to perpetual peace on substantially Western terms—with a rapidly wasting asset. The proposed international agency would have involved a revolutionary transformation of the world order, hardly less than what is implied by present-day proposals for general and complete disarmament and raising all the difficulties that now make general and complete disarmament seem so unattainable. Had America been sure of retaining the monopoly indefinitely, the price would still have been insufficient for securing so stupendous a result. But the United States knew that the asset was dwindling with every passing year. One should not have expected to purchase perpetuity with so ephemeral a coin.

The Russians could afford to wait and did so. Winston Churchill lent his support to the widely held belief that it was the American monopoly alone that dissuaded the Soviet Union from sweeping Western Europe with its conventional Red Army battalions; but like other of that great statesman's insights, this was certainly an oversimplification. In later years there has been little to suggest that Stalin's policy ever seriously contemplated a military conquest of Western Europe, and even less to indicate that the bomb monopoly, while it lasted, had any important effect on Russia's immediate military calculations. The bombs released on the Japanese were a terrible portent for the future, but they were far from representing an operational weapons system. Thereafter the

United States allowed the atomic development to lag for a year or two; and by the time the Russians punctured the monopoly in 1949, America's arsenal was still insufficient in numbers and insufficiently supported by tactical and strategic "doctrine" to be a reliable instrument of immediate war. If the Russians had wanted to sweep Western Europe with their conventional forces at any time before 1950, they would have risked some savage losses, but it seems unlikely that the American atomic arsenal could have brought the Red Army forcibly to a halt. The Russians, however, had no real reason for such an adventure; while it must have been amply clear to them that the capitalistic West, whatever its ultimate purposes and despite its possession of the bombs, had no immediate intention of assaulting the Soviet Union. They could afford to wait; and, as they no doubt knew, they did not have to wait long.

The fact seems to be that during the brief period of the monopoly purely strategic considerations were of relatively little consequence. This circumstance was fortunate: if they had been—if the responsible political leaderships had responded to strategic calculations in the way our students of strategy and of the utterances of opposing military theorists assume that they will—the results would have been disastrous. The existence of the monopoly created a situation almost ideal for a massive preventive war. In strict military logic the West should have made an all-out effort to perfect the atomic arsenal and employ it to crush Soviet conventional power before the Soviet Union achieved an atomic riposte. Equally, the Red Army should have been released upon Western Europe in an all-out effort to secure "mastery" before the atomic arsenals rendered conventional military power nugatory. Nothing of the kind happened; in our complicated world the logic of the military strategists is not in total control. The only actual effect of the monopoly was to create a situation in which the weaponry on both sides—conventional no less than atomic—was actually good only for a preventive war that neither side had the foolhardiness, immorality or plain stupidity even to contemplate. The weaponry of both kinds was not used in the only way in which by that time it was usable. Nor has it been used since.

In the autumn of 1949 the monopoly passed into history with the explosion of the first Soviet atomic bomb. In this explosion went up together all Western policies based, consciously or only implicitly, on the West's monopoly possession of the "absolute weapon." The foundations were removed from under the Baruch Plan, and little has been heard of it since except as a counter in the polemics. Under the idea (which Stimson in 1945 had seen to be fallacious) that the American bomb monopoly would provide a kind of general "offset" to Soviet influence on the Continent, the North Atlantic Treaty Organization (NATO) had been established in the spring of 1949 as a defensive alliance mainly political and economic in character. In the echoes of the Soviet bomb, it was soon to be apparent that the organization's crassly military content would have to be given attention. In a military sense the world was suddenly back where it had started, only on a much higher level of potential terror and destruction. There was no "absolute weapon," and in the brief period in which America had appeared to hold one in her hands, she had been able to put it to no effective use. The failure of the Baruch Plan epitomizes the whole course of disarmament negotiation before and since; here were, in magnified form, the same kinds of miscalculation, the same self-defeating factors and forces, that have characterized "arms control" from its beginnings at the turn of the century. The Baruch Plan meant nothing to the Russians except that it assured them the time to redress the military balance; and when they had done so, the new balance meant nothing to the Americans and their partners except that they would have to take up the arms race in the old pattern but on a new, more dreadful, scale.

The immediate American response to the Soviet atomic bomb was the "crash program" to develop a thermonuclear superbomb. It was apparent to the thoughtful that such a program was no answer to the basic problem; and the scientists on the Atomic Energy Commission's General Advisory Committee recommended against it, believing that with the Russians now able to negotiate from a strength of their own, a final effort should be made to get agreement with them before plunging into this dubious adventure. The Truman Administration did not accept the suggestion; limited in the political means at its disposal by the psychology of the times, it probably could not have done so. The point was already academic. With both great powers now gripped by the baleful hand of military technology, the issue was beyond control of either, and no American decision could have importantly affected it. In point of fact, the Russians (though the United States did not know it) were already about as close to a hydrogen bomb as were the Americans, and the anguished secret debate in late 1949 and early 1950 was to a considerable extent beside the point.[6] With American, no less than Russian, statesmanship incapable of seeing any alternative to the arms race, the race would have swept on to its new heights of terror much as it did regardless of temporary decisions. The net outcome of the monopoly was to put the world back in the old disastrous pattern of military rivalry, though on a much higher level of potential catastrophe. What had seemed in the grim dawn of Hiroshima an unparalleled opportunity for the better ordering of international affairs had been irretrievably lost. The pattern was the same. Yet the fact remains that some two decades later all that had emerged from it was not supercolossal disaster, but only the cold war.

In retrospect the Korean War may well seem to have been a far more decisive turning point in world history than was recognized at the time. It came at a singularly critical juncture; perhaps, indeed, it was the result of it. Russia had just produced her own atomic bomb; the United States had not yet developed a working strategic "doctrine" for nuclear warfare. In Europe most of the consequences of World War II had in reality simmered down to a fairly "stable state," though few could recognize the fact. In the Far East in 1949 Chinese Communism had, independently and with no more than the mistrustful support of Moscow, completed the conquest of mainland China and so brought a new, potentially

[6] Actually, the "super" then under discussion was never achieved. The project flagged, and not until June, 1951, with the Korean War already in stalemate, did a "new approach" revive it. The first practical American thermonuclear "device," not yet an operable bomb, was fired in mid-1952; the Russians produced a thermonuclear explosion in August, 1953, six months before America tested her first "droppable" multimegaton thermonuclear bomb.

great power onto the world stage. The United States had established an island empire right across the empty expanses of the Pacific, pushing its "defense perimeter" up to, but not onto, the Asian mainland. The American power structure in the Pacific was impressive, but the United States had little idea of what in practice it might do with it. The political, diplomatic and ideological situations, like the military situation, were uncertain, "fluid," at a critical point—and from this juncture the Korean war was precipitated. When that war ended in 1953 the international order had been significantly transformed.

We know too little about Russian, Chinese and North Korean policy in early 1950 to speak dogmatically about it. The inference is that when Stalin instigated, or authorized, the North Korean attack in June, 1950, he was making no more than an obvious play in the conventional game of military power politics. Halted, at least temporarily, in the West, he saw in Korea an apparent opportunity to pick up at small cost a useful bit of small change in the Pacific. The United States had withdrawn her troops from the peninsula and had excluded it (as was noted in Acheson's subsequently notorious speech of early 1950) from its "defense perimeter." Korea was hardly essential to Russian policy at that time, but it was a position that could be very valuable. And its value would lie not only against the West; already the Kremlin no doubt saw its potential against the Chinese Communists. Moscow had a much firmer control over the North Koreans than over the Chinese in Peking; and the Kremlin must have seen much promise in the possibility of North Korea's overrunning the peninsula without seriously involving the Red Army.

But as with many other calculations in military power politics, matters did not turn out as had, presumably, been anticipated. Truman's unexpectedly energetic response, both in the field and in the United Nations, clearly took the Russians by surprise, since they had incautiously left the U.N. flank for once unguarded. After their brilliant initial successes, the North Korean forces proved unequal to the assignment given them. Their debacle in October, 1950, must, had no other factor intervened, have faced the Kremlin with a choice between writing off the enterprise or accepting a major war with the United States. The whole course of Russian policy after 1945 suggests that the Soviet Union would probably have chosen to write it off. But a new factor did come into play: the Communist Chinese.

By massively intervening in November, 1950, Peking successfully restored the position to one of military stalemate along substantially the original demarcation line; and in the spring of 1951 the United States opened negotiations for a "peace without victory"—the first it had sought, in a long and active military history, since 1814. The basic war aim became the *status quo ante bellum;* and while it was to take two more years of diplomatic maneuver, backed at times by bloody fighting, to convince both sides that neither could significantly improve the situation in its own favor, the *status quo ante* finally emerged. It was peace without victory for anyone. Moscow's adventure in military power politics had failed in its presumed objects. Neither China nor the United States won more than defensive victories, leaving the underlying international power patterns unchanged. Organized war on the old models was not, as Bismarck's wars or the Russo-Japanese War had been, a usable instrument of positive policy; and in the decade that has since elapsed, a whole new system of international politics, markedly different from that which had obtained before 1914 or before 1939, has in fact emerged.

The new system has been characterized by the retirement of the mass-destruction weapons systems into the purely defensive strategy of "deterrence," by the transformation of the two monolithic power centers once represented by Washington and Moscow into much more complex (and more flexible) coalitions and by the absence of any large-scale war or any real threat of one remotely comparable to the threat which hung over Europe in 1939. International violence has by no means been eliminated, but it has consistently taken the form of guerilla warfare; of the incitement, the promotion or the support of guerilla warfare and revolution elsewhere; of subversive and propaganda "wars"; to some extent of economic pressure; or simply of riot and mass protest. The fiasco of the Anglo-French descent upon Egypt in 1956 seemed to demonstrate that the world order had developed beyond the point at which this kind of military adventurousness was practicable or held out any promise of reward; and we are unlikely to see another example. International politics under the new conditions has not been bloodless and is certainly not easy or comfortable, but it appears to work successfully toward tolerable and nondisastrous ends.

All these developments were implicit in the Korean War and its aftermath. Despite some pressures to that end, atomic weapons were not used in Korea, thus lending strong support to the view that they were not usable, even then, in any situation containing a threat of major war. In the Indochina crisis a couple of years later, it was to appear that they were not usable even in a peripheral context. The idea of employing a few atomic bombs for the relief of the beleaguered fortress of Dien Bien Phu was seriously advanced; but it was laid aside, for practical military reasons as well as those of high policy. As the nuclear arsenals continued to mushroom in numbers and terror, they were to become less, not more, employable as the bases of operative military power. Yet by their very existence they were at the same time to involve the great conventional armaments in the same paradox.

In the first shock, the Korean surprise was widely read as a signal that the Russians were at last upon the march. The supposed peril to Western Europe dominated the actual problem in the Far East. When in the latter part of 1950 the United States quadrupled its defense appropriations, most of the increase went, not to waging the war in progress in Korea, but to buttressing the conventional defenses of Western Europe against the Red Army. American occupation forces in Germany were tripled and reorganized into fighting formations. NATO was transformed from a largely political coalition into a hard-shell military alliance, its forces integrated under an American supreme commander at Rocquencourt, France, and with plans to form some hundred quickly mobilizable ground divisions, with full air and naval support, on the World War II pattern. But by 1953, as the Korean War was ending, these visions were already fading. It was obvious that the Russians were not on the march after all, and that the whole grand scheme was going to cost too much. Given the protections of the American nu-

clear arsenal and the Strategic Air Command, were out-
lays on such a scale really necessary? The existence of
the nuclear arsenal tended to eviscerate the conventional
defense systems. The difficulty was that nothing practically employable was put in their place.

It would be useless to attempt to follow all the confusions, primarily strategic in the first instance but growing increasingly political as fears of any immediate war
began to dwindle, that flowed from the dilemma. The
effort to escape it by getting "a bigger bang for a buck"
(in the phrase of the American Defense Secretary,
Charles E. Wilson), through substituting "tactical" nuclear weapons for manpower in the conventional forces,
was unpromising from the start. No good answer has
been found for De Gaulle's claim to an independent
nuclear force; or to the assertion of a similar claim
by China. A decade later (in early 1964) no solution
had been worked out for the problem of a "NATO nuclear capability," which is far more of a problem in the
political relationships than it is in the military ones of
the nations concerned. In spite of the ingenious efforts
of the theorists of "first strike" and "second strike" thermonuclear war, of the "balance of terror" and the offen-
sive potentialities of civil defense, no real way has been
found to introduce the giant weapons systems into the
military relations of the states. And they have tended to
take the great conventional forces along with them into
desuetude. Throughout the decade the one real answer
to all such problems has been more and more clearly
emerging: it is the strategy of "deterrence," to which the
major conventional forces have been more and more
assimilated along with the thermonuclear weapons, and

which has actually been evolving into what might be called the antistrategy, not simply of deterrence, but of absolute prevention.

Armaments have always, of course, been justified on the ground that they are deterrents to war. "If you wish for peace, prepare for war" is a maxim that goes back to Roman times if not before. But in the past, war had always been a practicable and acceptable alternative to peace. As President Eisenhower once pointed out, it is so no longer. Even ten or fifteen years ago designers of the military posture would use the ancient phrase: their plans were intended "to prevent war if possible, to win it if not." The addendum is rarely heard any longer. The idea of "victory" in a major war was pretty well dissipated after Korea; and the most the military experts now offer us is somewhat to mitigate the costs of the common defeat in which another major war must involve all parties.

The new situation was rather plainly, if perhaps a trifle disingenuously, announced by the then Secretary of State, John Foster Dulles, when in January, 1954, he declared that the United States would thereafter rely upon "a capacity for massive retaliation, at times and places of our own choosing." This statement really gave the whole program away. It was produced in the hope of controlling Chinese operations in Vietnam (possibly in Korea as well). Fundamentally it was a bold attempt to hypothecate the actual, tangible explosive content of the nuclear arsenal into a structure of working "credit" on the international exchanges, much as a banker hypothecates his gold reserves (in themselves unusable) to sustain the great edifices of operative paper built upon them.

As such it could not succeed. There is no valid evidence whatever that actual Chinese policy in Southeast Asia was deflected by the Dulles statement. It informed Peking that in Vietnam the United States had no intention of again employing the conventional war that had been used unsuccessfully in Korea. American policy would henceforth be "retaliatory" only; and retaliation is ineffective without something to retaliate against. So far as military considerations are concerned, the whole issue is left in the hands of the opponent, who can gauge for himself what will invite retaliation and proceed to secure his political objectives by all other available means. This is the canker at the heart of any policy of retaliation —especially of "massive" retaliation—that has eroded policy ever since.

The attitude has caused endless questions over the past decade. How, with the available giant weapons, is the United States to prevent the "piecemeal" destruction of its national interests? Neither the British thinkers, with their theory of "graduated" deterrence, nor Herman Kahn, with his own theory of graduated "provocation," have ever really met the problem. Would the United States really risk retaliation with the giant weapons in order to preserve Europe? Where does a retaliatory policy leave the French—or the British, for that matter—vis-à-vis their own responsibility for their own national defense? All these problems were implicit in the Dulles statement of 1954, but he made them virtually explicit by introducing the key (and weasel) word, "capacity." It was not massive retaliation itself that was to do the job, but only the "capacity" for it. The Chinese knew as well as everyone else that Mr. Dulles had no expectation of actually employing the nuclear power on which he was founding American military policy. This was not a proclamation of power, but only of a simulacrum of power, which could be of slight effect in the actual course of international politics.

Most of these paradoxes were to come out in the wash, and backwash, of the Suez crisis two years later. Neither conventional war nor massive retaliation nor any other military solution proved practicable. The solutions finally found were of a nonmilitary character.[7] And so they have been in the main ever since. The United States has never actually threatened to retaliate massively on anyone. Neither has the Soviet Union. In two situations Khrushchev has indulged in "bomb rattling"—in the Suez crisis and in connection with Castro's rise to power in Cuba. In neither have the threats been of any more practical significance than was Mr. Dulles' very similar bomb rattling in 1954; and when a potentially serious crisis appeared in the Cuban situation in October, 1962, the threats were very carefully muted by both sides.

Since the conclusion of the Korean War the power struggle has been conducted by other means than war or even threats of the mutual suicide, which is all that great-power war today can come to. This turn of events, too, was implicit in Korea. The long and tortuous negotia-

[7] A recent book, Herman Finer's *Dulles over Suez* (Quadrangle Books, 1964), makes a savage attack upon the sanctimonious policies of the Secretary of State. They are certainly not above criticism, and in early 1964 they came home to roost over the United States with a vengeance in Panama. But the case is not conclusive that any other policies would in fact have worked better. The underlying fact is that the old pre-1939 war system was unworkable in Suez in 1956, as it is unworkable in Panama today. It is no longer possible just to call out the Marines in the old, grand manner; and it is most unlikely that Lyndon Johnson will ever repeat anything remotely resembling Theodore Roosevelt's boast: "I took Panama."

tions at Panmunjom not only announced the end of the old warfare of "victory" but adumbrated many of the substitutes that are being found for it—in propaganda, infiltration, political pressures, "vicarious" and guerilla conflict. The fighting that went on after the negotiations began was at times very heavy, but was never for more than limited objectives and for political rather than military effect. The results were not intended to be recorded on the battle ground but at the conference tables, in "world opinion" and in the politics of distant capitals. The Chinese were without the military strength to recapture South Korea; but by ruthlessly sacrificing their troops to these essentially political ends, they successfully confirmed their new status as one of the world's great powers. There were many elements of political and guerilla warfare in the Korean conflict, which badly baffled the American regular soldiers to whom its conduct was entrusted, and added to the distaste of the soldiers as well as the American public for the idea of getting involved in another formal war on the Korean pattern in Indochina.

On the two occasions since on which the United States has deployed significant forces of conventional troops abroad—in Lebanon and Thailand—it was careful to do so only in areas where no actual fighting was going on and where, given the precautionary intervention at the request of the local government, there was unlikely to be any. In Vietnam, where war had been endemic for years, there was no organized intervention. Although America ultimately put some 15,000 uniformed personnel in the area, they were confined to the roles of leadership, instructors, air transport and

supply troops. Too many have been lost in these operations, but this is not war in any conventional sense.
American officers and administrators in the area have
clung to the principle that if the war is to be won at all,
it will have to be won by the Vietnamese themselves;
and as progress has been slower and the reports more
pessimistic, there has still been no suggestion that the
United States should intervene by military means to reverse an adverse outcome. "Saving" Southeast Asia from
Communism remained an important American objective;
but it was not important enough to risk a major war,
while no lesser one gave much hope of controlling the
situation.

Since Korea, American strategy has taken a great interest in "indirect aggression" and guerilla and "coun-
terguerilla" war. While the Air Force has generally continued to withdraw into its unmanageable mystique of
the giant weapons systems, the Army and Navy have
been devouring the works of Mao Tse-tung, Che Gue-
vara, the French theorists of the Algerian war and other
exponents of "peoples'" and guerilla warfare. A decade
ago the whole war problem seemed to revolve around
the giant weapons systems. These have since tended to
recede into the background, with conventional forces
appearing more and more prominently to the fore. The
Kennedy Administration spent much money and energy
on developing conventional forces for "limited" war; yet
there was never much consideration of the question of
just how and where such large-scale yet limited war could
in fact arise. Some theorists maintain that today we are
grossly overweaponed to fight conventional wars (outside of Europe) that will never occur. The fact is, as

Charles W. Thayer observes, that since World War II guerilla wars have gradually become "the predominant form of armed conflict throughout the world." [8] In the frequently bloody shambles of Vietnam or the Congo or elsewhere our theorists have learned a lot about "popular" and guerilla war. What they have not learned is how to convert conflict of this kind to useful political ends. Whatever the future in Vietnam, it seems clear that America can no longer determine it by military means alone.

Korea announced, however dimly, that organized war had lost its function as *ultima ratio* in international society. Suez supported the conclusion. A dozen crises since have confirmed it. In the result, American military policy has come down to the bare, defensive base stated by President Johnson in his budget message of January, 1964:

> We have chosen not to concede our opponents' supremacy in any type of potential conflict, be it nuclear war, conventional warfare, or guerilla conflict. We have now increased the strength of our forces so that, faced with any threat of aggression, we can make a response which is appropriate to the situation.

This statement announces hardly more than the Dulles policy of a "capacity for massive retaliation" updated to accord with the facts of the contemporary world. It suffers from the same defects, and is actually an abrogation of purely military power as an instrument of a working international politics. It raises questions as to

[8] Charles W. Thayer, *Guerilla* (Harper & Row, 1963), p. xvi.

what "response" may really be "appropriate" to the
many kinds of threat raised by the advance of the global
social, political and economic revolution in which the
American democratic system finds itself. It is not really a
military policy at all, but might better be described as an
antimilitary policy, embodying the antistrategy of deterrence and leading logically to no other end than the
general demilitarization of the world system.

Since 1945 there have been any number of crises,
any one of which might well have been sufficient to destroy a world order constituted like that of 1914. There
was the "rape" of Czechoslovakia (1948), the Berlin
blockade of the same year, Korea (1950), the Arab-
Israel war and its climax at Suez in 1956, Indochina (in
1954 and since), the East German and Polish revolts,
with the climax in Hungary in 1956, the Algerian
war for national independence, the several and prolonged crises over sub-Saharan Africa, the U-2 affair in
May, 1960, the two Cuban crises (the Bay of Pigs in
1961 and the missile crisis in October, 1962), and not
a few more of lesser significance. But the world order,
as it was established after 1945 and thereafter symbolized in the "cold war," has withstood them all with
what to many may seem a rather remarkable degree of
toughness.

Accompanying these material conflicts on the world
stage there have been constitutional crises as well. Here
one must include most of the conflicts over disarmament,
which were actually concerned much less with armaments than with the political positions of the great armed
powers. Here one must include the Soviet efforts to convert the U.N. Secretariat to the "troika" principle, the

arguments over U.N. intervention in the Congo and the refusal of the iron-curtain countries (and France) to meet their assessments for the purpose. The long series of conflicts over the status of West Berlin and the threats to the Western position there were really constitutional in nature; and so, one should perhaps add, is the growing power conflict between Moscow and Peking. In 1964 it was impossible to foresee the end of these issues, but they seemed to be working out toward a world system, or constitution, that would allow for both the continued ideological division of the globe and its effective demilitarization.

But if it was Korea that began to step the cold war down to the less dangerous levels of the "hot peace," it is in Cuba that the lineaments of "coexistence" seem most clearly to have appeared. They may not be pleasant, and it may seem odd to advance the Cuban case, where warlike threat and military mobilizations have so often filled the air, as a foundation for nonmilitary coexistence; yet the contention can be made. In the seemingly most dangerous of the crises—that over the Soviet missiles in October, 1962—there was no actual resort to arms, either thermonuclear or conventional, while it ended, as all such crises must in a world demilitarized, in "peace without victory" for any one of the three major participants. It is significant that the successful surmounting of the missile crisis was followed by the achievement of the partial thermonuclear test ban. As a concrete step toward disarmament, this treaty was a very small achievement; but its significance was great in that it was the first instance—at least since the Washington naval treaty of the early 1920's—in which even a small measure of

arms control was attainable, not through a precise balancing of the military strengths and hazards, but through
a recognition that in this particular context the military
factors were irrelevant. The United States was willing to
abandon its insistence on inspection for underground
tests because the possible military advantages to be
gained by "cheating" were so small as to be negligible
beside the political advantages of the treaty; the Soviet
Union was willing to abandon its insistence that any nuclear treaty must be total because the weaponry itself
offered an insufficient leverage to obtain so revolutionary a consummation. Extreme arguments were advanced
in the United States to show the perils to military security
to which the unpoliced underground test ban could conceivably lead. The Kennedy Administration wisely disregarded them, as Khrushchev disregarded the vociferous
Chinese objections on the same order. The missile crisis
revealed the real inutility of the weaponry in practical
international politics; the partial test ban was a first,
tentative, application of the lesson.

Cuba has, however, had a good many more implications. Tad Szulc observes:

> The explosion whose successive shock waves
> staggered Latin America was the victory of Fidel
> Castro's revolution on January 1, 1959. The col-
> lapse and disappearance of the Batista dictatorship
> fulfilled the political revolution . . . but without
> stopping to catch a breath, Castro plunged into a
> social revolution of a violence and thoroughness
> never seen before in Latin America. In fact, it was
> the most rapid, radical and complete revolution to

occur in the world since the Communists had taken over China, ten years earlier.[9]

The revolution had other striking characteristics. Since the original Bolshevik seizure of power in 1917, all Communist revolutions had been the direct outgrowths of war, of war situations, of military occupations, until this one. In 1958 there was no international war in Cuba (as there was in China during the long and bloody rise of Mao Tse-tung to power); the Cuban revolution was certainly not made by the Red Army, nor even by the Cuban Communists and the Communist infiltrators, who were a minority in the Castro ranks. It was not the Communists who took over Castro, but Castro who, for his own political and demagogic ends, took over the Communists—a turn that seems nowhere else to have happened, except possibly in Yugoslavia. (There are now evidences of it, on a much smaller scale, in Africa.) The process was quite contrary to the established cold-war concept of a Moscow-directed infiltrative drive "to conquer the world" and at many points has seemed to cause as many headaches for the strategists in the Kremlin as for those in the White House and the Pentagon.

It seems quite possible that it was, at bottom, Castro who blackmailed the missile weapons out of the Kremlin; and that they were sent, to begin with, more in response to the internal difficulties of the Soviet system than to the requirements of its external political-military relations with the West. It is, at least, difficult to explain their withdrawal on any other grounds. The point is that the Castro revolution was not a typical Communist "seizure

9 Tad Szulc, *The Winds of Revolution* (Praeger, 1963), p. 118.

of power" but was a genuine revolution, feeding on the forces from below rather than on those imposed from the top, representing one possible kind of response to the basic political, social and economic revolution that is irreversibly sweeping the world. But as such it presents problems, not only to the heirs of the American and French revolutions, but also to those of the long-completed Bolshevik revolution in Russia. Nor is what happened in Cuba the only possible response. Szulc thinks it quite possible that Castro's revolution will "never find imitators" even in Latin America. Russian-dominated Communism is by no means the sole answer. There is Nasser socialism; there are the beginnings made by Perónism in the Argentine; there are the military dictatorships, arising under officers drawn from the generally liberal middle classes rather than from the aristocratic and reactionary elites of the past. The United States has already passed the point at which it can condemn military dictatorship as in itself bad—America has relied on too many military dictators in too many situations in which they appeared to offer the only alternative to chaos. When the political parties fail in their responsibilities to freedom and justice, the disciplined cadres of the army often remain as the sole focus around which a viable national life can be reconstructed.

The possibilities are endless. They are certainly far too various and complex to be contained within the barren frame of a "cold war" between the United States and the Soviet Union, with "victory" going to the winner. There is no longer any "victory," but only a difficult political process, in which organized war has retired into the background, from which no one—neither Communists nor democrats—is certain to emerge with complete success but out of which a demilitarized world politics appears to be emerging.

In 1964 we had before us the picture of two giant states, each in varying degrees of difficulty with its allies and supporters, each armed with a colossal weaponry that neither either wished, intended or even dared to employ, but each resolved to maintain its own security, its own power and prestige position in the global order by all means "short of war" available to it. Neither seriously believes that it can independently "dominate" a world order that holds many pitfalls and difficulties for each; but neither will passively yield such domination to the other or refrain from taking any casual opportunity that may offer to improve its own power position. The post-1945 world has afforded each a wide range of maneuver short of war to attain these ends (including the display, though not the employment, of the giant weapons systems); and each has maneuvered politically, peripherally and vicariously to influence history in directions favorable to it. In the missile crisis, however, they at last came, if not "eyeball to eyeball," at least face to face. For such a situation there could be but one of two outcomes: either a full-scale war or "peace without victory." The missile crisis, like the Korean War, was resolved in a peace without victory. There has been no final solution for anyone, not even Castro. But the situation, in remaining fluid, remains manageable. That the world order attained by the end of 1964 is a type of order that makes peace without victory possible in a situation such as this attests to its toughness and very considerable degree of viability.

So far as this book is concerned, history reaches its conclusion at the end of 1964. One must turn to the future to ask what it may be possible to build upon it.

FOUR

THE LANGUAGE

A MAJOR DIFFICULTY CONFRONTING ANY SOCIAL, historical or economic analysis resides in the fact that any social or cultural system, great or small, is always a product both of experience and of the ways in which that experience is perceived. In this respect the international order is no different from any lesser one. At any given point in its development it is always a product, not only of the previous history, but also of men's apperceptions of that history; it has unquestionably grown out of the "facts" of human experience, but it is more significantly shaped by the ways in which men see, think about and talk about those facts and by the concepts of "language" in which they state their "lessons" and seek to apply them as guides to policy and action.

It is for this reason that every generation must, as it has been said, rewrite history for itself. It is not so much the "facts" that are rewritten (though later research may always bring to light factual material unknown to earlier historians) as it is the way in which the facts are perceived. In the light of later insight, even more than of later knowledge, the previous generation's history becomes, not so much "wrong" or mistaken, as unusable for present purposes. It emphasizes events that no longer seem significant; it neglects factual materials which to the eye of the new generation seem of primary relevance. The language in which the older history speaks seems not even to refer to the kind of problem for which the new generation seeks guidance from experience. In the end, the new generation rewrites its own history into forms not necessarily any more "true" than the old, but more usable for its own ends. Westerners look with contempt upon the efficiency with which this process is carried out in totalitarian societies; nor can one condone the deliberate distortion of history into propaganda in Moscow any more than on Madison Avenue. The Western historian cannot escape, any more than the Communist, the necessity for rearranging the infinitely variable and complicated data of the past into forms suitable to his own purposes and the purposes of his times. Each generation must make its own translation of the vast and obscure record into language intelligible to it.

A knowledge of the history of the present international order would seem indispensable to any useful discussion of it; consequently the preceding chapters have been devoted to a preliminary historical survey, trying to give a condensed account of the history, or experience, available to us since the rise of the modern nation-state. No doubt many will object to this version as distorted or misleading, but not, I think, on the ground that anything in it is factually wrong. Objection will all come down in one way or another to a contention that the conceptual system, or "language," in which the record is reviewed is imperfect or inadmissible. Factors of great significance, it will be said, have been neglected; others of little relevance have been magnified. Concepts—such as that of power, for example—have been loosely loaded with unacceptable content; others, such as that of "Communism," have been recklessly stripped of the connotative baggage they ordinarily carry. But all this is not to say that the history itself is mistaken; it charges only that the *ideas about it,* the language in which it is here read and reported, are mistaken. Such charges may be sustainable; the argument here is not as to their validity but as to their nature, their gravamen. They focus attention upon the overwhelming importance to the discussion of the language, the conceptual systems, in which it is carried on.

Since the history has been reviewed only as a basis for further analysis, it is unavoidably reviewed or rewritten in a language usable to us who are its present heirs. And it will be, again unavoidably, objectionable to those dominated by older conceptual systems, just as the Copernican cosmology was long (and by no means irrationally) resisted by those accustomed to the geocentric view of the universe. The way in which the experience of the cold war has here been reviewed may have no more final or absolute validity than a number of other ways. It does claim to present a system of ideas or concepts that are more practically applicable than many established conceptual systems to the problems of our times.

One cannot escape the fact that most of the language commonly used in the current discussion of international affairs is essentially worthless for our purposes. We can understand readily enough that when a Communist statesman sees international politics exclusively in terms of capitalistic ruling classes being driven by ineluctable historic-economic forces into aggressive imperialistic war upon all "peace-loving" and "socialist" peoples he is using notions without applicable content. It is more difficult to see the defects in our own conceptual systems. Yet again and again we find ourselves involved by our language in seemingly unanswerable paradox and insoluble dilemma. For three quarters of a century, to take the most obvious example, statesmen of all ideologies have stood baffled before the great paradox of disarmament. Disarmament is impossible without prior adjustment of the political and power issues that are expressed by the arms; but adjustment of the political and power issues is impossible without prior abolition of the armaments out of which in great measure they arise. The dilemma is of long standing. And since no approach to an answer for it has ever been found, one cannot help feeling that it is a conceptual difficulty, rather than one springing from some deep inconsistency in the nature of human social organization. We are not being driven to our own destruction by some inexplicable and inescapable Fate, but by our faulty apperceptions—the defective language—in which we try to understand the realities of the international system.

This primary importance of the language, of the way things seem to us rather than of the way they are, can be illustrated in many ways. In the days of the great depression we stood baffled and helpless before the paradox of "want in the midst of plenty," which Fate, or "something inexplicable" in the total system, had apparently presented to us. But the paradox itself was conceptual; it could have been dissolved by closer analysis of what was really meant *in this particular context* by the notions of "want" and "plenty." And the dissipation of the over-all paradox in this way would have brought to light the host of subordinate conceptual dilemmas—like those involved in our notions of what was appropriate to governmental and to private action —that seemed to render the over-all paradox insoluble. It was not, in fact, insoluble, any more, one suspects, than is the armaments paradox; but it was not resolved until countless philosophers and administrators, from John Maynard Keynes to Franklin Roosevelt, had sufficiently succeeded in modifying the established conceptual systems to make resolution possible.

A somewhat different example is afforded by the terminology of the cold war. It is all but universally accepted that the period between 1871 and 1914 was a period of European "peace"; it is equally accepted that the period since 1945 has been, in Europe and in the now enlarged global system, a period of "war." Yet it is difficult to see in what way the one period differed from the other. The topography of the power structures, alliance systems and so on altered, but the topology was the same. The mechanics of competitive armament, military threat, diplomatic power plays, "indirect aggression," the use of ideological conflict for political and power ends would seem to have been more or less invariant from one period to the other. If what has been going on since 1945 is "war," so was what went on after 1871; if the condition after 1871 was one of "peace," so is the condition obtaining since 1945. It may be said that

the name given to either is irrelevant. This statement
would be true—except that the terminology itself exer-
cises so powerful a determination. The invention of the
phrase "cold war" was to give a warlike cast to everything that followed; and under the spell of the words,
men, groups and nations have reacted to situations and
events since 1945 in ways rather markedly different
from those in which they reacted to closely similar events
and situations after 1871. It is not the external "facts"
that have changed, but our ways of looking at them and
the language in which we discuss them.[1]

One could multiply indefinitely the paradoxes and dilemmas presented in this way by contemporary international politics. They arise out of the conceptual framework commonly applied to them; and "there is no way,"
as Anatol Rapoport has observed, "to resolve a genuine
dilemma within the conceptual framework in which
it arose." Most of the major international problems—of
war, of disarmament, of freedom for small nations or for
minorities within the greater ones, of adequate economic
opportunity for the underdeveloped—are of this char-

[1] One could draw some parallels, not too far-fetched, between the
Boer War of 1899 and the Korean War of 1950. In both, a major power
found itself involved with a minor power in a peripheral theater, not
primarily because of the economic or other concrete "interests" at stake
in the theater, but in defense of its power position on the global stage.
The German Kaiser's intervention with the celebrated "Kruger telegram" represented an impulse to exploit the local problem to Britain's
global disadvantage, much as Stalin's support of the North Koreans
seems to have been an attempt to exploit the local situation to the
global disadvantage of the United States. By 1950 matters had become
much more brutal and bloody than they were in the more gentlemanly
atmospheres of 1899, but it is not clear that this represented any substantive change. The point is that because of the differing conceptual systems, no one regarded the Kruger telegram as the declaration of war that
it later, one might say, turned out to have been; while everybody regarded the North Korean attack as the declaration of a general war that
has not occurred and, one hopes, never will.

acter. In *the terms in which they are stated* they are insoluble, in a sense as precise as that in which we say that the problem of squaring the circle can, demonstrably, have no answer. A question for which there is no possible answer is a question without meaning. The hackneyed example, "Have you stopped beating your wife?" is unanswerable because it has no meaning to begin with. The difficulties it seems to present are unreal because they arise out of a confusion of incompatible conceptual systems and concealed assumptions.

Genuine dilemmas of this kind in socio-political life can, as Rapoport says, be dealt with in at least three ways: they can be ignored (as most people today simply ignore the implications of the nuclear arsenals); they can somehow be compromised (as the advocates of "arms control" look for a compromise that will suspend the issue without settling it—they will emphatically declare that they have stopped beating their wives because they never started, a position that is logically flawed); or they can be "won" by brute force (as advocates of preventive war would "win" the armaments issue) without thereby in any way overcoming the underlying dilemma. The dilemma can be dealt with in these ways; but it can only be resolved by "a critical re-examination of the modes of thought which had led to the dilemma in the first place." Speaking (in 1961) of the test-ban negotiations in the stage they had then reached, Rapoport remarks that "the strategic recommendation, i.e., to resume testing, is obviously bad even though strategically irreproachable, because it leads to an outcome that is bad for both parties. The inescapable conclusion is that strategic thinking simply cannot cope with situations of the sort described." It is "irrelevant to the solution of our dilemma." [2] Like most of the other "modes of thought" we apply to international problems, it is not so much wrong as useless; it gets us nowhere, but rather commits us simply to vicious circles from which there is no exit.

If this is the only result to which the language, the conceptual systems, we apply to international politics can lead, then it seems essential that we change the conceptual systems, since—difficult though that may be—it is not so difficult as changing the basic mechanics of the political system. Beginning with the Hague Permanent Court of Arbitration, and going down through Wilson's Covenant of the League of Nations, the Kellogg-Briand Pact to outlaw war, the Charter of the United Nations, its later amendment to put "peace-keeping" authority in the General Assembly, the plans for further amendments such as that of Clark and Sohn for "world peace through world law," the approach by way of the mechanics of international order has been unfruitful. The same cannot be said of the approach by way of the ideology, the conceptual systems, underlying the mechanics. Both Khrushchev and Kennedy addressed the international problem in terms that would have been somewhat foreign to Stalin or Truman; they tended to modify old and cherished concepts that no longer seem applicable to present contexts. Pope John XXIII was speaking of the international problem, at the time of his death, in language that Pius XII did not use and might not fully have understood; the great reverence accorded not only by the Catholic but also by the non-Catholic world to Pope

[2] Anatol Rapoport, "New Logic for the Test Ban," *The Nation*, April 1, 1961.

John reflected a feeling that here was a man who had "said" something; he had intervened, not in the mechanics of the world order (as many of the politically powerful among his predecessors had done), but in the language, the conceptual system, in which the world order was being conducted. The language not only can, but does, change. It is true that if we are to escape our great international dilemmas the changes in the conceptual systems out of which they arise will have to be much more far-reaching. But even that is not as impossible as it often seems.

The language in which contemporary international relations are conducted and discussed is open at nearly every point to devastating criticism, which it is certain increasingly to receive. As an explanation of the international order and a means of dealing with it, it is hardly better than the mythologies invented by the ancients to explain and deal with the natural order. Indeed, it rather strikingly resembles them. It has created a new Olympus (called, curiously enough, "the summit") and peopled it with the greater and lesser deities of the nation-states. There they war with each other—usually, like their Olympian prototypes, for the most disreputable of reasons. They fling their thunderbolts against one another, and incidentally on the hapless humanity that serves them, by a caprice that ordinary mortals cannot hope to understand or control. At best these gods may be placated; and by offering them the propitiatory sacrifice of devoted patriotism and colossal arms expenditures, by standing ready to offer the human sacrifice of millions of battle dead, their vagaries may be somewhat restrained. But this is uncertain; the conceptual system itself is ill-adapted to the understanding and control of the international order.

For want of any better models, the ancients not unnaturally endowed their gods and goddesses with the attributes of men; they were motivated, like men, by greed, ambitions, sexual desire, jealousy, self-defense. Because we have lacked the wit (and we are only beginning to acquire the knowledge) to devise more workable explanations, our modern pantheon is similarly anthropomorphic. The nation-gods war with each other for motives of greed ("economic interest"), aggrandizement ("conquest"), jealousy ("prestige") and self-defense ("national security" or "protection of the national interest"). It may be a little difficult to work the sexual motif into the nation-state scenario, but even that is not wholly impossible, as is evidenced by the legendary material from Helen of Troy or Cleopatra down to Mata Hari or Christine Keeler and John Profumo. But while such concepts of the "causes" of war and motivations of states dominate the general discussion, no careful study of the origins of any modern war finds them applicable to the problem or is able to make much use of them. The modern international mythology is not only increasingly involving us in insoluble dilemmas; it is also increasingly failing to fit observable facts. Such is the beginning of the end for any conceptual system, foreshadowing its replacement by another and more workable one.

Men must always, no doubt, live by myth systems—and perhaps any conceptual system may be so described, since it is never more than a statement of our apperceptions of reality, rather than a description of reality itself. But the working myth systems have to be both useful and persuasive. The mythology of contemporary international relations is neither, and it is thus laying itself open to more and more destructive attack. The ancient pantheons, fantastic as they may seem to us, were just as logical—indeed, unavoidable—by the light of the knowledge and concepts available to their creators as are our modern notions of "perpetual conflict" and inevitable thermonuclear war. Once established, they were supported (as is the modern war system) by masses of seemingly incontrovertible evidence gradually accumulated by their high priests and professors. Yet they fell in the end under the weight of the shocking moral and practical dilemmas to which they led, to be replaced by monotheistic concepts that were both much more believable and far superior as means of meeting the emotional and spiritual needs of human society. That the basic concept of the One World may develop in much the same way as did that of the One God does not seem to be a totally absurd prediction.

Conceptual systems do change as the insoluble dilemmas to which they lead are recognized and as improved knowledge reveals their inconsistency with observable experience. An even more apposite example can be found in the fate of the crystalline spheres that once propelled the heavenly bodies in their orbits around the earth. These again seem to us a very odd notion; we forget that they were originally not only a logical but an *inescapable* deduction from the known data and the available concepts.[3] They ultimately collapsed because

---

[3] The ancients had no concepts of "action at a distance" or "fields of force"; force was to them physical force imparting motion to solid, tangible objects. The heavenly bodies moved, apparently in circles; there must be something imparting this motion to them, as the bowstring im-

of the accumulation of observable inconsistencies they produced and because a series of great scientists culminating in Newton developed new concepts of force, mass and motion that allowed the spheres to be laid aside and that provided a far more consistent, useful and productive view of the universe. Equipped with this new view, science and technology advanced with giant strides to their staggering achievements in the nineteenth and twentieth centuries.

It is at least suggestive that the Newtonian achievement rested basically upon its revision of the once established concepts of physical "force," for in our modern international mythology "force" (usually thought of as armed force) is one of the central as well as one of the most baffling and inapplicable of the controlling concepts. It is constantly involving us in seemingly insoluble dilemmas of the kind discussed above. There is, for example, one very familiar problem: The maintenance of order always rests ultimately on the presence of a superior coercive "force" of some kind; it follows that to maintain international peace there must be a supranational "force" capable of coercing the recalcitrant; yet the employment of this peace-keeping force can only lead, under our established systems of ideas, to the war

---

parted motion to an arrow; since they moved in circles the moving element must be circular or spherical in shape, and since it was undetectable it must be crystalline or transparent in structure. The notion of concentric, crystalline spheres was the only one that met all the observed data. Its foundations were as intellectually respectable as those on which eighteenth-century physicists erected the "luminiferous ether," which had to be postulated since nothing else seemed to meet the observed facts. The luminiferous ether had a far briefer, more inglorious, history than the crystalline spheres, but both were overthrown in the same way —through the development of conceptual systems that rendered them no longer *necessary*.

which it is its business to prevent. This paradox, more than anything else, was the rock on which Woodrow Wilson's battle for Article X, "the heart" of the Covenant of the League of Nations, foundered. Wilson, for his part, escaped it no more successfully than did his opponents. Neither was "right"; nor could the most exhaustive restudy and remeasurement of the experiential data —restudies, say, of the effects of the actual employment of armed force in international affairs—decide between them, so long as the underlying conceptual system remained unchanged.

In the Newtonian era it was not the observational data that were rewritten, though they were, of course, continuously being reduced to more precise measurement and statement; it was the way in which men found it possible to look at them. Improved observation, more precise and sophisticated historical or economic research, usually serves only to buttress and confirm the conceptual system in the light of which it has been undertaken until, sometimes quite dramatically, it opens the possibility, even the necessity, of looking at the whole problem in a new way. Then advance becomes possible, often rapid and far-reaching. Then the older conceptual systems are ultimately doomed, even though those brought up to these ways of thinking may fight long and desperate battles in their behalf. The experience is so common in history as to leave no grounds to suppose that it will not happen in regard to the "insoluble" problems of international relations as it has happened in regard to so many of the "insoluble" problems of the past.[4]

---

[4] The experience is symbolized for us in a number of great names: Newton, Marx, Darwin, Freud, Keynes, Einstein. None of these men produced "final" truths; all were bitterly attacked by contemporaries, not

Processes of this kind begin, I think, in the observed deficiencies of the vocabulary. The ancient Greek philosopher would have had difficulty in understanding a thermonuclear bomb because his vocabulary would have been unequal to the task. Our difficulties in understanding and controlling the international system are of a similar kind. We do not have the words in which to discuss experiences that force themselves upon us; as a result, we use older and unserviceable words and ideas, emotional tags and conventional misrepresentations of past history, and so we fall into utter confusion. A good illustration would seem to be the problem of a "nuclear force for NATO." What this phrase means is completely lost in the inadequacy of the words. One can, of course, understand that in a general way a going international "force," such as NATO is supposed to be, must have its "own" nuclear "capability." Beyond this visible headland, an impenetrable fog shuts down, compounded of the rival political aims of France, Germany, Britain and Italy; of the total uncertainty as to what nuclear forces are good for or how they can be fitted into a working pattern of international politics; of the American desire to control the deployment of the weaponry, which the other nations are demanding precisely because they resent American control; as well as of technical complications that indicate that the "mixed crew" force of surface ships

infrequently on grounds that were later to seem well-based, and their contributions have been modified by later students. What each did—and this much has not been modified—was to open the way to essentially new ways of thinking about old familiar facts of experience. That someone of similar stature will arise in the area of international relations may seem a great deal to hope, yet we have already seen his prototype— in Norman Angell or Ivan Bloch—and the hope is undoubtedly sustained by history.

carrying nuclear weapons, as proposed by the United States as a solution for the political difficulties, is militarily as well as politically impracticable. It is all much like the old argument over a European Common Army (ECA), which in the end proved incapable of meeting either the military or the political requirements of the situation to which American theorists sought to apply it. It may be possible to patch up the technology of the mixed-crew nuclear surface naval force; but there is still the political difficulty represented by the Soviet Union's insistence that any Western policy that places nuclear weaponry in German hands will be regarded as an unfriendly act and as such may destroy all the political and military advantages that the mixed-crew NATO fleet was designed to provide. Hamstrung by an unsuitable vocabulary, the Kennedy-Johnson Administration did not give up; and in early 1965 it seemed possible that a NATO nuclear force might ultimately emerge. But with the French and the growing British insurgence, with Graeco-Turkish relations coming to a critical point over Cyprus, NATO itself appeared likely to undergo transformations to which the existence or nonexistence of a nuclear-armed surface fleet was more or less irrelevant. The vocabulary of international relations had simply failed to provide (by early 1965) a solution for the dilemma of "a nuclear force for NATO."

There are numerous words, constantly employed in diplomatic as well as popular discussions of international affairs, that are almost if not quite devoid of operable meaning. Everyone has heard about the difficulty of talking with the Russians because they use such standard words as "democracy," "freedom," "aggression" in opposite senses to those in which the West employs them. But this difficulty is a simple semantic one. The trouble resides in the fact that the words really have no meaning at all, regardless of which side may be using them. It is harder for a Western democrat to define what he means by "democracy" than it is for a Russian. The words are like battleflags, valuable emotional symbols, but no more useful than the design on the flag as tools for the understanding of international politics.

But if such words as "democracy"—which appears in practice to be defined as what the West has and the Russians don't, or vice versa—are unhelpful, so in a deeper sense are other words, going to the heart of the international process, which the Americans and the Russians, or the Chinese or Western Europeans, all use in the same way but with an equal lack of operable content. These are the great words that enshrine the international mythology, the conceptual system in which international relations are conducted, to which all respond in essentially the same way and to which few, if any, have attempted to attach a working meaning.

They are such words as "force," which has been discussed above. We constantly talk about "the forces" operative in the international system and the use of "force" within it, although we do not know what we mean by the term in either sense. They are such words as "power"; the entire scenario revolves around this concept: the actors are "the powers," engaged in "the struggle for power," limited by "the balance of power" or driven by the rise or decline of their relative "power." Yet there is no usable or agreed definition of "power" itself. The notion carries innumerable different connotations in differing contexts, without the user's ever explaining (even, or especially, to himself) with what particular connotations he is loading it.[5] They are such words as "law." We commonly think of a state of "law and order" as the antithesis of a state of violence; to have a peaceful, nonviolent international order, we must therefore institute a system of international "law." That this is a simplistic definition of law should be obvious from the long tale of history, in which very advanced systems of law have coexisted with extremes of violence. Our concepts of the actual functions of "law," in the international as in domestic systems, demand revision.

There are other great operative words of the same kind that call for re-examination. The notion of "national security," for example, seems one of the most obvious and unassailable in our conceptual system; but when the pursuit of national security promises the possible, even probable, death of three quarters of our population, the destruction of the ecology and of a large part of our technological equipment, the whole concept is brought in question. The concept of "the national interest"—which must at all costs be defended—is in somewhat the same category. The notion of "aggression" has been embedded in existing international law as the one unpardonable international sin. But no one has ever been able adequately to define the crime. There is an almost total vagueness as to what does or does not constitute "aggression"; and while the concept has undoubtedly been helpful in the regulation of international politics, it has seldom had much practical application.

[5] The problem of "power" and its meanings is so critical that it will be necessary to return to it in greater detail. See Chapter Five.

There is still another notion, not quite in the same class as the foregoing perhaps, but possibly even more basic to the whole of our contemporary international mythology. It is the notion that there must be ascertainable (and therefore remediable) "causes of war." In every aspect of our daily lives, cause and effect are immediately linked (if one wakes up with a hangover, it is *because* he drank too much the night before); and, faced with such shattering effects as those of a major war, it is only natural to look for the "causes" that produced it. Many acres of good paper have been wasted upon the search for the causes of war by those who never realized that the causal relationship may simply not offer a serviceable concept in dealing with the phenomena under consideration. A century after the end of the American Civil War there is no agreement among its historians as to the "causes" that produced it. There is rather a tendency to dispense with the notion of "cause" altogether and to recast the conceptual system into one much more indeterminate—a system concerned not with fixed "causes" but with elusive parameters enclosing many variables of chance, conflict, probability, in which the outcome, the war itself, is the only determinable fact.

This difficulty over "causes" suggests another one. We are virtually compelled by our conceptual system to personify the nation-states, as the ancients were compelled to personify the forces of nature, and for the same reason. The paucity of our language of international politics makes it too hard to deal with them in any other way. We know very well that such complex socio-political entities as "the United States," "Russia," "India," "Ghana" and so on, though creations of men, are not in fact simply superindividuals; but we are forced by the language to treat them *as if* they were, without realizing how misleading such a process can be. We assign to the nations the motivations of individuals; we try to regulate or predict their behavior on the assumption that their acts are "caused" as are the acts of an individual person, only to find that a nation is not in fact a person, that it is not motivated and does not behave in the same way as an individual person.

One repeatedly encounters national policies designed —quite rationally, it would seem—to influence the behavior of another nation that collapse upon the fact that nations do not behave like persons. If we extend foreign aid, we expect of the recipient a certain amount of gratitude and a certain willingness to identify its interests with our own, as we would in the case of a neighbor whom we might befriend. We are astonished when this does not happen. The foreign aid becomes a right, not a benefice (in early 1964 Panama accused the United States of "aggression" before the Organization of American States, in part because America had suspended aid payments), and our claim to the recipient's support in international politics does not run one iota beyond its own calculation of the advantages to be derived in the international political drama from our support. Miscalculations of the opposite kind are no less frequent. The American attempt to achieve the economic isolation of Cuba makes no sense except on the theory that by destroying the ability of the Castro regime to feed and clothe the "Cuban people," the latter can be goaded into destroying the Castro regime. Such a course has been tried over and over again in international politics, and it has never worked. It is possible to control an individual by isolating him from all sources of economic support except those one may command; with a nation, this action is not effective. In Cuba today, as many times before, the only result is to consolidate the people behind the dictator; while the nation—a highly compound animal with many tentacles throughout the world—can find many ways of surviving not open to an individual. With a nation one is not dealing with a person, and cause-and-effect relationships derived from the study of behavioral psychology are seldom applicable.

A common response to such difficulties is to try to break down the concept of the "nation" into hopefully more manageable sub-elements—such as the "government," the "ruling classes," the "workers," the "people," the "masses" and so on. Thus Woodrow Wilson went to war against the Imperial German Government alone, explicitly excluding the "German people." Thus the Soviet Union has enlarged its power at the expense only of "fascists," "capitalists," "imperialists" or "aggressors," and never, in theory, at the expense of the "workers" or the "masses." It was seriously expected that the "workers" everywhere would, like Wilson's "German people," arise and assist in their own liberation—or subjugation, according to the point of view. But they did not. The drama, from 1918 down to such complicated affairs as were going on in early 1965 in Vietnam, has never fitted the scenario. The actors have consistently failed to speak the lines that the conventional language of international politics required of them. The sub-elements, as they were conceived, were as anthropomorphic and mislead-

ing as the nation-state concept itself. They were, moreover, subtly interrelated with each other and with the concept of the nation in ways the vocabulary could not take
into account. So far from improving the language of international politics, this refinement of the concept has
reduced it to more complete confusion.

One needs only to look dispassionately at almost any
important international crisis to realize how inadequate
and inapplicable is the language employed. In 1914 the
common picture of a "little Serbia" heroically resisting
the brutal and unprovoked assault of the Austro-Hun-
gary giant materially affected events. It has taken much
subsequent reflection and research to reveal how completely this picture was at variance with the actual processes and motivations involved. It is true that in the days
of formal warfare among the organized nation-states the
great anthropomorphic entities—"France," "Germany"
and the rest—were reasonably serviceable conceptual devices. In the post-1945 era, when "indirect aggression,"
guerilla and political warfare have become the chief ve-
hicles of international conflict, we are beginning to realize
how far these gross concepts fail before the true intricacies
of international politics.

In the 1956 Hungarian crisis, for example, the conventional Western scenario presents the "Hungarian people" rising against Communist brutality and oppression;
momentarily successful, they are bloodily put down by
Russia's tank divisions and so are returned to bondage.
The Soviet scenario, needless to say, differs from this
picture in every essential. The point is not that one is
right and the other wrong; the point is that *neither* is an
adequate or practically useful description of what took

place. Both versions are poetry—as are our accounts of the siege of ancient Troy—appropriate to their poetic and emotional purpose, but without validity for analysis or prediction. It was not the "Hungarian people" who rose in revolt, but a fraction—perhaps only a small fraction—of the inhabitants of that state; their revolt was not a counterrevolution against Communism—most of the rebels seem to have been more or less convinced Communists, and there was certainly no question of restoring an *ancien régime*—but rather a revolt by Magyar nationalism against Slav (Russian) domination; the Soviet tank columns restored order—in other words, restored a *status quo ante*—but to describe this as a "re-enslavement of a people" is pure poetic metaphor. Some Hungarians no doubt felt themselves again in bondage; others felt themselves released from turmoil and destruction; what the "Hungarian people" felt there is no way of knowing, since there is no way of consulting so elusive an entity.

The language employed in the Hungarian crisis of 1956 was as misleading and unserviceable as that employed in the Austro-Serbian crisis of 1914; but experience has taught us much since 1914. The old conceptual systems are no longer persuasive, and this lack of conviction may be the main reason why policies based on the old concepts fell so flat in 1956. The West should have come to the rescue of the "Hungarian people," but it very carefully refrained from doing so. The West should have been able to turn Hungary into a powerful offset to its own fiasco in Suez; it tried to do this and was a bit bewildered by the fact that so few paid any attention. Many in the West emerged from the Hungarian episode with a bad conscience; but this was a consequence, not of the complicated and brutal realities in that situation, but of the language and conceptual systems they were applying to it.

As we advance into even more complicated issues in international politics—such as those presented by the rise of Nasser's Egypt, of the many African succession states, of Castro's Cuba—we become more and more conscious of the utter inadequacy of the language and the concepts we have to deal with them. It is surely almost grotesque to attempt to describe a situation like that in Algeria as a "war" between "France" and the "Algerian people"— there were too many and various conflicting interests involved; there were too few regular military operations, while the gruesome terrorism that largely substituted for them was not what is usually thought of as "war." The highly complicated situation in which we are involved in Vietnam (in early 1965) had never been intelligibly reported in the United States, largely because of the inadequacy of the language and the concepts available.

Indeed, our involvement may be said to have begun in a conceptual failure. As the end of World War II approached, Franklin Roosevelt was convinced that "France has had Indo-China for nearly one hundred years, and the people are worse off than they were at the beginning. . . . France has milked it for one hundred years. The people of Indo-China are entitled to something better than that." The French consequently should not be allowed to return after the expulsion of the Japanese.[6] Aside from the factual error (the French had exercised control for no more than half a century),

6 Bernard B. Fall, *The Two Viet-Nams* (Praeger, 1963), p. 27.

the conceptual system here was simply inapplicable to the problems of Indochina; it led Roosevelt into the wholly impracticable proposal of a trusteeship in which both China and Russia were to have prominent parts and diverted American policy into courses which, more than anything else, gave Ho Chi-minh, the hard-core Communist leader of North Vietnam, his chance. Roosevelt's ideas of this tangled situation were totally at variance with the realities and were consequently inoperable. The proposed trusteeship was a fantasy impossible of realization; the French in fact returned—there was no workable alternative—but with their authority so undermined that ten years later it had collapsed; it would be hard to demonstrate that the twenty years of violent and bloody political warfare which ensued brought the Indochinese peoples (there were several, not one) anything "better" than they had known before. This is not to say that what they experienced was "worse." Such a judgment would call for a computation of incompatibles and incalculables into which I would not wish to enter. The argument is that if Roosevelt, and the other leaders as well, had commanded a conceptual system better adjusted to the human, social and political realities in the Indochina of 1945, an enormous amount of misery, as well as an enormous amount of international political difference and difficulty, might well have been averted.

Here, as in many another international crisis, we simply cannot apply the concept of the anthropomorphic god-states, advancing upon one another like pugilists with "victory" or "the knock-out blow," as the final answer to all the issues involved. Here, rather, is the far more intricate pattern of violence as it now appears in contemporary international politics. It is by no means new in the world. But, steeped as we are in the traditions of the eighteenth- and nineteenth-century organized war systems, it is new and baffling to us to find it appearing as a central fact in the international power struggle. One is reminded of the fate which overtook Admiral Mahan's theory of "sea power" as the supreme determinant in the affairs of nations. He carried it to the quite logical conclusion that "sea power" rested on the battle fleet "in being," and that the battle fleet was therefore the beginning and end of "power" on the world stage. But the German development of submarine warfare in World War I simply slipped beneath the keels of Mahan's battleships, and those of their descendants that survived are all in "mothballs" now.

We do not have the language, the laws or the conceptual systems adequate to deal with the problems of international violence in the world created by the development of the thermonuclear arsenals. In Vietnam, in Cuba and Latin America, in sub-Saharan Africa and in many other places we are learning how poverty-stricken is our vocabulary for dealing with the actualities of contemporary international life. It must, and undoubtedly will be, improved. There is no hope of advance toward the entirely practicable and realizable visions of a more stable, more peaceful and less bloody world order that are already before our eyes unless and until the underlying conceptual systems we bring to international politics are so modified as to make these visions attainable. As has been suggested, each generation must rewrite the experiential evidence into language intelligible to itself and usable for its own purposes. This is always a gradual and multiple task—one cannot call in a governmental commission, no matter on how high a level, to do it. But it is a job that usually gets itself done. The work is now visibly under way. Pope John XXIII's last encyclical, *Pacem in Terris,* was a major contribution to the task. President Kennedy introduced a new "tone" into American foreign policy not recognizable in the speeches of Truman or Eisenhower. The Russian and Chinese Communist ideologies appear to have fallen afoul of each other, not over specific policy issues, but over this more basic question of remaking the underlying language of international politics. But the issue (if it is the issue) between them of possible "coexistence" or "protracted conflict" represents only the beginning of the essential critical process. We have plenty of advocates among ourselves of "protracted conflict" and should examine their arguments no less critically than the Russians now seem to be examining the arguments of the Chinese. In every specific international crisis, no less than in the larger and more general issues, we should look as closely as possible for the realities behind the excited verbiage; all intelligent and vocal men should ask themselves constantly what the effective factors are, what the words really mean, where our old established concepts of international politics are in fact leading us.

The Bay of Pigs invasion was bungled because it represented essentially an attempt to apply conventional military methods to a highly unconventional military-political situation. The Cuban missile crisis was surmounted basically because of a realization in both Moscow and Washington that the long-range rockets did not carry the unanswerable values attaching to great military systems in the past; the politics was more important than the explosive power. Both Khrushchev and Kennedy tended to talk the old language of military power, but neither acted upon it because neither at bottom any longer believed in its applicability to the concrete situation. The click-beetles emerging afterward from the woodwork imply that they still do; but these are voices out of a past no longer of any practical utility in the present.

If we are to reach an already plainly attainable future, the language of international politics must be revised. There can be really little doubt that this will happen; that the current international mythology will give way, as have so many past mythologies, to one perhaps no more "true," but better suited to human purposes. This process of revision cannot be sudden; it must be slow and continuous, and all thoughtful men must give themselves to the labor. Each new day's headline and its accompanying editorial should be subjected to critical scrutiny; none should feel himself free of the obligation of asking constantly: "What does this story, what does this comment, really mean?" Is the man really saying anything, or is he (to borrow an old parable from H. G. Wells) just another of the wild asses of the devil braying to the moon?

For this revision to proceed, however, it is necessary that men look more carefully than they usually do at two or three of the great central concepts underlying the existing international political system. Two are of primary importance: the notion of "power" and the notion of "law." To these, one may now turn.

FIVE

THE PROBLEM OF POWER

ANYONE INVESTIGATING THE POSSIBILITY OF A DE-
militarized international politics is immediately
confronted with the problem of power. This
concept, as has been said, is central to the whole operation of the existing militarized international political system, and the problem raises the great obstacle before all
hopes of general disarmament. Disputes among nations
over material goods or concrete benefits are subject to
negotiation and, in fact, are usually settled in this way;
but "power" is nonnegotiable, and among sovereign states
power issues, it is argued, can be decided, in the last analysis, only by arms. "International politics," as Hans Morgenthau has observed, "like all politics, is a struggle for
power"; and in a political system composed of sovereign
states "peace can be maintained only by two devices": by
a "balance of power" or by "normative limitations" (in
the form of international law or public opinion) on the
power struggle.[1] The statement seems quite valid under
the presently accepted international mythology and may

[1] Hans J. Morgenthau, *Politics Among Nations* (Knopf, 1961), pp.
27 and 23.

sufficiently sustain Morgenthau's generally pessimistic view of the international future.

Yet it raises many difficulties. What is meant by "power" —or by "peace" either, for that matter? How, in fact, is "power" balanced, if it ever is? Can one legitimately distinguish between the "balance of power" and the "normative limitations" when it is apparent that the state of the balance has much to do with establishing the normative rules, and that the normative rules play an important role in the weighting of the balance? Like so many similar statements of the kind, Morgenthau's seems to leave the concepts of "power," "military force" and "law" in a state of confusion that plainly calls for clarification.

The notion of "power" appears prominently in almost every study of social organization, on every level from the family unit up to the international order. But the idea is usually as vague as it is omnipresent. For the purposes of the present discussion, I have tried to develop some more applicable definitions, or assumptions. It will be apparent that they underlie the historical review attempted in the second and third chapters, where they seemed to supply a useful way of looking at the history. The question is whether they will be equally useful in looking at the future.

For present purposes, then, "power" is defined as "the ability or capacity to influence or determine decision in others." Objection can, of course, be raised to this on various grounds, but I have found no narrower definition that seems to serve. It has the merit that "power," so understood, may equally be military, economic or legal power; it may equally use violent, threatening, suasive or ideological means; it may equally reside in, or be used to influence decision by, individuals, groups, states or nations. With this definition we are at least dealing with the same stuff throughout the whole social spectrum; we are talking about the same phenomenon, however varied its manifestations and effects. The "power" of a father over his children, for example, is of the same kind as the power of the Soviet Union over its satellites; each is a capacity to influence or determine decision in others, though the scenarios in which the "power" appears may differ enormously.

"Politics" is to me the active organization and reorganization of power. In any social order, great or small, the power structures are innumerable and subtly interrelated, ranging from the "pecking order" in a university to the prestige positions of the great armed states on the international stage. It is the basic task of politics to keep them all in some workable relationship. For this task, politics has at its disposal a wide variety of mechanisms, ranging from the absolute of brute violence (war) at one end of the scale to the absolute of a perfect justice (law) at the other. In human societies, of course, neither extreme occurs in a pure form; no political system is wholly controlled by either violence or justice. The politics of the system stands between these two extremes, mediating, as it were, between war and law in the organization and reorganization of the power structures.[2] Political systems vary enormously in their means of carrying out this function. Their politics can be of the most

[2] Politics itself is neither war nor law. In the hackneyed Clausewitzian dictum that "war is a continuation of policy by other means," the accent should fall more often than it does on the word "other." Law, it might be said, is equally a continuation of policy or politics by "other" means. Both war and law, in the present view, are alike instruments of politics.

bloody and savage kind—as lately in the Congo, for example, or in the great crises of the international political system—or they can be of the most law-abiding sort, as in the settled Scandinavian countries. In either case, the politics still consists of the organization and reorganization of the power structures involved.

From such a point of view a "war," or a similar display of brute violence on a lesser scale, becomes an extreme test of the actual power relationships of the parties concerned. "The law" as it may stand at any given point is, similarly, a kind of statement or diagram of the way in which power is organized at that time. Law as a generalized concept is obviously one of the great, creative and controlling forces in human affairs. But in any political system the specific corpus of effective law is always changing in accordance with changing power relationships. It is one of the commonest lessons of experience that the mere enactment of a law is insufficient in itself to organize the power structure. Established law is a reflection of established power relationship; the enactment of any new law will be nugatory unless the power structure has changed or is changing into forms that will support it. While it is not difficult to draft excellent and seemingly quite workable laws for securing general disarmament or world peace or even world prosperity, it has so far proved impossible to secure their adoption because it has been impossible to develop an international organization of power that would sustain them.

But new organizations of power can appear. The breakup (in the summer of 1963) of the persistent log jam over a nuclear test ban was quite clearly related to new concepts of the international power problem in both

Washington and Moscow. The change came at the same time as the open break between China and Russia. This "great dispute," as Edward Crankshaw observed, "which has been in full swing since 1958, is at bottom a quarrel about power." It may be difficult to distinguish the power issues underlying it from the ideological differences in which they have been expressed, but Crankshaw has shown persuasively how the shifting Communist ideologies have responded to changing appreciations of the power structure. When Khrushchev rewrote Lenin with the doctrine of coexistence, he was "bowing to necessity"; for a number of subtle reasons, he had to. But the open split that resulted must either fracture the Communist movement completely or force it to "find a new ideology, more exactly in accordance with the facts of life"—in other words, with the actualities of the international power structure.[3] The achievement of the partial test ban can be regarded as striking evidence of this development. From Washington it was reported at the time that in "official diplomatic talk" there was "increasing speculation that something much more profound [than the test ban] may be happening in the world. . . . Men are beginning to wonder whether the design of the postwar world is being shattered beyond recognition."[4] The speculations may have been gloomy, as they usually are in diplomatic talk, but many will see such a reorganization of the international power structure as having great promise.

The development of an international power politics that will proceed with far less savagery and threat and

[3] Edward Crankshaw, "Two Dogmas Shake the Communist World," *The New York Times Magazine*, July 21, 1963.

[4] Max Frankel, *The New York Times*, July 23, 1963.

far more law in its operation than is now the case does not seem an obvious impossibility. The great obstacle, as has been said, is the "power struggle." "Power," in the sense in which the word is here used, is ultimately non-negotiable because it is an abstract concept, dealing with future possibilities that are unpredictable and with future contingencies that are unforeseeable and therefore cannot be laid on the bargaining tables of the present. It is the deepest impulse of a statesman never to sacrifice his "freedom of action." He is always engaged in withdrawing or modifying or sacrificing his acts, but his "freedom" (or power) to act must, as far as he can manage it, remain inviolate.

It is often said that power in the abstract is a meaningless concept, that power takes on significance only as it is applied to definite ends. This is, I think, to overlook the distinction—so necessary in mechanics—between "kinetic" and "potential" energy. The energy, or power, stored up in the waters behind a hydroelectric dam is a very real quantity, even though for the time being it may remain unused. It is a potential power, applicable by those who command and control it to any one of many different possible ends. The power that is the bone of contention in the power struggle proper is of this kind.

Men, as individuals or organized in groups, communities and nations, have always struggled for power in this sense and doubtless always will. In most social conflicts there seem to be two distinguishable elements, which occur with varying prominence. Normally there is some concrete issue over goods or benefits (or ideologies), but beyond that and often engulfing it entirely there is the power issue, springing from the fact that the way in which the specific dispute is settled will go far toward determining how all future issues will be settled and who will hold control in future settlements. So long as the first element is predominant, the question will usually be capable of resolution by bargaining, collective bargaining or diplomatic negotiation. But as the second, or power, element takes command of the situation, the bargaining will tend to end in individual violence and collective bargaining will break down in a seemingly unavoidable strike, while diplomatic negotiation will tend to collapse in "inevitable" war and disaster.[5]

The struggle over the organization of power is going on continuously on all levels of social life; for most of the world's peoples most of the time, however, it is conducted in an "orderly" fashion, with a minimum of bloodshed. It is commonly said that such is the case because on all levels below the international order there exists government of some kind, legally sovereign and possessing a legal monopoly of armed force, capable of restraining the power struggles over which it has jurisdiction to nonwarlike or nonviolent methods. In this task, government is assisted by the equity and efficiency of its legal and juridical systems. It is the function of the laws and the courts to provide decisions in power issues

---

[5] Hitler, by using the power of his military threat much as a union leader uses the power of his strike threat, was able to negotiate one successful settlement in Europe after another. But as the fact of his successes began to dominate the concrete gains and losses involved in each, the "bargaining" process progressively failed. The British and French, having abandoned positions intrinsically of greater importance to them, finally arrived in Poland at a position which, although they could not defend it militarily, they felt they could not surrender without being reduced to "second class powers." World War II was the result. Earlier chapters have described the process in connection with the Franco-Prussian War and the war with Japan.

that will seem more acceptable to those concerned than the decisions attainable through brute force alone, and so will render the peace-keeping work of the police, the militia and the other armed forces of the state easier than it would otherwise be. It seems plain, in the common view, that the persistence of armed violence on the international stage results from the fact that there is no world government, little world law to govern in international power struggles and no world police to enforce peace—to constrain such struggles to nonmilitary or substantially nonviolent modes of resolution. The conclusion, seemingly as unchallengeable as it is depressing, is that only after a world government, the world police and the body of world law have been created can one hope for a demilitarized world politics.

Yet one suspects that the whole problem is rather more complex than this popular form of analysis suggests. The view raises a number of difficult facts. No political system, even the most just and orderly, has ever excluded violence altogether from its affairs. Murder (a form of violent protest against the power relations established by law and custom) is never wholly eradicable from the most peaceful of societies.[6] The simple existence of a sovereign government, with its legal monopoly of the police power and its judicial and legal system, does not, in fact, prevent resort to violent rebellion, riot or guerilla warfare in any save the most highly organized nations, and not wholly even in them. It is true that some states have confined the domestic power struggle to much less violent means

[6] Lewis F. Richardson, in his curious mathematical treatment, *The Statistics of Deadly Quarrels* (Quadrangle Books, 1960), estimates that between 1820 and 1945 murder caused more violent deaths than any of the wars, with the exception of the two world wars.

than have others; but if, as it is often said, the more peaceful ones are the states with "strong" governments, whereas government in the more turbulent states is "weak," one is forced to further question. What political, social or psychological basis exists on which it would be possible to erect a similarly "strong" government over all the three billion inhabitants of the globe? If the power struggle on the international stage is to be reduced to less lethal forms than it now assumes, there must, it would seem, be some less simple prescription for "strong" global government.

The United States, with the impressive police powers at its disposal and the subtle and intricate system of laws and traditions it has built up, has successfully confined the industrial struggle for power to nonviolent means. Great strikes no longer involve the arson, gunfire and bloodshed that they once did. The country has found a substitute for violence in these struggles, but with all the law available it has not yet found a substitute for force. Collective bargaining will suffice through all the concrete issues of wages and working conditions; but when the naked struggle for power is joined, there seems no resolution except in a strike—a trial of brute force which, if less destructive than a war would be, is still similarly destructive to *all* the interests involved: of management, labor and the public, none of whom can gain anything but a possibly empty power position from the outcome. The international world now finds itself in an approximately identical situation.

In the American industrial conflict there seems to be a tendency toward an impasse for which there is no solution short of confiding to government and its police power the authority to decide the power issue itself. This tendency corresponds to the proffered solution on the international plane of an all-powerful world government, a world court and a world police; and it is about equally unattractive to all the parties involved. On the American industrial stage no one really wants the power issue to be decided by higher authority; all parties would rather that it be left open, under the proviso that actual violence, riot and bloodshed continue to be excluded. The probable result must be a kind of rough compromise between government and the contenders. In the threatened American rail strike in the summer of 1963, for example, collective bargaining finally broke down over a "power issue"—the issue over control of job security involved in the "featherbedding" dispute—and Congress had to exert its own power, not simply to avert bloodshed, but to constrain even the nonviolent power struggle that would have been represented by a great strike. Thus in the end it was government which, claiming an overriding power to avert a strike, enforced terms under which the power issue could be resolved without one. Both unions and management retained their power positions, however, although abandoning the "war" that in theory was the only possible means of settling the power issue.

It is not fantastic to predict that in general the power struggle on the international level will increasingly be handled in an analogous manner. A global government, competent to decide all the innumerable power issues likely to arise among all the innumerable states, communities, associations, corporations and individuals involved in our world order, and capable of enforcing its decisions by the armed might of a global police, seems to me to lie beyond the range of any present possibility. A modicum of world order, not competent to decide basic power issues but capable of insuring that they be decided in the main by nonmilitary and nonviolent means, is a goal more immediately realizable.

The basic argument against world order can, I think, be summarized by saying that on the international stage there is no equivalent for the strike—which, though nonviolent, is still a naked test of force or power, in which the outcome, though not attended by physical violence, is acceptable to the parties concerned. On the international stage, it is said, there is no such final solution and determinant, no such *ultima ratio,* except that provided by organized war and bloodshed. In our definition, "power" is the ability to determine decision in others. In a well-ordered society a union and its members will accept a decision defined by its power to strike, without taking further recourse to violence; if the union's strike power is insufficient to extort a desired decision from management, the union must and will accept its failure. But how can nations accept an adverse decision in the power struggle without appeal to war? How can statesmanship in the long run trust the security of its people to anything less than their armed might to make it good? How can their future, their destiny, be left to anything short of the final arbitration of organized bloodshed? Nations cannot establish their rights or their power by going on strike against the international order. When their power and security are finally involved, war is the only recourse open to them. The power struggle, controlled, adjusted, modified as it is in many ways on the local and national levels, finally "heads up" into the international power struggle. There one has run out of law, of government or of police. Even serious power problems can be, and normally are, compromised; but sooner or later there arrives the ultimate moment of decision. It becomes a matter of "either we or they," and war—the maximum of violence, with every resource of the community mobilized to insure success—inevitably follows, however catastrophic the results are likely to be for everyone concerned.

Such is the grim picture commonly advanced. Yet, like most of our other concepts of international politics, it is too doctrinaire. In fact, nations do "go on strike" against each other, with results often more dramatic, and more conclusive, than those obtained by large-scale war. In much of the guerilla fighting of recent years there has been more of the "strike" than of "war." It might be said that President De Gaulle has conducted a prolonged "strike" against the kind of power structure that the United States and many European nations have tried to organize in the West. In this instance the issues are almost purely those of power. Yet it is hardly conceivable that they will or even could be resolved by war among the NATO nations; and the circumstance scarcely justifies the view that in international politics there is no ultimate resolution for the power struggle save in organized bloodshed. In Bismarck's Europe the prize of "power" could only, perhaps, be won by war; a hundred years later alternative means seem available. A working, generally accepted and recognized power structure within the Atlantic world seems a quite probable development without further great wars among the member nations.

Such a power structure will not be permanent or unchangeable; nor is it likely at any given time to accord exactly with any one government's ideas as to how power should be organized. Some putative solutions will be discarded by experience. It is already clear, for example, that a "united Europe" dominated and dictated to by American thermonuclear power is unfeasible as the basis of the power organization of the Atlantic world. But so, in the long run, must be a disunited Europe fractured under French or other claims to national power—claims that in the modern situation can assume no real significance except in the context of a combined Atlantic community. The power struggle within the West will go on; but it will eventuate in working compromises between such extremes and not, certainly, in an intra-NATO war. De Gaulle is, of course, aware that it is quite impossible for France today to achieve power or "hegemony" in Europe, in the manner of Bismarck, by actually going to war with anyone, just as the Johnson Administration knows that it cannot dominate Europe, in the manner of Hitler, by deploying military force against any European states. It is still obvious that the United States is very powerful in Europe—it can influence or determine decision there in many fields and in many ways—and that De Gaulle, without even threatening to go to war, has markedly enhanced French power in the world and in the United States. The French decision in early 1964 to open diplomatic relations with China was an arresting exercise of power, though with no military accompaniments or implications, likely to have more far-reaching influence in world politics than any action France could have taken while involved with her soldiery in Indochina.

Here are the outlines of a nonmilitary international politics within the Atlantic world: an organization and reorganization of international power structures without recourse to war or the threat of it. It is often argued that such a development has been possible only because of the overriding military power threat of the Soviet Union. If the Communist threat were eliminated, it is said, the Atlantic community would fall apart in a conventional military power struggle, and the old internecine war on the 1914 pattern would again soon be upon us. But this is a cliché of the discourse that really seems to have very little substance behind it. It is more and more widely recognized today that military power is not everything in international politics, as it once seemed to be, and that this is true even in those areas where the Communist problem is remote or absent. Assuming the simple excision from the globe of that one third which is now Communist, leaving the Western and "uncommitted" two thirds as they now are, with their present distribution of economic, political, nuclear and other military power factors, it is not easy to picture just how another great war could arise. Dangerous local situations would continue to exist, but hardly as triggers to a general explosion. Power shifts would continue to take place; some nations would become more, some less, influential in determining international decision, but whence would come that desperate conviction that the whole future of a great state, the preservation of its "way of life" and its liberties, turn upon the defense of an abstract power position through resort to major war?

The Communist menace is not the only, and perhaps it is not even the most important, factor that has kept the Western powers from mutual self-destruction. Since 1945 the Communist menace (or the West's apperceptions of that menace) has supplied strong reinforcement for many

other factors that would in any event have been molding
the Western world into a community capable of manag-
ing its power problems by a nonmilitary form of international politics; it is less the fear of Communism than
the nature of the modern world society that has tended
toward the elimination of militarism from Western relations. Major organized war seems obsolete today; it would
seem not less but more so if the Communist issue did not
exist in international politics.[7]

It is not simply the Communist menace that has brought
the Western great powers to confine their power struggles
to a nonmilitary form of politics; basically it is the overwhelming menace of war itself, together with its patent
inutility. And these factors have operated equally behind
the iron and the bamboo curtains, leading upon the
global stage to the substantially nonmilitary international
politics that has in fact ruled throughout the world over
the past two decades. If the United States knows that it
has become impossible to impose any useful "dominance"
or "hegemony" over Europe by a great war, so—judging
from the whole course of its policy and its actions—does
the Soviet Union. Not only the great thermonuclear "deterrents" but also the conventional military establishments themselves have been reduced to an almost purely
defensive role. They are not, in fact, "instruments of
policy"; in a dozen corners of the earth—Vietnam, Cyprus, Cuba and elsewhere—policy wages difficult struggles
for power and position in almost total disregard of the

---

[7] It is at least suggestive to recall that during the interwar period,
when the threat of Communism was felt acutely in the West, it operated, not to impose, but to disrupt Western unity. It was an important
factor in precipitating the intra-Western power struggle that broke in
1939.

nuclear weapons and their physical firepower. And the present trend seems so definitely away from another great war that many observers have concluded that the only danger of one now lies in technological or political "accident." [8]

All this speculation does not imply that the international power struggle, nonnegotiable though it may be, has been suspended in the larger world any more than it has been suspended within the North Atlantic system. Enormous power shifts have been, and are, taking place without the ultimate test of all-out bloodshed. The virtual disappearance of the old colonial empires; the shifting power relationships among the United States, Britain, France and the other Continental European powers; the rise of the new nations in Africa and Southeast Asia; the painful yet hopefully creative shifts in interracial power relationships; the even more arresting shifts going on within what we once too simply regarded as the Communist monolith—all these represent tremendous readjustments of the world's national and international power structures. They have by no means proceeded without vio-

[8] Is it symptomatic that the science-fiction writers now so often concentrate their fantasies on "accident" (as in Burdick and Wheeler's *Fail-Safe*) rather than on a war which could realistically be believed to grow out of actual political-military relationships in the actual world? Even Neville Shute (*On the Beach*), fictionally obliterating the entire human race, felt it unnecessary to offer any political, social or psychological reasons as to why nations should resort to these extremes of destruction. Older practitioners usually took some care to provide a credible war to sustain their forecasts of disaster. H. G. Wells (*The Shape of Things to Come*) started his fictional second world war in the Polish Corridor, where in fact the real one subsequently began. Other prophecies, both good and bad, of the future of war have at least set up the war. The weaponry has become so awesome that this seems no longer necessary in science fiction. But if the war is no longer relevant to science fiction, is it possible that the science fiction of weaponry is no longer relevant to the political problem of war?

lence, but they have been carried out without that grand-scale and gruesome explosion to which the system of armed sovereign states, each having gathered into its own hands complete control over all lesser power struggles, was thought inevitably to lead.

The problem of the international power struggle is central to the problem of a viable world order. We have learned, I believe, that those who used to pour out their fear and moral opprobrium on "power politics" were misguided in their target. In a sense, all politics is power politics; what matters is the form and the sources of the power. It is difficult to imagine a single global authority, however completely empowered to make and enforce law, that could have controlled the international power struggles of the past two decades, or regulated the great shifts of power they have recorded, with anything like the same economy of life and the same rough justice that we have actually witnessed. Thanks in part—but only in part—to the supergiant weaponry, we have achieved a substantially nonmilitary form of international politics, which has shown a remarkable capacity to deal with the problem of the power struggle—the one problem that has always been advanced as insoluble in any demilitarized system. On the contemporary international stage power is still in theory organized around the huge military establishments, the giant weapons, war offices, war industries and the military threats they imply. But these fearful panoplies are in fact largely inoperative. The significant elements of the power struggle are today largely conducted "by other means."

This situation has come about, not only through the fear of war in its hypertrophied modern form, but also, somewhat paradoxically, through the real security of the great modern states against it. It is a security deriving less from the strength of the colossal deterrents than from their irrelevance. The United States may be secure today because it maintains a capacity to annihilate the Russians if they attack it; but it is even more secure because the Russians could gain nothing of consequence by a military attack in the first place. We can see that the situation obtains for the United States in respect to the Soviet Union —and for reasons having nothing to do with the self-supposed American "peace-loving" character—and we should not so persistently overlook its equal truth for the Russians in respect to the United States. The present world order is one in which significant power, both military and other, has accumulated in no more than four great centers: the United States, the Western European complex, the Soviet Union and China. Whatever their propagandists may say, these are in fact mutually almost invulnerable, and would have been had the nucleus never been unlocked. The kind of fear for the future instilled a century ago in the France of the Second Empire by the rise of Prussian military power cannot seriously affect these great and highly stabilized triumphs of socio-political organization. Only the ignorant victims of long-outworn concepts can talk (except, of course, for propaganda effect) about "preventive war" between these powers. Even the current bellicosity of the Chinese against the "imperialists" is to be ascribed much more to their power struggle with Moscow than to any intention of themselves resorting to major war.

On the eve of World War I the rise in Serbia of pan-Slav nationalism was a very real and dire threat to the shaky power structure of the polyglot Austro-Hungarian Empire—a threat to which there seemed to be no answer except in war, however disastrous such an eventuality might prove. Such perilous situations do not exist today. The major power centers are far more secure in their power; and where threats of this kind may seem to arise, they know that world war, or even any considerable organized war, cannot cure, and is likely only to compound, the difficulty.[9] The four major power centers in the contemporary world are, in fact, almost unassailably secure in their basic power positions, and they can watch the rise and fall and shifts of power on the world stage without being driven into the final death trap of "we or they," "now or never," "survive or perish," "liberty or death." Their wordmongers continue to be fond of such slogans, but they do not really get much response from the huge and substantially secure nation-state organizations within which they operate.

By and large a citizen of any one of these great power organizations will expect to get what liberty or profit he can from his own government, rather than looking abroad for external assistance. He demands of his rulers that they insure his subsistence and survival, but not, in the great stabilized states, that they do so through foreign adventures unlikely to contribute much to either. This situation is obviously much less prevalent in the new under-

[9] It can, I think, be argued that the Soviet Union faced a threat of this kind in the Hungarian nationalist rising in 1956, and that the United States faced a similar one in Castro's commitment of Cuba to Communism and the arrival of the Soviet missiles. Both were, of course, of a much less lethal kind than that which the Serbs presented to Franz Josef's empire; it is still significant that both were handled by the threatened great powers without precipitating a world war and with a noticeably careful avoidance of positions that would have made one inevitable.

developed and revolutionary states; and it is no doubt the case that the power-hungry everywhere will always seek to employ the enormous powers of the state, as they employ the power of groups and corporations, to their own greater puissance. But the medium of international politics grows increasingly viscous and resistant; such individuals and groups must increasingly look elsewhere than to international war for the satisfaction of their personal or group ambitions. Sir Francis Drake made a very good thing out of his piratical war with the Spanish Empire. The head of a great modern oil corporation may still make a very good thing out of international politics; but he no longer, like earlier entrepreneurs, relies on fire power. He eschews both local war and international conflict, but he still makes money—and wields much power.

This new condition has come about basically because power organization in the modern world has progressed far beyond the primitive military systems that for so long seemed to be the *ultima ratio,* the be-all and end-all, of international politics. The sovereign nation-state, so often cast as the villain in the international drama, has in fact, as was argued earlier, performed a tremendous and indispensable role in the modern organization of power. What would we, or what would the world as a whole, do with the 200 million Russians or the 800 million Chinese if the political bonds that have organized them into cohesive and responsible entities were suddenly dissolved? The world society has suffered far more from division and chaos among them in the past than it is ever likely to suffer in the future from their unification. It is true that their repressive and police methods have played an unpleasantly prominent role in holding these great aggregations of human beings together; but to demand their destruction, for that reason, as mere "police states" is to take a very shallow view both of the problem of power and the problems of policing in a world of three billion human beings, not many of whom are shaped in the likeness of a Kennedy liberal or even a British parliamentarian. As a *military* entity the sovereign nation-state is reaching the end of its scope, but as a power organization it has not only contributed enormously to the creation of our modern world, but also provides the basis for advance toward a demilitarized world politics much more clearly than do plans for universal, "free" and democratic world government.

Among the great states the struggle for power continues, but in nonmilitary forms. In that third of the world, more or less, beyond their direct command—the world of the underdeveloped, unstable, revolutionary small powers, both new and old—it also continues, often with bloodshed and violence. Here the power-hungry military and political patriot or adventurer finds a scope now elsewhere denied him. If one can say with some confidence that another Hitler has become impossible in the great stable states, this less ordered segment of the great community abounds with little Hitlers. They may, to be sure, have nobler social aims than the ex-corporal ever achieved, but their basic politics, their basic concepts of the mechanisms of power, are the same, and within their arenas of action they present much the same problems in the international organization of power. How difficult these problems are the United States has learned in its often fumbling policies in Latin America and elsewhere; while they are, of course, immensely complicated by the effects of great-power rivalry upon them.

In these turmoils the local leaders and movements constantly appeal for great-power support against their own internal (or external) opposition; the great powers respond by fishing for advantage, backing one or another guerilla leader or "popular" movement against those supported by their great-power rivals. But they do so always without risking the naked power confrontation for which the only outcome would be world war. To see this process in the stark terms of a "war" between the Soviet Union and the United States, or even between Communism and democracy, is to stultify one's whole approach to power issues in fact much more subtle, permitting much more flexibility of response, than American policy has usually achieved. When in early 1964 President De Gaulle moved to the recognition of China, the United States was trapped in a situation in Indochina for which there seemed to be no practicable military solution; for which no viable political solution could be found either within or without Vietnam; for which costly politico-military defeat seemed the only probable outcome; but from which the United States could not extricate itself because it was paralyzed in the cold-war psychology. De Gaulle, a statesman who from long experience probably knows more about the facts of life and politics than most of his peers, has opened up the possibility of realistic and viable solutions, to which the United States will probably have to accede sooner or later. Here, as so often in the past, the only question seems to be whether the United States will accede soon enough to gather some benefit from the outcome or, imprisoned in cold-war ideology, will wait so long as to insure the worst possible outcome from the American point of view.

But in the world as it is now organized the outcome, whether soon or late, will be less than catastrophic for the United States and certainly far less catastrophic than a thermonuclear war. The whole history of the past twenty years points, not to the ultimate triumph of "Communism" or the ultimate triumph of "democracy" in the global system, but to a fairly certain prediction that neither the Communist East nor the democratic West is ever going to organize the globe on its own exclusive pattern. The actualities are far too complex for such crude, "Manichean" concepts of international politics. Both "Communism" and "democracy" are fluid, changing words for working forms of social organization. The West has often backed "democratic" spokesmen only to find them turning into dictators of the totalitarian type; but the Russians have as often backed "Communist" leaders only to find them turning into very independent, and often pro-Western, Communists. Power-hungry individuals—such as Nasser, Nkrumah, Castro and the Vietnamese generals—have found their own avenues to authority, often playing the great powers against each other in the process. The power hunger of populations—such as the native African, Indian and Indonesian—has not proved unmanageable even under our existing world system. Throughout the whole process the final, nonnegotiable power crisis of "we or they" has not arisen.

The power struggle proper—the struggle to control, not any immediate division of goods or benefits, but future divisions of goods and benefits under unpredictable future circumstances—is inherent at all levels of social organization. The sovereign nation-state, through its developed apparatus of law, government and the police power, has largely reduced it to generally nonviolent expression except upon the international stage. There no global law, no global government and no global police— none, that is, adequate to suppress violence wherever it may occur—exist. But even in their absence, the working organization of international power has been tending toward the development of an international politics that, while adequately serving the inordinately complex needs of society for the adjustment and readjustment of power structures, has been doing so without necessitating recourse to major military action or superorganized war.

The power struggle proper is not, as it is usually assumed to be, an insuperable barrier to a relatively peaceful system of international relations. In the world even as it is now organized we are reaching a point at which the great states and the smaller can live, as most of the smaller have been living for many years, without the corroding fear that the winning or the loss of the prize of military power will determine their fates as communities and nations throughout all time to come. The Scandinavians and to a large extent the Latin Americans learned this lesson long ago, and they have been living substantially at peace, dealing more or less successfully with their own internal power problems without appeal to the international power complex and consequently without great concern as to the rise or fall of their own power positions in the world as a whole. The international great-power struggle is in itself of not much interest to them, except as it may involve them in the gigantic catastrophes, not of their own making, to which it gives rise.

This circumstance explains the spread of "neutralism"

through the world power structure—a phenomenon at once so exasperating, so inexplicable, so baffling to the great protagonists of the international power struggle. "Neutralism" is no product of the post-1945 cold war but has been a stumbling block for a military organization of world power at least since the "armed neutrality" of the late eighteenth century or American neutrality toward the European power struggle in Napoleonic times. Winston Churchill inveighed against the neutrality of Sweden, Ireland and Turkey in World War II; the Russians forcibly and bluntly denied neutral status to the central European states such as Poland and Hungary, just as American policy tried to deny it to the Middle East, India and Southeast Asia in the postwar period. But neutralism can neither be denied nor suppressed, fundamentally for the reason that the quarrels of the great power centers do not immediately concern the peoples or the local politics of those considerable areas that still lie beyond direct control of Washington, Moscow or perhaps Peking.

Americans have often been dismayed to discover that in such places as Cuba, for example, or Vietnam the war between the Communist and the non-Communist worlds, which engrosses the whole imagination of many Americans, either means very little to the people on the ground (where the war must in fact be won or lost) or means something quite different from what we imagine it to mean. In Vietnam at the beginning of 1964 America found herself involved in a bitter, bloody and destructive form of local politics and factional fighting, to which the great symbols of democracy and Communism had about as much relevance as the elephant and the donkey on American electoral banners. They are symbols much less of ideological commitment than of the sources from which the several factions expect to draw their power and their support. The ideological battle, if there is any, is of the slightest consequence, and whether success ultimately resides with the Communists or the anti-Communists will have only minimal effect upon the real power positions of both Washington and Moscow. The Eisenhower-Dulles theory of the "row of dominoes" as an explication of Southeast Asian politics was probably the most lamentable example of misleadingly false analogy to occur in recent times. Great national organisms do not go over at a push, as a domino does; change in one will, of course, affect conditions in a neighbor, but not with anything like the inevitability of a second domino's collapse; while dominoes, which have but two positions, "up" or "down," offer no analogue to the complex variations of power in the real world. It is simply self-defeating to look at the contemporary international world as presenting a cold-war problem. The labels do not fit; the clichés are inapplicable; this approach gives no hint of the answers that will in all probability emerge. De Gaulle's initiative toward the neutralization of all Indochina reflects the strength of the neutralist position on contemporary international politics, but that in turn reflects the weakness and emptiness of a cold-war concept, in which neutralism is impossible and to which it is ultimately destructive.

Neutralism has grown throughout the uncommitted world because the cold war makes no sense to most of it. Neutralism has been rejected, fiercely and often bloodily, by the cold warriors because it exposes the practical political emptiness of the war concept when applied to the facts of contemporary international life. The neutralist nation, or the neutralist statesman, is somewhat in the position of an atheist amid an intense religious war. His very existence demonstrates the folly of both the great contenders; he must be exterminated if the war is to go on. But neutralism is beyond extermination today and is one important reason why a new and essentially nonmilitary form of power politics is today controlling in the international world.

The prevailing politics is by no means always pretty. It involves such elements as savage guerilla wars and assassination campaigns; the brutalities in the Congo; the unsettling consequences of Castro's importation of Communism into Latin America; the long and bloody tragedy in Vietnam; the potentially even more tragic and bloody situation in South Africa; riots and rebellions and injustices in many other areas. What it has not involved, and does not now seem likely to involve, is the all-out struggle for military power, on 1914 and 1939 models, among the great and stable military states. In a world that has reached the degree of order and organization revealed by the contemporary scene, the power problem is not insoluble. It is not, in fact, the barrier to a more rational international system that it has often seemed to be. All this seems evident in the experience of a half-century of world war and in the attitudes of the great states as they now stand face to face with each other. But to understand how this situation has come about, and why it is likely to be prolonged indefinitely, one must turn from the problem of power to the problem of law, of order and of legal coercion.

SIX

LAW AND ORDER

THE PROBLEM OF THE POWER STRUGGLE ON THE international level is by no means insoluble, since through the past twenty years we have again and again found solutions for it by "means short of war." The fact must still be faced, however, that we have found them only under the frightful threat and the coercive power of the giant weaponry; it may be true that the weapons alone have made these solutions possible. Like Faust, who sold his soul, we have sold our souls to the devil of hypertrophied military power; and the relatively considerable measure of order, peace and prosperity that world society has enjoyed under the contract implies an appalling day of reckoning. If mankind is to escape the consequences of the bond, it can only be through the development of a world system of "law and order" that does not, like the existing system, include the great armaments as elements apparently essential to its functioning.

The consideration forces one to return to the whole question of law, order and coercion in human society. It is certainly not as simple a matter as it often seems. The notion, entertained by many, that we need only

to enact a global system of "law and order" to void
the devil's contract and evade the reckoning is not persuasive. It has clearly proved unavailing so far; and it is
likely to help us as little in the end as did Faust's despair-
ing protestations when the bill was presented, unless we
can in the meantime acquire a firmer understanding of
the terms and ideas involved.

In all human societies, from the family group up to the
state and even the "anarchic" international system,
there is law, order and coercion. The legislator, the priest
and the policeman appear to be the basic atoms of social
organization, much as the atoms of hydrogen and carbon
are basic to all organic matter. And it is the structural
relationship among the three that determines the character of the society, much as it is the arrangement of the
hydrogen and carbon atoms in their complex chains
that determines the nature or the characteristics of the
particular organic compound that results. In social, no
less than in chemical, organization these arrangements of
the basic stuff can vary widely. In the great and stable
nation-states of today—such as the Soviet Union and the
United States—they follow patterns which, although in
some ways quite similar, are obviously not the same; in
the more chaotic lesser states the differences may become
extreme. Plainly, there are many possible kinds of "law
and order." In contemplating a demilitarized international system, it is not enough simply to ask for a world
"order"; it is necessary also to consider what kind of
order it will be and how it will operate.

Most Western thought appears to take the answer here
as obvious. For a demilitarized international order there
is but one model conceivable—that provided by the West-

ern democratic, free-enterprise state, which has solved its own internal problems of order with remarkable success. For most, this model appears to be the meaning of "law and order." No world system of law and order will exist until we have translated to the global setting the essential institutional arrangements of Western democracy: free popular voting, representative legislatures, a strong but responsible executive, an independent judiciary and an international police to enforce the laws and uphold the court decisions. At least since Woodrow Wilson proposed to make the world "safe for democracy," this view seems to have been taken as almost axiomatic by Western liberal thought. Unfortunately it raises difficulties.

One such difficulty is that the model is not in fact the only possible one. The Communist nation-state has been about as successful as has Western democracy in regulating the power struggle and eliminating violence over vast areas of the globe, including countless disparate peoples and races. If "order" is the only object, the Communist model can, as in fact it does, compete quite favorably with the democratic one. However much we may dislike the idea, there is nothing to show, in the abstract, that a wholly Communist world would not be quite as "law-abiding" and "orderly" as a world wholly organized on Western democratic principles. If the future is in fact to belong to the latter, their superiority must be demonstrated by something more than their success in eliminating violence from the power struggle.

A more serious difficulty lies in the implicit assumption that it is possible simply to expand the Western democratic system from a national to a global level, with the expectation that it would operate for the world as a whole as well as it does within a great nation-state.[1] The Western democratic system of law and order is a more subtle, more delicately balanced social mechanism than this assumption suggests; and its magnification and transposition into a global order raises problems not always fully appreciated and certainly not easily resolved. Every mechanical engineer knows that one cannot develop a small power plant into one delivering ten or twenty times the horsepower merely by "blowing up" the original drawings. The large engine may run on the same underlying principles as does the small one, but there still has to be a complete redesign to take account of the new stresses involved, the new relation between the strains and the metallurgy, the "scale factor." To do this, the engineer must understand, not only the broad principles of the engine, but also how it works in detail, where the stresses fall, where the old parts will serve and where new ones must be developed. To expand the Western democratic system of law and order into a global system, one must have a similar grasp of how in fact it operates.

This consideration returns us to the essentials of the Western democratic system of law and order as it operates in practice. One may take the United States as a good example.[2] It is the basic function of government—in the United States as everywhere else—so to regulate the

[1] See "Preliminary Draft of a World Constitution," *Common Cause*, March, 1948, pp. 325 ff.

[2] It is a particularly good example, no doubt, because it is, in constitutional theory at least, a federal system, and therefore seems to many to offer an especially apposite model for a federal world. Actually, one may doubt whether this circumstance is much more relevant to its successful functioning than is the similarly federal form to the functioning of the Union of Soviet Socialist Republics. But as a federal structure would be unavoidable in a world system, American experience with the device may well be illuminating.

power struggle among the individuals, groups and communities subject to it as to insure that the struggle will not destroy or disrupt the whole system and will be continuously resolved with a minimum of violence or, if one chooses, with a maximum of "order" and justice. To this end, as has been said, government, here as elsewhere, has at its disposal the instrumentalities of law, emotional allegiance or consent (order) and coercion. The laws represent the normative rules and regulations under which the power struggle may be carried on. They are general statements, describing in necessarily general or universal terms the rights, duties and mutual obligations of all subject to them, and they are in their nature equally applicable to all.[3] By the same token, they are also a crystallization or diagram of the power structure as it exists at any given time. And at any given time the basic force of the law derives, not from the coercive power it holds in reserve, but from the extent to which the community accepts its normative rules as right and just; this in turn depends upon the extent to which the community accepts the basic power structure that is reflected in the laws.

As normative rules for the regulation of the power struggle, the laws will in general be successful in the degree that the power structure underlying them is accepted as right and just. We are apt to experience a mild astonishment today at the insouciance with which past

[3] The declaration in the Fourteenth Amendment that "no state shall deny to any person the equal protection of the laws" introduced no new principle of jurisprudence; it was simply the necessary corollary to the opening clause, which abolished slavery and made all "persons"—that is, the former slaves—full citizens. Just or unjust, the law must apply equally. The present revolt of our Negro citizens is less against unequal *treatment* under the law, although that of course occurs, than against the fundamental inequity of the laws themselves.

generations, even the most enlightened, accepted miseries, exploitations and cruelties that to us seem utterly barbaric. It is hard to believe that the humane men who founded our republic in the conviction that "all men are created equal" and with the expressed object of securing "a more perfect justice" and "the blessings of liberty" could have accepted chattel slavery and indentured servitude without a qualm and could even have constitutionally equated a Negro slave at only three-fifths the worth of a free white man. But this attitude accorded with the accepted power structure of the time; it seemed no less "just" to the men of the age than did the exploitation of the factory worker, the unskilled immigrant and the domestic servant to the upright citizens of the nineteenth century or the savage discriminations in jobs, opportunity, housing and education entailed by racial segregation to the upright Supreme Court judges who handed down the "separate but equal" decision in the case of *Plessy* v. *Ferguson* in 1896.

The laws will reflect the power structure and they will command respect, allegiance and obedience so long as the power structure itself is generally seen as "right" and "natural"—an expression of the "way things are." Laws are, however, general; they lay down broad rules, within which it is permissible to struggle for power, but they cannot control in any specific power issue. For that, the courts are indispensable as providing an alternative to violence. Here administration normally carries by far the greatest burden of routine decision; but when a naked struggle for power arises, only the courts (or their equivalents) can provide a resolution that will seem to the contenders at least as just as anything they could ob-

tain by resort to violence and less destructive to their own
interests than a violent solution would be. Standing, as in
a sense they do, between the lawmakers and their police
power, the courts perform a vital social function. By interpreting and applying the necessarily general laws to
specific power issues as they arise, they protect and preserve the legislators from their own illusions of omnipo-
tence and at the same time greatly facilitate the task of
the police in maintaining order—in maintaining, that is
to say, the accepted power structure and insuring that the
conflicts that arise are resolved by nonviolent means. In
most specific situations a court writ can be substituted for
the policeman's nightstick or pistol; the writ (or its
equivalent) usually serves, and the nightstick only rarely
has to be employed.

As the agent of law and order in a stable society (as
the embodiment, that is, of government's legal monopoly
of coercive force), the policeman has a double duty. He
must see that the general rules and regulations are generally observed—that people do not murder or steal or
disobey traffic laws or misconduct themselves in the parks
and so on—a sometimes dangerous but relatively simple
task, since in this he has the overwhelming weight of
community assent behind him. But when a bitter power
issue arises, about which there is often no general agreement in the community, he must also see that it is resolved by "legal" or nonviolent means—that the verdicts
of the courts or the acts of the administrators and legislators are accepted. Here the role of governmental coercion
becomes far more complicated, as is illustrated by the
difficulties encountered by the various federal and state
police forces in dealing with the verdicts of the federal

courts in regard to the racial power struggle in the South.

This much is common to all stable governmental systems, regardless of their constitutional form. The "police state" is a comparative, not an absolute, term; the mixture of law, allegiance and coercion is always present, however widely the proportions may vary. Also common to all differing constitutional systems is the basic problem of government—the problem of how to keep the power structure, as expressed in the laws and coercively enforced regulations, in accordance with the actual power relations within the community. The latter are always changing and in any given social organization must continue to change if the society is not to be reduced to a totally static condition analogous to that of the social insects. "Revolution," in some sense or another, is indispensable to social growth and vitality—a fact that Jefferson set forth, perhaps overdramatically, in his celebrated remark that the "tree of liberty must be watered by the blood of martyrs." What Jefferson failed to add was that the "blood" could be as figurative as the "tree"; but the figure, in any case, is true. Many of the greatest revolutions in our affairs—the industrial revolution, for example—have been largely bloodless, but they have claimed their martyrs, their toil and suffering, nevertheless. It is the task of any government of "law and order" to permit the necessary revolutions to take place, to readjust the legal framework to the developing realities of the power structure, with a minimum of violence and disruption.

Even in a "police state" such adjustment is not impossible, as the Communist empire demonstrates, not only in the obviously shifting power relationships between various groups and classes within the Soviet Union, but also in the Soviet Union's shifting power relationships with China, Yugoslavia, Poland and other elements in the Communist organization. But the adjustment is never easy and seems to carry a constant risk of violent and unmanageable breakdown, such as that which overtook the old Czarist Empire, or the Austro-Hungarian Empire or other imperial systems that have relied primarily on their police power. It is the boast of Western democracy that it provides far more subtle, more efficacious and safer mechanisms for dealing with underlying shifts in the power structure.

The whole system of laws and administrative rules, backed by coercive police power, will work so long as the power structure it reflects is generally accepted as right and just. The "normative" institutions will suffice so long as they reflect what is accepted as "normal." When abnormal conditions arise—when the real power structure, that is to say, is no longer in accordance with the "normative" rules—it is necessary either to modify the normative rules or coercively and violently to impose new ones. The first recourse of the "police state" is to the latter method.[4] Western democracy has developed more subtle institutions through which to utilize the advantages of the former. The popular vote and the representative legislature are devices through which it is possible to adjust the laws to new power relationships

---

[4] Its claim is, of course, that it is merely restoring "law and order"; it is simply returning everything to the *status quo ante*. But except in the most minor of fracases, police repression never restores the old order. The fact that the challenge has been made in itself demonstrates that the old order is unrecoverable. Even when it is most successful, police repression is compelled to impose new rules; it cannot simply revive the old ones. The successful repression of the Hungarian revolt of 1956 did not restore pre-1956 Hungary; it created a new situation, with new power relationships.

without resort to violence. A citizen voting for his Congressman may have no more than an infinitesimal influence over the conduct of great affairs; but he has "participated," he is to some extent morally bound to the consequences of his vote and will be less a revolutionary in the degree to which he is responsible for the outcome. This is no doubt the deepest motive for "get out the vote" campaigns promoted by democratic elites. Laws constructed by popularly elected legislators will seem to him more just and on the whole more acceptable than those handed down by fiat from a dictatorial executive. In the American democratic system, the executive branch has a power often only a little less absolute than that of a Communist chief of state; but it is again limited in ways that make its exercise more acceptable. The President must stand for re-election once every four years. In the interval he is almost as much beyond popular control as a Communist prime minister or party secretary; while even the quadrennial accounting is diluted by the President's command over the party machinery and by the course of events he himself in some measure manipulates. Yet the necessity for the accounting does put limits on his actions; it makes him sensitive to public opinion and to the power of the voters and at the same time makes the citizenry more acquiescent in the acts of the executive. The whole arrangement is another of democracy's devices to keep "law" in accordance with the actual power structure; it does not so much protect the people from the President as protect the President from the people. The electoral requirement has the effect of warning him in time of basic shifts in the power structure; to these he must either accommodate his policies or see the governmental system destroyed. It seems plain from recent history that Soviet dictatorship also has "feedback" mechanisms of the same kind to which the top command is responsive; they serve the same purpose of protecting the dictatorship against overly drastic changes in the power structure over which it presides, but they seem much less efficient and reliable than the "feedbacks" built into the democratic system.

The popular vote and the ultimate responsibility of the executive are two basic pillars of democratic order. The independence of the judiciary is the third. Subservient judges can fulfill—and throughout history often have fulfilled—the basic social requirement for judgments that will be accepted as an alternative to violence. But their efficiency in this function declines in direct proportion to their subservience. The Russian judges who conducted the purge trials in the middle 1930's gave a necessary color of law to Stalin's tyranny; Stalin had to have trials and had to have judges who would conduct them, but the purge trials, as a social instrument, were not notably efficient; they were weak links in the Soviet chain of law and order. The independence of the democratic judiciary gives it a far more powerful role in the maintenance of order. It is not, of course, an arbitrary independence but is limited by the whole body of law and of social institutions within which it operates, and judges are as responsive as other men to the accepted power relationships within the society they serve. The most upright of judges have repeatedly put the coercive power of the state at the service of power structures that to later times seem grossly unjust. But their freedom, in the democratic system, from direct political control allows them a sensitivity to changing power relations not always present in the legislator or the political executive. The court that in 1896 believed that the doctrine of "separate but equal" was a just and workable statement of racial power relations in the United States could come in two generations to a realization that the doctrine was no longer either just or workable and so could demolish it. To segregationists the reversal seemed a travesty of law; they could not see that in fact it served to preserve the authority and continuity of law and order in face of changing power relationships.

The subtlety of the Western democratic system of law and order in dealing, as it does, with an enormously complicated system of interrelated power struggles goes far beyond this crude exposition. Its balances are many and delicate; they are never more than partially success-ful, and to maintain the system at all calls not only for "eternal vigilance," but also for eternal patience and an ever more sophisticated grasp of the real nature of the power relationships it controls. Simply to enlarge it to global proportions seems an impossible task. In the world as a whole there exist almost none of the energy sources, the levers and linkages on which the system's operation depends. There is no world law—none, that is, capable of standing as a general statement of the rights, duties and obligations of all, including all groups, cor-porations, communities and higher power organizations in a population of three billion souls. There is no world legislature capable of attempting such a statement, or diagram, of the almost infinitely complicated power re-lationships involved. And there is certainly no possibility of developing such a legislature through the essential democratic devices of the popular vote and equal representation.

There are no available linkages through which a global executive could be held responsible to the global community as a whole and could thus function (as the American President does, broadly speaking, with a considerable measure of success) in the interests of the total community. In the absence of a generally accepted system of world law, there is nothing on which a global judiciary could sustain a position of independence in applying the general law to the specific power conflicts that must continually arise. And without either a representative legislature or an independent judiciary, a world police becomes almost a contradiction in terms. As the embodiment of the total coercive force of a society, the policeman maintains order only by enforcing its general laws and seeing that its specific judicial decisions are respected. In the absence of either, he ceases to function as a policeman; the police becomes (as did Hitler's SS) an occupying army, a *condottiere* or a Praetorian guard, using its monopoly of armed force not to keep order, but to establish its own prestige and power position in the community. A global dictatorship is perhaps conceivable; but a global democracy appears to be quite beyond the range of the possible. If a demilitarized international political system is to be established, its structure of law and order will have to modify considerably the principles underlying Western democratic law and order.

The core of the problem appears to lie in the question

of coercive force. All proposals for general disarmament or demilitarization recognize the continuing necessity for coercion; all include provision for large national police forces; all provide in one way or another for an international or supranational police force; all assume a global society in which the policeman shall have replaced the soldier. Yet none has gone more than very superficially into the problem of this proposal's implications—of how the coercive police power is to be organized, controlled or applied, of where its functions will begin or end. And because all the power problems of a global society come to a focus, as it were, upon this issue of coercive power, the problem of the police forces must, if we ever begin to take effective steps toward disarmament, soon appear as presenting the great difficulty.

There is a difference between the function of the policeman and the soldier which, although not always recognized, seems here to be basic. It can be put most simply by saying that the policeman enforces a law that it is no business of his to make; the soldier makes law that it is not primarily his business to enforce. The instrument of both is armed force—that is, violence or the threat of violence. The same individuals may at one time or another act in either capacity, but the capacities themselves remain distinct. When the soldier is engaged in enforcing generally accepted law, he becomes a policeman; equally, when a policeman is engaged in making law (as suggested by the aphorism about there being "a lot of law at the end of a nightstick"), he becomes a soldier. Both the soldier and the policeman are embodiments of the coercive force of the community as a whole; neither a private army nor a private police is compatible with modern social organization.[5] But they embody it in different ways.

It has already been argued that one of the greatest triumphs of the modern nation-state organization is its successful accumulation in its own hands of a monopoly over the coercive force of the society as a whole. It was not simply that it imposed order upon the warring feudal barons. Gradually it established the principle that *any* exercise of armed violence, if justified on the ground that it was in the interest of the community, or in accordance with community law or in furtherance of community power, must be under the control of the whole community. If the violence were done in the name of the community, it must be under the responsible control, not of one or another special interest, but of the community itself. A public police was gradually substituted for the private armies; a national armed power gradually replaced, in foreign relations, the adventurous operations of the private entrepreneur.

In 1589, the year after the defeat of the Spanish Armada, Sir Francis Drake led a retaliatory expedition to Cadiz. Sailing in the name of England, it was an expression of English *national* power and prestige, but it was organized as a joint-stock enterprise of London merchant-adventurers in which Elizabeth I took shares along with the other financiers. The first great age of Western European imperial expansion (in which so

[5] Privately maintained police and "security" forces are of course commonplace in the West; but they are permissible only to the extent that they enforce generally accepted public law. A private police enforcing the privately decreed laws of their employers would take us back to the Middle Ages. Even as it is, the private security guard, the private detective, the plant policeman raise enough difficult questions of public policy.

much of contemporary international politics was forged) was dominated by the great private trading companies, utilizing a national thirst for national power and glory to sustain the more private interest of the great banking and ship-owning families in personal profit. Such enterprises could not continue; the total power of a great nation in its external relations could not be left to the service of a small group of its wealthy and elite families, any more than its internal power could be left forever at the disposal of the Tory landlords and the owners of the rotten boroughs. The slow liberalization of Britain's domestic institutions implied an assertion of community or national power over the lesser composite groups and interests. It was accompanied by a similar assertion in external affairs. In the Indian Mutiny of 1854 the "John Company" reached its end; just as domestic affairs were effectively "nationalized" by the Reform Act in 1832, so foreign affairs were finally nationalized after the Mutiny. The trading company and the private entrepreneur were to exert considerable influence on foreign affairs thereafter, but the nation—the total community —had established its dominance, which was expressed in the state's command of the total coercive power in the community: in the development of an effective internal police and a genuinely national military power.

Thereafter the state was in effective command of both the police and the soldiery. Neither could any longer act as agents of particularist or private interests. Both were embodiments of the coercive power of the community as a whole; and each found its *raison d'être* only in that role. It was still true that the policeman was the enforcer of accepted domestic law; it was still the soldier's function to make law in the international field, where it either did not exist or was inadequate to control those power struggles that rose to the international level. The soldier, it may be observed, has always regarded himself as a maker of law; he is never an anarchist. He is a "freedom fighter"; he dies to impose a "new order," which will be more just and right than the old; he sacrifices himself to make a world "safe for democracy" or, as a hundred years ago, in the name of "states' rights" or the "preservation of the Union"—none of these being an anarchic end but all implying a new order, which is to say a new law, a new and nonviolent order in the affairs of men. Even Hitler's *Sturmabteilung,* which came as close as anything our times have seen to embodying a naked thrust for power for power's sake, a "revolution of nihilism," had to be inspired by visions of a new order —an order to last "a thousand years" through the perfection of its justice, an order in which Germans would have the power rightfully due to a master race and Jews would be, again rightfully, deprived of their insidious capacity for harm. The horrible picture of the Third Reich with which Hitler inflamed his followers was still a picture of peace, order, law and "justice." But it was Hitler's own irresponsible version of peace and justice.

This "nationalization" of the total coercive force of the community as a whole was the great contribution of the modern nation-state to international order. Under it, the policeman acquired the ability to enforce an established structure of domestic law and the power relations it reflected. The soldier could make law (where it did not exist), or set up new power relationships, only as the agent of the total community he represented. It was a

useful and creative regularization and ordering of coercive force in the global system. Nor was the law as
made by the soldiery necessarily bad; if the test of "good"
law is the accuracy with which it reflects the power structure that it controls, one must admit that the verdicts
returned by military coercion in international politics
often conformed to reality. The fundamental revision of
the American Constitution, imposed by military coercion
in the Civil War and recorded thereafter in the Thir-
teenth, Fourteenth and Fifteenth Amendments, is accepted by most people today as not only essentially "just,"
but also as unavoidable if the nation was to deal with the
changing power problems of the age.[6] The military verdict returned in World War I may be open to much question; but few persons will now deny that the verdicts
returned in World War II represented a working statement of the going power relationships in the present age.

It is not the injustice or the unworkability of the results
achieved by military coercion in the modern age that has
condemned the militarized nation-state system. It is the
ever more colossal human costs of military coercion and
its ever dwindling efficiency as a means of achieving
these results. Coercion cannot be absent from a global
system any more than it can from any lesser one; but
when it can be supplied, in the last analysis, only through
the huge and mutually hostile modern military estab-

[6] The point is confirmed in an interesting way by the savage and near-
treasonable opposition which descended upon the Confederate government from its own internal "states' righters." Having begun the war in
the name of states' rights, the Confederacy found itself driven to the
same measures of centralized control, conscription, suspension of *habeas
corpus* and so on that the North was employing. In its resort to war the
South, no less than the North, was making a law for itself; had it won
its independence, it might well have emerged with a constitution not materially different from that of the North.

lishments, it defeats its own social purpose. It is the function of the coercive element in any social organization to maintain established power structures, or permit their transformation into new ones, with a minimum of violence and social disruption. The coercive element in existing international society is so supplied and so organized as in the long run to maximize both aims. Major war is no longer an efficient way of maintaining or adjusting a power structure, and its costs have become insupportable.[7]

For this reason so many today hope ardently to substitute the policeman for the soldier in the international society. But the legal and emotional devices that have made such a substitution possible within the great Western democratic states appear to be quite inapplicable to a global society. For that matter, so do the rather different devices that have made the change possible in the great Communist states. A global dictatorship may be more readily conceivable than a global democracy; but the prospect is not actually very realistic and seems less so as one observes the difficulties accumulating within the Communist empire. If it cannot do better than it is doing with the one third of the world over which it

[7] The reader should perhaps be reminded that in this concept "power" is much more than command over the agents and instrumentalities of physical force; it is intricately compounded of political, economic, psychological and emotional forces as well. The "power structure" at any given time relates all these in complex ways. In the process either of maintaining or transforming such a structure, even in the case of great wars, actual coercion—physical force—seldom seems to play more than a secondary part. Possibly this is one of the reasons why the coercions of war so uniformly fail to produce the results expected by those who resort to it. Hitler's seizure of power in Germany was "war" only in a metaphorical sense; it relied on many elements other than those of brute coercion and for that reason produced exactly the result he had intended, as his later wars did not.

claims command, how well would it succeed with the entire globe? But if neither global democracy nor global dictatorship supplies a practicable answer to the question of coercion in a global society, one must look farther than either to discover it. And one may begin, perhaps, by looking first into the actual operation of the international political order since 1945.

Modern politics has, as has been argued earlier, recorded vast changes in the national and international power structures of the global society. It has done so with a rather surprising minimum (taking the world as a whole) of war, bloodshed and violence. The coercions necessary to bring about the present situation have to a considerable extent been applied, not by the soldiers making their own law, but by the policemen (or their equivalents) in both the great and lesser states upholding established law and legal institutions—mainly those of their own national states but at times those of "international law" as well. The results, of course, have been anything but perfect. There has been more than enough of bloodshed, and the coercions employed have by no means always had even the color of law behind them. But, far from taking on the pattern of organized international war, they have taken the forms of riot, rebellion, guerilla war (which is essentially a form more of political than of military conflict), propaganda war and mass movement. Individuals, group interests and communities have resorted to physical coercion to secure rights or freedoms to which they believed themselves entitled; and our attention has naturally been focused on the violence attendant upon such efforts. We tend to overlook the vastly greater areas in which international and national politics have gone on, peaceably in the main, by the aid of such law and order as is available. Coercion of some kind is a necessary element in any social order. But the more it can be removed from the hands of the soldiers and put into those of the police, acting under at least some kind of legal sanction, the more hopeful becomes the answer to the world problem.

Such, at any rate, has been the clear tendency of modern times. The notion of a world "policed" rather than left "militarized" and at the mercy of its soldiers is anything but new. The partition of Africa by the European great powers after 1880 was in considerable measure a "police action," and one may usefully compare it with the many others that have since taken place, down to the U.N. intervention in the Congo. Theodore Roosevelt proclaimed a "police power" in the Caribbean; Woodrow Wilson proclaimed a world so policed that it would be "safe for democracy," and he attempted with ill success to police the Caribbean and Mexico; the Korean War was in theory a "police action." In all such cases the police idea broke down, of course, because the coercive force it entailed was in the hands of the great-power military establishments, with no adequate body of law to sustain their police work or to preserve it from the savage fears and rivalries among the would-be policemen. The partition of Africa was as much a gambit in the disastrous game of European power politics as it was a response to the growing problems in Africa that undoubtedly demanded policing. Three quarters of a century later, the United Nations is again trying to police Africa. Its methods and approach represent an enormous advance over those of the late nineteenth century; yet they are still bedeviled by the power rivalries of the policemen and by that absence of an established law that inevitably turns the simplest police act of keeping law and order into a political act of making it. The efforts of the U.N. in the Congo are only a beginning on the inordinately difficult complications of an international police force. What is important is that they are, unlike previous efforts of the kind, a real beginning.

Looking at the world order as a whole, it is evident that the necessary element of coercion is today supplied overwhelmingly by the national police forces of the stable states. In this context, the distinction between the internal and the international power struggle is not particularly relevant. The power conflicts arising within a state are intimately related to the power conflicts between states. The success with which the domestic police deal with internal power problems has a powerful effect upon the international power problem, where we can, as yet, rely ultimately only on the soldier. It is probably true to say that World War II was largely generated out of the Weimar Republic's inability to settle its internal power struggles by the "normal" methods of police coercion under the law. For present purposes, there is no real division between the social functions of coercion on the national and on the international level. In this sense, coercion presents us with a kind of continuum throughout the social order, and by far the largest portion of the spectrum is today occupied by the legal (or accepted) coercions of the national police forces.

The same situation would obtain under any system of demilitarized world politics now imaginable. The task of policing the globe is so huge and so complex that it

would necessarily devolve, as it does largely devolve today, upon the several national police forces. Under all
suggested plans for disarmament, the national police
forces would continue to exist; and they would continue
to carry, as they now do, the primary burden of world
order. For nine tenths of the global requirement for coercive force they are already, as it were, the agents of
deputies of the international order and must, it would
seem, remain so. The point is often overlooked that no
international police force presently conceivable could
assume more than a small fraction of the coercive responsibilities now discharged by the national police.

Through most of the present-day global society the
national police forces perform their basic function—to
minimize violence in the prosecution of the power struggle—very well. By "nationalizing" internal violence
they have, as has been suggested, contributed materially
to its elimination from international politics. In relation
to its present population, the world as a whole has probably enjoyed more peace and less bloodshed than ever
before in its history. It is, I think, a mistake to see the
problem of a demilitarized or "policed" international
politics as one primarily of policing the national police
forces. It is, rather, one of strengthening, supporting and
utilizing them to secure their maximum contribution
toward the requirements for coercive force in a global
society.

Today the police forces fail, or threaten to fail, in several ways. Inevitably revolution at least tends to put
them in an ambiguous position. Within any state or society, a revolution represents a readjustment of established power structures. Individuals, groups, economic

classes and racial or national minorities arise to claim
privileges, rights or power positions denied them under
the existing regime. It is the function of legal coercion
—the police force—to insure that such situations are
worked out with a minimum of violence. To this end
the police must at the same time defend the established
power structure from violence on the part of the revolutionaries and also defend the revolutionaries from violence on the part of the established powers. If the situation is really revolutionary, the latter task is as essential
as the former to avert general breakdown, and the police
are left in a position of conflicting responsibilities to
which they are often unequal.

Substantially or even wholly nonviolent revolutions
do of course take place; and the depth and permanence
of the revolution are usually in inverse proportion to the
amount of violence entailed. Even in the "police state,"
where legal coercion is without the political, psychological and traditional supports provided by the democratic
system, major readjustments of the power structure can
take place without violence; and in the stabilized state
system of today—among which one must include not
only the Western democracies but also the Soviet Union,
probably China and smaller Communist states such as
Yugoslavia and Poland—violent revolution seems unlikely. It seems probable that among the great majority
of the world's peoples the domestic police powers will
continue adequately to meet most of the needs of the
international order for coercive force.

They are not doing so now, however, in some of the
new and more disordered states, and the possibility of a
breakdown of the police power over much larger areas

of the earth must, it would seem, remain. Since the success of a demilitarized or nonviolent international order would appear to depend in considerable degree upon the maintenance of a substantially nonviolent order within the constituent national units, such possibilities pose difficult issues as to the role of coercion in the global system as a whole. Proposals for general disarmament usually begin by allotting to each state an internal police force of such numbers and so weaponed as to be able to maintain domestic order, suppress rebellion, patrol the frontiers, enforce customs and immigration regulations and prevent border raids and forays. These are large specifications (although it is difficult to see how they could be reduced); if all national police forces met them successfully, the world society might be distressingly drab, static and oppressive, but at least the problem of coercion for *international* politics would be largely solved. There are, actually, few conflicts of interest among the stable national units, and those that do arise are not susceptible to resolution by war or organized violence. The dangerous conflicts are those, not of interest, but of military power; they are engendered by the fears, threats and illusory ambitions inherent in the militarized system, and if the military coercions could be eliminated, a series of more or less perfectly functioning national police forces would provide all the coercive power necessary to make the international politics of a global system workable. Unfortunately, however, even the best national police forces operate with something less than perfection; and the likelihood of their complete collapse, either in such local areas as the Congo or, much worse, in the great and presently stable states, poses what is perhaps the central problem of "law and order" in a demilitarized global society.

The appalling difficulties encountered by the United Nations in its attempt to introduce an international police force into the Congo situation are instructive. When the appeal of the Congolese government for U.N. assistance in "repelling aggression" was received, a good deal had already been learned from experience; the repulsion of aggression is (as Korea sufficiently demonstrated) a military, not a police, function, and the General Assembly was as unwilling as it was inherently unable to involve itself in a war in support of Leopoldville against Katanga. The most it could do was to send police forces, not to decide such political issues, but only to insure that the decision was attended by a minimum of violence. Contingents from the great armed states were excluded, in order to "localize" the whole problem and avoid its entanglement in the great-power rivalries. Only the smaller or "neutralist" states, not directly involved in the great-power struggle, were invited to send troops; and as these became available, they were to avert violence, not by arms, but by their presence. They were under orders to use their weapons only in the extremity of self-defense. They were to "keep order" but to have nothing to do with the political issues amid which order had collapsed.

It immediately appeared, however, that there was no generally agreed "order" to be kept. Both the Soviet Union and France refused their financial support of the effort, for reasons related, not to their interests in the Congo, but to their power position on the world stage. Some of the African contingents were withdrawn because the states were less interested in keeping "order" than in seeing that the kind of order to be imposed would further their own national calculations. And the U.N. police forces that remained soon found that they could not simply eliminate violence without taking essentially political positions in regard to the politics out of which the violence had arisen. Before the end, they were fighting a small war to make a law that had not before existed— that is, to impose a readjustment of a power structure that had collapsed. They were left in the ambiguous position always occupied by the policeman in a revolutionary situation; and only the astuteness and high political sense of Dag Hammarskjold and his successor, U Thant, made it possible to resolve the situation with some measure of success. If violence disappeared at least temporarily from the politics of the Congo, it was because the U.N. police helped to impose a new power structure in the Congo —something that lies outside the proper province of the policeman, but to which he was in this case forced by circumstance.

In a static situation the policeman simply enforces the law; in an unstable and dynamic one he can hardly help making law as he attempts to maintain a nonviolent politics. Politics is the organization of power—that is, the adjustment of rival claims to power. Simply to forbid violence in the process of adjustment—the function of legal coercion and of the police who embody it—is inevitably to sustain the claims of those in power against the claims of those who seek it, unless other than violent means are available (as in democratic societies they normally are) for exerting leverage upon the power balance. In this sense, the police can never be impartial; and

a completely impartial international police, even if sustained by treaty and juridical systems reflecting an established international power structure, would seem to be
an impossibility save on one condition: that adequate
and generally accepted nonviolent means should exist
for resolving power struggles on the international level.
Legal coercion will succeed in its basic task of eliminating violence from the power struggles of men only as
acceptable alternatives to violence are available. In the
ordinary concept of a condition of "law and order,"
the "law" is a statement of these alternatives; the "order"
is the operation of coercive force compelling resort to
them.

The problem of creating an international politics that
will be "policed" rather than left to the vagaries of military coercion clearly calls for something more than
merely "outlawing" war and establishing an international
police to enforce such a statute. In the United States we
have made it a crime to attempt (or even to advocate)
"the overthrow of the government by force or violence."
In this proscription there is a certain naiveté; it may ex-
press our sublime confidence in the perfection of our
legal and political institutions, but it is evident from experience that a legal act is very far from meeting all the
problems of law, order and coercion that may arise even
within a Western democratic society. We have had
troubles enough of our own; but Adolf Hitler's destruction of the Weimar Republic by "legal" means, followed by his destruction of the international order
through means that, if without legal authority, were at
bottom no different from those accepted as legitimate
by its defenders, is our best as well as most appalling

lesson in the problem of coercion in the international power struggle.

Adolf Hitler exemplifies the power struggle almost absolutely. Alan Bullock finds the key to his character in a "will to power in its crudest and purest form." [8] From beginning to end, his one discoverable objective was power—power for himself, power for the party on which he arose, power for the state his party captured, the retention of his own power amid the crumbling of the empire he had created. Party, people, state, nation and in the end his own life were all in turn sacrificed to this goal of power without purpose. It was with insight that Rauschning described his revolution (and there is no doubt that it was a major revolution) as the "revolution of nihilism"—the revolution of nothing. From the beginning, neither he nor his followers propounded any rational or even intelligible goals of the power they demanded. The object was power itself; the goals were subsequent inventions.

The early Nazi party program was never amended —and never observed, except when it was useful as a propagandist weapon. As he was approaching power in Germany by "legal" means, Hitler scorned to offer any program; the only element wanting, he argued, in the Germany of the early 1930's was centralized "power"; this he would supply in himself, but how he was to employ it was no business of the society from which he demanded it. Once he had the whole formidable power of the German state at his command, he employed it in the same way upon the world stage. His object was to break the "power" of Russia, of France, of Britain in inter-

[8] Alan Bullock, *Hitler* (Pelican Books, 1962 ed.), p. 382.

national affairs and to establish the dominance of Germany (and thereby himself) on the world stage. But his ideas of how this dominance would be used were even more witless than those of his far more amiable predecessor, Wilhelm II, for whom German power and prestige were vital objects in themselves but who could never fit them into a workable pattern of international politics.

The main difference between the two situations lies in the fact that the Kaiser sincerely wanted to do so; Hitler, the revolutionary, did not care. The objectives of an international system of peace and reason, which he frequently proclaimed in the immediate prewar years, were purely tactical; they were devices to make good Hitler's power position, and in no sense analyses of the world's *malaise* that he had so powerfully helped to promote. Even in the latter half of World War II, when the whole tremendous exploit was beginning to go wrong and Mussolini tried to suggest to him that the only salvation lay in putting some real political and social content into the grandiose vision of a "New World Order," to which he was sacrificing such rivers of blood, Hitler's response was negative. Power cannot be put at the mercy of concessions. Just as he had offered no program to the Germans to justify his appeal to them for power, so he would offer the peoples of Europe no program to hold their support for a power already collapsing.

Where in all this colossal tragedy were the police? The question has repeatedly been asked—usually, perhaps, in somewhat different terms, but coming down to the same thing in the end. Where were the global community's resources of law, order and legal coercion? Why were they so totally unable to limit the bloodshed and devastation attendant upon a shift in many underlying power balances that had become more or less inevitable? To package the answer into the statement that there was no world law and no international police to enforce it is an obvious oversimplification. There was a very considerable corpus of world law, embodied in the Versailles Treaty (and the attendant treaties), modified by the Dawes Plan and the Locarno Treaty (1925) and the Washington pacts of 1922. War had even been "outlawed" by the Briand-Kellogg Pact. The police—or legal coercive forces—within all the great states seemed quite capable of keeping domestic order in conformity with the requirements of the international order. Where coercion might be called for in the international area, it had been left in the hands of the national military forces; these were, however, in the main stable and responsible, nowhere given to adventure and in general more interested in keeping the peace than in disrupting it.[9] The international society of the late 1920's was in the main well policed, reasonably orderly, its multifarious power struggles generally constrained to nonviolent mechanisms of adjustment. In Europe, as A. J. P. Taylor puts it, "it looked as though treaty-revision would go on gradually, almost imperceptibly, and that a new European system would emerge without anyone noticing the exact moment when the watershed was crossed." [10] Yet the

[9] Both in his advance to power in Germany and in his use of that power on the world stage, Hitler found in the German army one of his more difficult obstacles. The story may have been somewhat different in Italy and Japan, but it is hardly deniable that World War II was not, primarily, made by the soldiers.

[10] A. J. P. Taylor, *The Origins of the Second World War* (Atheneum, 1962), p. 59.

warless world of the Briand-Kellogg Pact collapsed. It
seems significant that the collapse began, not in the failure of international coercive power, but in the failure of
the national police powers, especially in Germany.

Hitler's whole success was founded upon the subversion or paralysis of the domestic police power, as embodied in the police, the army (in its role as guardian
of domestic order) and the political and military heads
who controlled them. After the tawdry failure of the
"beer-hall putsch" Hitler clung to "legality"; he never
thereafter directly challenged the police power. Instead,
he first paralyzed it by exacerbating every available
power conflict within the distressed community and then
captured it for himself. The violence, brutality and intim-
idations of his brown-shirt armies were "political"; they
were directed, not toward resolving particular power
struggles, but simply toward rendering any resolution
impossible. He skillfully brought government in Germany to an impasse from which there was no exit except
by endowing Adolf Hitler with supreme, and irresponsible, command over all agencies of coercive power in
the community.

Both before and since, this grim process has been repeated many times in many communities. In the case of
Germany, it took place in one of the comparatively few
great and organized states upon which the fabric of international order must depend; and—by what may be no
more than a tragic accident—it took place in a way that
made it most disruptive to the established order of international politics. Many others have risen to seize dictatorial power in lesser states with little, if any, impact
upon the international order as a whole. Hitler, however,

found his major weapon for the capture of power in Germany in his assault upon the international system. The international system, as established by German defeat in 1918, as embodied in the "Diktat" of Versailles, as prolonged by reparations and German disarmament, could be made to account for all the ills under which Germans suffered. Hitler had only to make the vague and basically irrational promise that he would rescue Germany from Versailles in order to achieve total power over the Germans. It made no difference that the "Diktat" had been, and was being, amended in accordance with emerging power relationships. It made no difference that in the great depression the Germans were little, if any, worse off than other peoples who had not lost the war in 1918. The whole international system had to be destroyed in order to make Hitler personally powerful.

Hitler's anti-Semitism had the same basis, at once completely illogical and completely shrewd as an avenue to power. If there was such a thing as "the Jewish question," the rest of the civilized world—which is to say the going international system of the late 1920's and early 1930's —had adjusted to it. There may still have been wide discrimination against Jews in Western European societies, but to single out the Jewish communities for actual extermination was something that could no longer "be done" in international politics under the order that had been painfully worked out. Hitler's savage anti-Semitism was in itself a revolt against an established order that had developed to a point at which it forbade such means in the conduct of the power struggle. Hitler's appeal to racism, like his unilateral rearmament and his subsequent peremptory threats and annexations, was a mindless rebellion against the whole "system." Fantastically irrational in itself, it shrewdly served the one end of the "revolution of nihilism," which was, by wrecking all alternative solutions, to put Hitler, and under him his "Aryan" Germans, into total and illimitable power.

The end having been achieved in Germany largely by playing on issues of foreign policy, the revolution of nihilistic power had to be carried into the foreign field. There was nowhere else that power for power's sake could be exercised. The domestic success had been achieved on the simple promise to make Germany "strong." How else could it be fulfilled except by making Germany dominant over other nations? Hitler's idea of power could not encompass the notion of a Germany "strong" in her political, economic, social and cultural institutions. "Strength" meant irresponsible dominance. Already achieved in Germany, it could be applied only in the foreign field. Addressing himself to this end, Hitler proceeded to employ the same methods of "legality" that had already served him so well at home. He would paralyze and subvert the police, creating in international politics, as he had already done in German politics, an impasse from which there was no exit except to place untrammeled power in the hands of Adolf Hitler.[11]

In the international politics of the time, "the police"

[11] The issue as to how far this procedure was conscious design and how far simply the politician's expedient response to events as they arose may be of interest to students of Hitler but has little relevance for those interested in the total process. Hitler's thirst for power is undeniable, as is his failure to fill his concept of power with any concrete purpose. Even if he acted on no long-range calculation of where his course would take him, his perception of events and his responses to what he saw as opportunities were dictated by this brutal and impoverished view of world politics. Calculated or not, the results were the same.

is a term that must be expanded to include the whole body of coercive force available to the global community and the institutions by which it was controlled and applied. The force itself, as has been said, was distributed to the several national military establishments; it was controlled independently by the national governments, under a general law made up of the treaty and alliance systems and a few broader principles of international law, such as that which established the illegality of unprovoked aggression. Against this "system" Hitler had inveighed from the beginning, and now he set himself to destroy it, as he had destroyed the German political system, by "legal" means. Not until the Polish invasion in 1939 did he directly challenge it by force of arms. Instead, he simply rendered it unworkable.

He was careful never to move against it until it had first been paralyzed in its own internal divisions, fears and power conflicts. Perhaps his one most destructive move was the reoccupation of the Rhineland. The law and the treaties were against him; at the moment there was still ample "police" power in the hands of France, Britain and the rest to have ejected him summarily, and the whole international system might well have been saved had it been able to operate. But with his adroit and totally amoral mixture of threat and propaganda, Hitler had rendered it inoperable. He captured most of Central Europe, as he had captured Germany, without war; and he came close to taking Western Europe as well by similarly "legal" means. His appeals were always shrewdly legalistic—to "justice," to Germany's rights, to Germany's due—but he made good his own power by paralyzing the coercive forces within the international community that would otherwise have forced these claims to a nonviolent adjustment. The coercion was not available to impose upon him even a minimum of respect for the rights and the justice due to others. By subverting or neutralizing what coercive force the international community had at its disposal, he created a condition in which the power problem he raised was insoluble except by means of maximum violence, of blood and war.

But even the maximum of blood and iron provided no better a resolution of the power problem, for Hitler or for anyone else, than might otherwise have been achieved. It is noteworthy (as has been suggested in an earlier chapter) that so long as Hitler could manipulate the old system to his ends, his effective power rose in a geometrical progression; when at last he had maneuvered himself into a position in which he was compelled to destroy the system itself, the decline began. From the moment he released his armored divisions across the Polish frontier, Hitler began to lose his real control over events. He was to win many bloody victories thereafter, but they were never to restore to him the power, the command, he had exercised by nonviolent means. He was like the blackmailer, whose often great power depends upon the laws, the decencies, the accepted culture of the community in which he operates, but which totally evaporates in the moment that he flouts all law and decency by actually carrying out the threat he has been exploiting. Hitler in a real sense was a creature of the "Versailles" system—that is, of the whole system of international politics, law and morality that stemmed from World War I. He rose only by exploiting its every weakness to his own ends; when he destroyed the system, he destroyed himself. There was, in this result, a terrible and majestic justice. But the costs at which it was achieved were disproportionate.

Such costs are no longer acceptable to rational men. Even another World War II would be intolerable, to say nothing of a third war, waged with thermonuclear instruments of total destruction. To most thoughtful persons, the problem seems to turn upon the possibility of converting the international system into one that will be "policed" rather than one in which, as in the present system, the necessary elements of coercion are supplied by a police-*cum*-military structure. The power struggle, in all its infinite complexities, may be assumed to be ineradicable from the affairs of men. Coercion, like law and principle, may be taken as indispensable in the task of keeping the struggle within at least tolerably non-violent or "orderly" limits. The dilemma comes with the question of how a global system of coercion that will be of the police rather than of the military kind is to be organized. As the experience with Adolf Hitler seems to show (and it has been retraced only as the outstanding example of the difficulties that beset us in many less gruesome forms), the true role of coercion in a demilitarized international society presents problems of a formidable kind. One can hardly police the globe simply by creating a global police; that would be to leave unanswered all the issues concerning the role it would perform, the powers it would exercise, the controls it would be subject to. A demilitarized international political system that would be policed by policemen rather than regulated by soldiers presents theoretical and constitutional problems more difficult than any practical issues concerning the size, armament and command of an international police force.

SEVEN

A WORLD POLICED

POWER, LAW AND COERCION ARE THE BASIC STUFF of politics; and it is our vague, imperfect and often contradictory notions about them that constitute the great stumbling blocks in the way of a more rational and less destructive world political order. Clearly, a demilitarized world is not attainable merely by a general act of disarmament, merely by the creation of one great body of world law or merely through the substitution of a global police for the coercive soldiery. Disarmament, it seems, is impossible until a police has been set up; a police cannot be set up until there is an enforceable world law to empower it; a world law is impossible until the sovereign states have disarmed themselves. Over and over again one encounters the viciously circular argument. This circle will be broken only, it would seem, when our ideas about power, law and coercion are meshed into a self-consistent system, or world outlook, that will be workable—that will operate, that is, to meet the elemental needs of mankind rather than to insure its destruction. Such an eventuality cannot happen until our fundamental notions about power, law and force are subjected to more critical analysis than they ordinarily receive. The preceding chapters have attempted, however crudely, to initiate such an analysis. It remains to apply the theoretical discussion to the practical problem of a demilitarized international politics.

One can attack the question in various ways. It may be regarded as primarily cultural: can a demilitarized world culture evolve? It may be approached in a more mechanical way: can the military, economic and other material forces in the world be "balanced" into a tolerable equilibrium? It seems to me preferable to adopt the modern "systems" approach, which embraces both the cultural and the mechanical parameters. The world order as it exists today is, after all, an order—a system—of a highly complex kind, possessing an intricate "circuitry" that includes an endless variety of "feedbacks," "servomechanisms," "memory banks" and similar elements, all working with an amazing subtlety to maintain an order that is at least tolerable to the overwhelming majority of the world's inhabitants; while it offers to all of them, in at least some degree, the possibility of change and improvement. One could accept it, perhaps, more or less as it stands except for the ever-imminent possibility that it will run away into a supergiant explosion. The object of those who today hope for general disarmament and demilitarization is not basically to alter or reconstruct this marvelous total system; it is simply to remove its explosive potentials.

Such planners are not revolutionaries; indeed, it is this element that involves them in their deepest intellectual difficulties. It is the first principle of the genuine revolutionary utterly to destroy in order to rebuild. Because the goal of demilitarization is to destroy as little as possible in the existing international order, to retain all its immense utilities in the service of man, its advocates often find themselves in intellectual trouble. Perhaps they are not revolutionary enough. Rather, they are like the operators of an atomic reactor, seeking to push the control rods in to the point at which they will prevent a runaway destruction of the whole system but will not diminish its useful potentials. In an atomic reactor the control rods are made of an absorbent substance that will soak up the dangerous excess of energy. In the international system the control rods are made of less material elements—of law, analysis and understanding, for example—but their function is the same: to soak up dangerous excesses of energy in the system while allowing all its useful actions and reactions to continue. It is not easy or simple to modify an intricate and subtly interconnected system without rendering it inoperable. But it is less difficult to do so if one understands that one is dealing with a total system, not simply with one or another disagreeable aspect of it.

The idiom of the systems approach may be novel; but its essential content surely derives from the constitution makers of the late eighteenth century. Its "feedbacks" and "servomechanisms" are hardly more than their "checks and balances" in modern dress. Their object was to establish a system. The purpose of the American Constitution was, as its authors declared in the Preamble:

> . . . to form a more perfect Union, establish justice, insure domestic tranquillity, provide for the common defense, promote the general welfare, and se-

cure the blessings of liberty to ourselves and our posterity.

They did not, of course, propose themselves to accomplish these results, nor did they imagine that the written document in itself would do so. What they did attempt (and one need go no farther than *The Federalist* to confirm their attitude) was to establish a system so interconnected and powered alike by law and self-interest that it could be expected to work in general toward these ends. Just how it would work, in detail, was wisely left to the future. Their system itself was to undergo transformations they did not anticipate. The form and measure of justice, tranquillity, welfare and liberty it would promote could not be predicted. But that it did, in general, work to these ends is today hardly deniable.

Its authors, like all authors of operative constitutions, constructed it out of the ideological, political and legal material at hand. It had to take account of the institution of slavery as well as the passion for liberty, the sovereignty of the states as well as the need for union, the will of the people as well as the necessary instruments for their coercion. Its checks on and balances of power had to conform to the real power structures of the times; its "feedbacks" could retransmit only such ideological and social forces as were then in existence. The founding fathers were not, indeed, constructing a new system; they were taking an actual social system, as it was operating among the four million Americans of the time, and introducing into it only those minimal modifications in the circuitry that they thought necessary in order to make it work better toward the ends of man.

The existing world order, since it is an order, has a constitution—largely unwritten, to be sure, but no less effective in governing the working interrelationships of its peoples. If it is to develop a demilitarized international politics—a world "policed" rather than left to the coercions of military power—its present constitution must obviously undergo modification. It seems equally clear (even though the implications of the fact are often overlooked) that those through whose efforts this modification is to come about can work only, as did the Philadelphia Convention, with the ideological and social materials at hand. The long, persistent failure of the attempt at disarmament can be attributed to the fact that the disarmament conferences from the beginning had no materials of this kind with which to work. They were attempting to set the keystone in an arch for which no foundations existed; they were trying to design a machine, not to take account of the political and social forces available, but in defiance of them. Issues of disarmament never became urgent until the basic forces in international society were already running strongly against the possibility of disarming. The dilemma was similar to the difficulty with Keynesian economics: in times of prosperity no one wants to save for investment; in times of depression no one dares go into deficit spending for consumption. In times of relative tranquillity no one was interested in disarming; in times of increasing tensions no one dared divest himself of the arms that were the major cause of the tensions. Most efforts to meet the world problem by beginning with disarmament are like efforts to design a water turbine that will work only if water would run uphill. If Keynesian economics (speaking very roughly, of course) has become the accepted mode of thought among all the major peoples, it is because circumstance and experience have combined to exclude the older notions that contradicted it. If the demilitarization of international politics is ever to become an accepted element in the international system, it will be through a similar process.

Keynesian economics represents an important modification of the global economic "constitution." To realize the far-reaching nature of the modifications, one should go back further than the economics that were orthodox in 1930, back to those that were accepted in 1914, when it seemed to many that World War I could not long go on because of the breakdown it would bring to the whole necessary system of international exchange and finance. That the world's economic "constitution" has undergone immense change since then is obvious. That its political constitution will undergo (as today it is in fact undergoing) changes of similar proportions is not in any way incredible. But it must undergo them in the same way: through developing our basic materials— the basic ideas about power, law and coercion in a political society together with the basic institutions in which these ideas are now expressed—into a system less dangerous and less potentially destructive than that under which we now live.

The problem of a demilitarized world is not one of destroying the existing world system and then building anew; it is a problem in the modification of the system we have so that it will work to less destructive ends. If one looks at the matter in this way, one is forced first to take account of the virtues rather than the vices of the system as it now exists. Through its multitudinous "feedbacks" and control mechanisms the system normally deals with an almost infinitely complex series of power relationships, allowing power structures within its national units as well as among them to rise, fall and shift with, on the whole, a surprising minimum of violence and social disruption. Most of the world, most of the time, is already quite adequately policed by the existing national police forces; and these must survive as the main reliance of a demilitarized world politics for its coercive needs. This presumption is not because disarmament plans all provide for the continuance of internal police forces; the plans all include such provisions because, given the ideological and social materials with which we must work, there is no visible alternative. The national police forces (including in the United States and many other parts of the world semiautonomous state and local police forces) are an essential part of the "circuitry" of the existing system. To rip them out completely would reduce the system to chaos; to replace them, on the other hand, with a global police, or coercive, organization, reaching its centralized empowerment down through every state and community to supply on every street corner in the world the kind of coercive authority exercised, for example, by a New York traffic policeman is patently unfeasible. Even if such a plan could be carried out, it would wreck the delicate working of the present international system as thoroughly as would the elimination of all national coercive force.

The national police forces, varying enormously, as they do, in their local empowerment, their organization, their methods and their efficiency, must remain in a demili-

tarized international politics as the basic source of coercive power. "Order" must still depend primarily on them;
they are one of the indispensable elements in the existing
system available to those who would modify it into a less
perilous form. The modified system will continue to function through the kind of "circuitry" they represent because nothing as good seems available. They will remain,
as has been said, as the world society's chief agents of
coercion. The national governments, which control them,
will remain, as they are now, the world society's chief
sources of law—the world's agents, that is, for the control of the complex power struggles of men and their con-
straint into generally nonviolent means. In a demilitarized
international politics the national governments will operate in much the same way that they now do within the
mutually demilitarized politics of the North Atlantic
Treaty system.

Within the NATO system the independent and sovereign governments provide the laws and the supporting
coercive forces necessary to restrain the internal or domestic power struggles to substantially nonviolent means;
they are able to keep the internal power struggles in general from passing into the international field, and in the
comparatively rare cases in which these struggles do generate international issues beyond the competence of the
national government alone to decide, they are able to
secure their resolution through negotiatory, diplomatic or
other nonviolent means. Taking the North Atlantic powers as a single system, it is apparent that without the
coercive force supplied by the several national police
organs it could not function at all, but that no centralized
supranational coercive force is necessary to its generally

orderly and nonviolent operation as a viable order. A supranational NATO police force for the coercion of the individual member states has never been suggested. Within the alliance, coercive military "power" may still play a role, but it is an almost purely symbolic one. President De Gaulle, for example, seems much concerned with the desire to create a French military and nuclear "power," both to re-establish the "glory" of France and to secure a freedom of maneuver against the superior military "power" of the United States and Britain. But in this attempt the nuclear weapons, their carriers and their supporting troops are the merest symbols of a power structure that they do not and cannot themselves establish. No one, probably De Gaulle least of all, imagines that they will ever actually be used for the mass incineration of human beings—the only material use to which they can be put. The demilitarized politics of the Atlantic alliance reflects an international power structure that is not in fact determined by war or military threat and that would probably operate just about as successfully as it now does if no armies, navies or nuclear arsenals existed within it. The NATO system as a whole may still require military coercive forces to protect it against the outer world; it does not need (and could not use) a NATO police to carry out the coercive work within the system that its several national police organizations are doing very well.

The development of a global international politics operating in the same way is not only a possibility; it seems rather a probability, foreshadowed by what is going on around us. "Coexistence" has been making really remarkable strides in the past few years, not because any nation loves or "trusts" others any more than they ever did, but because it is gradually becoming apparent on all sides (not even excluding Red China) that coexistence is the only practicable mode for a working international political system. Since "coexistence" is rarely defined, one may venture a definition of one's own: a condition in which all the different forms of government—the democratic, the Communist, and the numerous intermediate forms of popular dictatorship, plebiscitary autocracy, oligarchy and so on—continue to exist, each primarily responsible for the regulation of the power struggle within its own areas, but all generally acquiescing in the nonviolent resolution of the power struggle on the international plane. Each will continue to keep its own law and its own order within its field of action. Each legal order will allow in its own way for unavoidable or desirable shifts in its own internal power structure, reducing or eliminating the violence that would otherwise be implicit in them. Where the international power structure demands modification, "coexistence" necessarily implies that it will be carried out by nonmilitary or nonviolent means. "Coexistence," if it means anything, can hardly mean less. And that such is the pattern into which international politics is now shaping seems undeniable. One hardly need labor again the obvious examples already cited— the increasingly intense power struggle between the Soviet Union and China, which seems most unlikely to erupt in a major war; the extremely difficult power struggle involved in the East-West confrontation in Germany, a struggle that has been waged for nearly two decades without a war but with no international coercive force to limit it to nonviolent means; the immense reorganization of the international power structure represented by the retreat of Western imperial colonialism, which was attended, nevertheless, by a minimum of bloodshed. The ratification in 1963 of the partial test-ban treaty, slight as its technical military effect may have been, will stand, I believe, as a major landmark in the development of a demilitarized international politics because it was perhaps the first faint recognition in the history of disarmament that the weaponry was becoming irrelevant to the real problems of the global order.

The treaty was attacked in the United States on the grounds that it would dangerously hamstring the country's potential weapons development. Significantly enough, it was attacked by the Chinese Communist government on essentially the same grounds. In the United States the Kennedy Administration felt itself forced to defend the treaty with the argument that it would leave American "superiority" in weapons development unimpaired. The Soviet government is not under the same compulsions to justify its actions as is the American, but its reply to its Chinese critics seems essentially the same: the test-ban treaty will leave Communist military power unimpaired and does not risk the destruction of the Communist system. Superficially, the replies alike of Washington and of Moscow to their critics would seem to leave the dangerous situation unaltered—both are still pinning their policies upon success and survival in an armaments race that neither can win. But this impression is superficial. The fact is that if either government had really believed that its own and its people's future turned upon technical superiority in the weaponry, the test-ban treaty could hardly have been written. It could be signed and ratified only because the precise balance of the weapons systems was seen on both sides to be no longer of first importance. In the present stage of world development it is apparent that no great power is going to divest itself of its military shields. But the military factor is no longer everything (except, perhaps, in those unfortunate interludes in which disarmament conferences place military considerations at the focus of all political thought), and statesmanship can accept accommodations and compromises in the military field without being too deeply concerned with precise adjustments in "the balance of terror."

The global system as it now stands, with its intricate legal, political, coercive and ideological circuitry, has brought most of humanity into a few great and seemingly stable subsystems within which the power struggle goes on with a minimum of blood and violence. Among these subsystems—the Atlantic system, the Soviet Russian system, China, India, the Latin American system—no issues remain that are susceptible to resolution by war or in regard to which a global coercive force could usefully be employed. Each subsystem is largely self-sufficient, reasonably confident of its own stability, with no pressing material demands (of a territorial or economic nature) upon the others. The only really dangerous issues that arise among them are those generated by their hypertrophied and mutually threatening military establishments. So long as these establishments exist, no global coercive force, operating on police rather than military principles, can conceivably regularize the resultant international power struggles. One can at least imagine a global army so weaponed as to be capable of fighting the national armies; but this would not and could not be an international would turn at once on the struggle to secure control of *police* force. Its sanctions would be those of the soldier, not of the policeman; the issues of international politics the global army to make a national variety of law for the world system, not upon the acceptance of a law generally controlling all. So long as the national armies remain, a global army could operate only to militarize every issue in international politics, and not to secure its demilitarization. But if the threatening national armies disappear, a true global police could take over the few remaining needs for coercion in the world system as a whole. Such a force would not represent a disassembling and complete rebuilding of the existing international system; it would represent simply a somewhat better and less dangerous rewiring of the complex circuits already built into it.

The perils of the existing circuitry seem rather easily identifiable. The greatest is probably the risk of "accidental" breakdown and explosion, though this can be exaggerated and, I think, usually is. The common notion that at the time of the Cuban missile crisis we were "within hours" of a Soviet-American thermonuclear war seems to me a bit of both foolish and dangerous historical mythology. As the event plainly showed, neither the Soviet dispatch of weapons to Cuba nor the answering American mobilization was intended as a prelude to war. Neither Moscow nor Washington had any desire for a war or any intention of precipitating one. The weaponry on both sides was being used for its symbolic (or communicational), not its military, value. The whole situation was in significant as well as striking contrast, for example, to that which arose in August, 1939, over the Polish Corridor. Hitler at that time apparently hoped to erase Polish power without a war, but he had no hesitation about accepting war, and in fact he deliberately put himself into a situation in which, with the failure of his peremptory demands, war was his only possible alternative. In October, 1962, the United States and the Soviet Union were never even remotely close to a crisis of this kind, and Kennedy no less than Khrushchev took great pains to avoid the development of such a situation. Even the existing international system is less "accident prone" than it often seems to be. But in the absence of any other presently visible reason why the great and stable power centers should fall upon and destroy each other, the danger of war by miscalculation or "accident" must remain high on the list.

A less immediate, but perhaps even more serious, danger in the existing circuitry lies in the possible breakdown of the legal-coercive mechanisms within one or more of the now stabilized major power centers. As has been argued in earlier chapters, the collapse of the international political order in 1939 began with the breakdown of the legal-coercive mechanisms within Germany. One may repeat that the function of a police is to minimize violence in the conduct of the power struggle; and the success with which it does so seems to turn, in the long run, upon the availability of nonviolent means for readjusting the power structure in accordance with the changing relationships of the men and groups involved in it. When revolution is too rigidly suppressed, or policed, it takes on violent forms, and its goal becomes the subversion or the capture of the police institutions of the state. The subtly complicated "feedbacks," monitoring systems and "servomechanisms" developed by the Western democratic systems seem to render violent revolution in any of them extremely unlikely, but certainly not impossible. In the stabilized totalitarian states, such as the Soviet Union and China, police control is very firm but to Westerners seems dangerously brittle as well. So it was in the old Czarist and Austro-Hungarian empires, with consequences that were calamitous to the world society. A revolutionary breakdown in either Russia or China would load the existing international system with stresses that it could deal with even less successfully than it dealt with the Nazi breakdown in Germany. While the coercive force available to the global system is concentrated entirely in the national armies, large-scale war among them would seem to be the unavoidable outcome of a situation of this kind.

A third perilous aspect of the existing system resides in the fact that it is stabilized only in part. The great power centers and many of their smaller components (for example, Yugoslavia, Sweden, Argentina) have established a degree of "law and order" sufficient not only to eliminate violence in large measure from their domestic power struggles, but also to make possible a substantially nonviolent international politics. The same situation does not hold for many of the new states and for the underdeveloped areas. Violence appears to be endemic in the politics of much of Africa, the Near East, some of Latin America and much of Southeast Asia. It is prominent in the internal affairs of these peoples; it is less so, as yet, in their international relations, but it is by no means absent from them. By a quaint paradox, only the poor and underdeveloped states can any longer afford the luxury of war.

The violence in such areas does not, however, assume

the extreme and catastrophic forms of war between the major armed powers. One encounters minor border affrays, guerilla wars, civil wars proceeding by political assassination, riot and propaganda rather than by the highly organized warfare of the great states. Most such conflicts are essentially political rather than military in character; it is politics in a violent and bloody form, but its outcome turns essentially on political factors rather than on such military factors as the destruction of the enemy's armies or the physical capture and occupation of his territory. The world has always known a good deal of this kind of action and the increasingly integrated and stabilized world system of today can probably accept a considerable residuum of this form of violent politics. The best of domestic police systems can never wholly suppress murder and mob violence; but they do not have to do so in order to maintain a generally working structure of domestic "law and order." In the global system a global coercive force could not suppress all violent rebellions or guerilla wars wherever they might occur; but it would not have to do so in order to maintain the world system in reasonably good working order. There was, for example, no international concern with the horrors of the Mau Mau war in Kenya, as there was over the horrors and disruptions of the civil war in the Congo. But this residuum of violence and bloodshed in the politics of the less developed areas of the globe presents two kinds of problem to the world order, in both of which a global, or supranational, police system seems necessary.

There are some limits to the amount of local violence and bloodshed that our integrated world system can accept. The old atrocities of the Czarist Russian pogroms;

the atrocities of the Turks against the Armenians; the
Nazi atrocities upon German Jews—all these shook the
fabric of the world society. The Mau Mau atrocities did
not, but those in the Congo did. There is a point beyond
which international intervention to police situations of this
character appears to become inescapable. There are some
situations of blood and social chaos that appear to demand a global or supranational coercive force; but in
these it is difficult for the world's existing coercive force
(made up of the separate national armies) to intervene
without risking the wreck of the global system as a whole.
Just where this point may lie is plainly one of the most
difficult of the theoretical problems of a world "policed."
Just how much local violence and bloodshed an otherwise well-policed world could accept is a problem perhaps basic to the whole issue of a police type of world
organization. Today we have no very good answer to the
question beyond the vague notion that in a policed world
violence and bloodshed must everywhere be put down.
This proposal seems obviously impracticable, and if it
were a possible answer it would be one that would lead
only to the rigidifying and stultification of all social and
cultural advance.

But the basic problem of violent revolution in the less
stable areas of the world is enormously complicated by
the interests of the great and relatively stable centers of
power. For the present, at least, it is apparent to all of
these major centers that they cannot contend for power
by military means. The international power struggle therefore takes the form of intervening in local situations.
Khrushchev, in his significant statement of October 26,
1963, reiterated the idea that the Russian policy of "co-

existence" did not repeal the Russian support of the "liberation struggles" of colonial peoples or of the "class struggle" in non-Communist systems. Few violent revolutions or guerilla wars can succeed without outside support; such support immediately involves the power interests of other states in the local power struggle, if, indeed, the local struggle has not been directly fomented by external power interests.

There is, of course, nothing new about such fomenting or support of local violence on behalf of larger interests in the international power struggle. The British conquered India mainly by setting the native princes against each other; the French monarchy supported the American Revolution in the interest of its power struggle with Britain; and similar actions have since occurred over and over again. But with major, organized war no longer practicable, this kind of support has become a salient element in the nonviolent power struggle among the major powers. The experiences of the United Nations in the Congo show the difficulty of policing a situation of local chaos in the interests of global law and order without becoming involved in an international power struggle, in the merits of which the world system as such can take no interest. The world system does not operate now, and probably can never operate, to apportion power among the various nations, states, groups and classes that struggle for power within it. The most it can hope for is to secure that these struggles continue so far as possible by substantially nonviolent means. But the United Nations was caught in the paradox that, to eliminate violence from the local power struggle in the Congo, it must in some measure make political decisions that would affect the

larger nonviolent international power struggle and thus
risk its relapse into international war.

Both Dag Hammarskjold and his successor, U Thant,
were to use great skill, patience and wisdom in their
efforts to develop a genuinely global, or supranational,
coercive force that would safely meet the needs of the
global system. It is easier to see the immense difficulties
they encountered than to measure the success they were to
attain. But the latter may in fact have been much greater
than is generally realized. The U.N. police forces have
certainly not established a global reign of nonviolent law
and order. They have had a powerful effect in reducing
the chaos in the Congo and in confining the Arab-Israeli
power struggle to nonviolent means. It may be that this
is the most which a global coercive force can be asked
or expected to do—that the U.N. police actions in Palestine and in the Congo represent, not a minimum, but a
maximum achievement. In a militarized world system
such controls as the United Nations has established may
seem feeble. In a demilitarized or policed world system
the kind of policing the United Nations has successfully
accomplished might well meet all the needs for a global
coercive force. In a policed world system we should expect a fair amount of local riot, bloodshed and "little
war," but in the absence of the huge panoplies of major
organized warfare, these events could be accepted much
as the continued prevalence of murder can be accepted
by the generally organized and law-abiding national systems in which most of the world's population lives today.

The problem of a demilitarized global society is basically a problem in the role and place of coercion in the
society as a whole. Coercion of some kind, under some

control, is necessary in order to prevent the power struggle from running away into total disruption and disaster. But with the very great measure of order that the national governmental and police systems have already introduced into the world system, the requirements for a supranational or global coercive force seem very modest. If the great organized military systems did not exist, these requirements would be of minimal proportions. It may be said, indeed, that the three sources of peril in the complex circuitry of the existing world system are all directly related to the existence within it of the massive, highly organized and heavily weaponed national military establishments. If these could be wholly replaced by national police forces, supplemented for certain purposes by a supranational or global police force under an accepted global authority, the system's needs for coercive force would be adequately met and the present risks of catastrophic breakdown would be eliminated. The international political order would continue to function very much as it does in "normal" times today. The power struggle would, of course, continue, on the international as well as on national levels, but it would be "policed" into relatively nonviolent modes. Violence would still exist in the world order, ranging from murder or political assassination through riot to civil or guerilla war, but it would be (as through most of the world it is today) the exceptional rather than the normal mode of international politics. The world order would remain at least as flexible, as changeable and as responsive to basic human needs as it is today; but it would be much safer and more secure for all involved in it. It would continue to use the sovereign nation-state—that really marvelous and subtle political invention—as the basis of world politics and world order, but by disarming it would draw the worst of its fangs.

No mere Utopian vision, this projection is implicit in the actual course of world politics since 1945; it is even more clearly implicit in the present plans for general and complete disarmament, to which statesmen as practical and realistic as Khrushchev and Kennedy formally committed themselves. This is the kind of system clearly described in both the Russian and the American draft treaties for general and complete disarmament (GCD). Both provide for the retention by all states of such national police forces "as are agreed to be necessary to maintain internal order and protect the personal security of citizens" (in the American wording); both envisage an international police force to police those aspects of the power struggle that cannot be dealt with by the national police; both imply international or supranational institutions to support this international police with a body of enforceable law adequate to "keep the peace"—to provide, in other words, for the nonviolent resolution of international power issues. It is true that neither the Soviet nor the American government has developed any really intelligible idea of what these proposals must involve or of how they expect the disarmed system of international politics to work. Possibly that is a basic reason why so little actual advance toward disarmament has been made. In proposing to eliminate the most dangerous feedbacks in the existing circuitry, the drafts have hardly even asked how the rest would operate or what new connections would have to be introduced into the system to insure its continued functioning. Both the

Soviet and the American drafts proceed as if simply disarming the existing system would bring into being a demilitarized world politics; there seems to be almost no realization that a modified system must be *designed,* as technological modifications always are, and that until the design of a demilitarized politics becomes clear, disarmament itself will remain an impossibility.

From the foregoing discussion of law, order and coercion in the great society, however, the nature of the design modification should become clearer; it should be easier to fill the general frame of the draft disarmament treaties with practical content and to discern the ideological and institutional patterns necessitated by the new circuitry. Too often the draft treaties and the negotiations based upon them seem to approach everything from the wrong end. In both versions, for example, the *national* police forces are dismissed with a line or two at most, as something too obvious for consideration. Yet if one looks at the global problem from the systems approach, it becomes clear that these are the really critical elements in the whole design. They are the energy sinks, or condensers, that are to soak up and control most of the energy of the power struggle; it is from them that most of the coercive force required by the world system is to come, and their size, armament, authority and functions are much more important to the total system than the precise shape and size of the military establishments that are to be dispensed with. The proposed *international* police arrangements, again, are hardly less sketchily dealt with. There is some tentative discussion in both plans of their composition, armament and control, but a complete vagueness as to their *function.* Indeed, ideas as to their function hardly go beyond the somewhat paradoxical notion that they will be relied on to "keep the peace" in a world from which war has already been excluded—a terminological confusion of what is really meant by "peace" and "war" that defines no concrete function whatever.

It should now be possible to reverse the approach. Others have pointed out that to a certain extent the problem of demilitarization is independent of the problem of disarmament. Discussions of disarmament are mainly technical, revolving around questions of "parity," inspection, stages and so on; discussions of a demilitarized world system are primarily political, revolving around questions of the total functioning of a total system. The former are unlikely to get far off the ground except as they are paralleled by advance in the latter. Disarmament begins, necessarily and unfortunately, with armaments. Demilitarization begins with the police. Specifically, it is here argued, it should begin with the national police forces. There would be some six score of them in the demilitarized world, variously armed, organized and sanctioned; but they would monopolize most of the legal coercive force in the world, and what they can be expected to do with it, what the feedbacks from the national policing into international policing will be, how they will in fact be interrelated, would seem to be the first subject for study in any consideration of a demilitarized international political system.

Above them will be set an international coercive force of some kind. Its functions, it is here argued, will not be so much those of "keeping the peace," in the style of police officers intervening to break up a bloody riot, as those of preventing a revival of war—in the style of police

officers performing their usual functions as traffic direc-
tors, regulators, supervisors of all those observances and
amenities that in ordinary life prevent conflicts of power
and personality from eventuating in riot and bloodshed.
A demilitarized world, after all, presupposes a general
act of disarmament; that in turn presupposes an acceptance by all the parties of the conviction that they will be
safer, more secure, more able to defend their real power
interests in a world devoid of major armaments than they
are in the present one. In such a world, the only function
of an *international* police would be to see that the international power struggle is confined to nonviolent forms.
The principal device for achieving this state is, obviously,
the elimination of the weapons and military establishments that are the means of organized war or international violence. Aside from a few minor regulatory duties
—such as policing sea and air lanes—the major task of
an international police would be to verify the fact that disarmament had been carried out in accordance with the
agreement and to insure that nowhere would the processes of rearmament again begin.

Police action is genuinely *police* action only as it is
taken in accordance with some generally accepted body
of law; in the absence of such a supporting body of law, or
if the police tries to make law for itself, the regulators
cease to be policemen and become soldiers or banditti. In
the task of verifying and sustaining disarmament, the
international police will need only a relatively simple
structure of law and regulatory provisions behind it. Since
the object of a demilitarized international politics is not
to decide the world's multiple power problems but simply
to insure their decision by nonviolent means, there should

be no insuperable obstacle to securing from peoples and governments a general agreement on such international laws and regulations as are necessary. International legislative and judicial institutions will be necessary to declare the requisite laws and support the global police; but such institutions would seem to enter the realm of practical possibility in the degree to which their powers are strictly limited to what is necessary, with no attempt to introduce into the total system any greater global coercion than the objects of demilitarization demand. In designing a modification of our world circuitry, one can make use only of such forces and applications as are available; one cannot turn men into angels, but one can see that their very human and fallible ideas and institutions work more smoothly and usefully than they now do.

The brief foregoing summary plainly leaves open many practical difficulties. It is advanced as a demonstration that, from what we already know about the actual operation of the notions of law, order and coercion in great human societies, a demilitarized international political system is entirely practicable. If the Russian and American leaders and their peoples—to say nothing of other statesmen and peoples—really want, as they say they do, a state of general and complete disarmament, there is nothing inherent in either human nature or the nature of politics to prevent their getting it. The declared goal is a *possible* goal. This is the overwhelmingly important demonstration; it is the "secret" of the international future— much as the greatest "secret" of the atomic bomb was, it was said, the fact that one could be made. Once that fact was known, the technical details of the manufacture were discoverable. The technical details of how a demilitarized or "warless" world will be established are of less present consequence than the fact that the matter can be accomplished; the technical details are discoverable—and that they will be discovered seems to me a very reasonable and conservative conclusion.

One might leave matters there, since there are different ways in which a demilitarized world might evolve and different possible shapes it might take, while the powers of even the best prophecy are limited. But it seems incumbent upon anyone who has come this far to grapple more directly with the remaining difficulties and to attempt a more concrete account of a possible evolution of a demilitarized international system. It is presented in the following chapter, not as a prophecy of what will happen, but as an indication of what might happen, and how.

EIGHT

FROM HERE TO THERE

IN THE SUMMER OF 1964 THE INTERNATIONAL WORLD
presented a scene already markedly different from
that of ten years before. Since the changes had been
gradual and cumulative, their real depth and scope were
not easily recognizable without an effort of memory. In
1954 the Korean War had hardly reached its uneasy close,
and the likelihood of its renewal seemed far more imminent than it does today. Having secured its Korean
rear, Communist rebellion, strongly supported by China,
was driving the French from Indochina, in the main opposed only by John Foster Dulles' announced policy of
"massive retaliation"—which, if it had really meant what
it seemed to say, would have been disastrous. The nuclear
arms race was at its height as the United States and the
Soviet Union vied to develop "droppable" thermonuclear,
or H, bombs, promising energy yields 2000 times those
of the weapons used against Japan, which had themselves
been 2000 times as destructive as all but a few of the
heaviest conventional bombs used in World War II. The
missile race and the terrors of the nonexistent "missile
gap" (the gift of the new "intelligence community" to in-

ternational insanity) still lay ahead; but the stage was set for them.

With the usually neglected exception of Yugoslavia, no visible rifts had yet appeared in the monolithic structure of the Communist empire, now reaching from the Elbe to Vladivostok and Canton and apparently pressing outward from this already huge land base to the conquest of the entire globe. Stalin had died in March, 1953, but the influence of this event on Communist policy was still obscure. The Communist Hukbalahaps were still active in the Philippines; the ambiguous Sukarno regime in Indonesia was scarcely a reliable defense; India was the leading exponent of what seemed an equally ambiguous "neutralism"; the rise of Nasser in Egypt appeared to be providing an open bridge for the Communist conquest of the whole of Africa; there were centers of Communist infection in Latin America and (to more heated imaginations) significant centers of the same kind within the American body politic itself. It is not surprising that a vulgar opportunist such as Joseph McCarthy flourished on these fears or that to millions of Americans the cold war with Communism seemed the one overwhelmingly important fact of international politics; just as to millions within the Communist bloc, defense against the machinations of Western capitalistic "imperialists" and "warmongers" appeared to be the beginning and end of international relations. To most Americans the picture of a vast, consolidated and essentially evil or immoral power, threatening the remainder of the globe with a huge army, on which great air and atomic power had now been superimposed, and advancing (when these military instruments seemed temporarily unserviceable for its purposes) by infiltrative means to which Western democracy could find no answer and which were irreversible in their nature, was overwhelming in its effect.[1]

Such was the rather grim scenario most of us were contemplating in the mid-1950's. Ten years later very little of it remained. The nuclear arms race had not only failed to produce the catastrophe that had seemed so horribly imminent; it was also showing quite definite signs of "leveling off" toward stability. The United States and the Soviet Union between them were still spending perhaps $100 billion a year or more on defense and the weapons race. But the weapons systems themselves appeared to be reaching a plateau of cost and complication (and unreliability) beyond which they were unlikely to go. Khrushchev's projected 100-million tonner aroused little competitive response in the Pentagon. The test-ban treaty, with its real promise of slowing the technological race, was successfully signed, ratified and delivered in 1963. The fantastic and horribly grotesque idea of orbiting weapons systems designed to rain multimegaton thermonuclear bombs on earth (to what possible ends?) appeared to be

[1] I believe that the apparent irreversibility of Communist conquest had more effect than almost any other of its aspects. Westerners were accustomed to the idea that if a reactionary or radical regime won at the polls, it could always be thrown out at the next election. If a nation lost one war, it had always open the possibility of winning the next one. Neither of these ideas was as well based in either constitutional or military fact as it seemed to be, but both were accepted as part of normal politics. The Communist and Nazi-Fascist revolutions eviscerated both of them. The "seizure of power" destroyed all the processes and machinery by which power might later be transferred to other hands; the winning of a war rendered the loser forever incapable of reversing the military verdict. This seemed to create an impossible situation. If a pro-Western regime (like that, for example, of Beneš in Czechoslovakia) held power, there was no way of protecting and continuing it in its position against the sapping tactics of the Communists; but if the Communists overthrew it, there was no way of sapping their regime in turn, because their first care was always to suppress any possibility of sapping.

fading before the saner light of economic, technological and even military reality. And the chances of some "technological breakthrough" that would disastrously alter all the military balances seemed to grow more remote as the weapons themselves grew more colossal and politically unusable.

The "delicate balance of terror" to which Albert Wohlstetter of RAND Corporation pointed in 1958 had in fact proved much sturdier and more stable than he had suggested. It may still be "delicate" enough if one thinks only in military factors; but it has been surrounded by political and moral factors—even those of plain common sense—that have severely damped its potential oscillations. The successful surmounting of the Cuban missile crisis in 1962 demonstrated the comparative inutility of the great weapons systems even in their symbolic role for the practical conduct of international politics; the subsequent test-ban treaty, probably for the first time in the whole history of disarmament, subordinated the strictly military balance to considerations of a more rational international politics. The continuing development of "deterrence" strategy was, in the minds of the soldiers and airmen themselves, undermining in a curious way the basic assumptions of the war system. By the opening of 1964 there seemed little likelihood of a major international war except, perhaps, by technological or, more importantly, political "accident." It is very doubtful that anyone, even the soldiers and technicians engaged upon the maintenance and development of the great weapons systems, could by 1964 really believe that a massive thermonuclear exchange would ever take place.

Great changes had taken place in both the Soviet

Union and the larger Communist empire; Communism was no longer the monolith it had seemed in the mid-1950's. Khrushchev had been in firm command through most of the ten years and had gradually developed new policies and new outlooks to a degree at which they could no longer be regarded as simply the old ones in a deceptive disguise. "De-Stalinization" had been announced in February, 1956, together with the doctrine that there might be "different roads to socialism." This event was apparently the beginning of the rift between Soviet and Chinese Communism—a rift that was to have a powerful effect in restoring to the international political process a flexibility and a genuine utility in adjusting the power struggles of men that were impossible in the rigid strait jackets of military threat. It was not simply that Khrushchev was different from Stalin; the truth was that he was both responding to and exemplifying political necessities that any Soviet regime would sooner or later have been forced to accept. As he gradually but persistently developed the policy of "coexistence," Khrushchev was accepting the inevitable: since neither the Soviet nor the Western power centers could any longer hope to take over the dominance of the world, coexistence became unavoidable. At the same time he was confronted with other pressures that compelled a policy of coexistence rather than one of total war. There was the rise of an educated, bureaucratic elite, which could not forever be kept as the mere puppets of old Communism, any more than the bourgeois bureaucracy of Alexander III's time could be kept forever as mere slavish clerks to the old empire. There was the rising pressure for more consumer goods and better food supplies, which no regime with claims to permanence could disregard. No longer could everything be sacrificed to capital goods and to "defense," and if coexistence was in fact a safe and practicable policy, it meant that these sacrifices to war were no longer justifiable. Khrushchev's sudden downfall in October, 1964, may have modified some of these trends, but can hardly have reversed them.

These circumstances introduced politics, rather than mere dictation, into the internal affairs of the Soviet Union. It was not, of course, a democratic form of politics; but Khrushchev was already a political leader, rather than merely a czar, in the Soviet state, as his dismissal would seem clearly to indicate. To continue to function, he had to keep behind him the Presidium and the Central Committee, the great technical bureaucracies and the "public opinion" that, if allowed little opportunity for vocal expression, plainly worked powerfully through these groups and classes and administrative structures to affect total policy. The Communist empire as a whole was proving too vast and varied an organism to be run centrally from Moscow. Tito's example had proved more profound in its effects than many in 1954 would have prophesied. Actual rebellion in the satellites still could, and would, be forcibly suppressed, as in East Germany and Hungary, but Poland, Czechoslovakia and even Hungary herself by the early 1960's were gradually asserting a political autonomy more and more resembling that of Yugoslavia.

Mao Tse-tung's China (like Tito's Yugoslavia and, it is believed, Ho Chi-minh's North Vietnam) had never properly been a satellite; and it was China that really revived politics within the empire. In the mid-1950's a power issue between Peking and Moscow began to develop, more serious because there was here no such ultimate disparity of force as there was between Moscow and Belgrade. Coexistence was the issue that finally brought the clash into the open. To make good a policy of coexistence, Khrushchev could not push expansionist or threatening moves beyond the situation the West could coexist with. To that extent he had to rewrite Lenin's theory of world revolution, and this revision in turn provided the Chinese Communists with a weapon against him in the power struggle. It may be doubted whether the Chinese, any more than the Russians, really envisage a third world war of universal destruction, leading to global Communism. But a certain parallel exists between the way in which the Chinese have used Khrushchev's "coexistentialism" as a means of weighting their own power in the internal Communist power balances and the way in which Hitler used the alleged spinelessness of the Weimar Republic toward the "Diktat" of Versailles as means of securing his power in Germany. The fact that there can hardly be any real question of a Sino-Soviet war here means that in an important area of the world's power relationship a nonviolent form of politics has been substituted for the crassly military forms that are usually thought to rule.

At the opening of 1964 both the Soviet Union and the Communist empire constructed around it revealed great and progressive changes from their structures of ten years before, and even greater changes from their appearance to the Western world. The United States and the Western community constructed around it had changed as well. For Americans, the cold war had been gradually losing the psychological and intensely emotional values that attached to it in the mid-1950's; and the phrase itself was less and less often heard. At the tragic climax of his career, President Kennedy was still talking about preserving the world for "freedom," but he was much less inclined than his predecessor had been to throw into his perorations the conventional tag about the unchanging Communist resolve "to conquer the world." Eisenhower had always, of course, been a sincere believer in peace and coexistence—if only the Russians would agree to coexist. It is hard to doubt that Kennedy and his advisers made a decision for coexistence that, because it was far more intelligent and perceptive than preceding policy had ever been, must rank with Khrushchev's in its historical importance. The Kennedy Administration (in part because of the necessities of domestic politics and the domestic power struggle) never relaxed its care for military defense; and on the eve of the assassination, the Secretary of Defense was declaring that American military power was in an unchallengeable position of superiority. But it was in its attention to the nonmilitary aspects of a genuine coexistence that the Kennedy Administration revealed the changes being recorded in the United States no less than in the Soviet Union.

It was a minor symbol, but a symbol nevertheless, when Robert Oppenheimer, whom Eisenhower had put behind "a blank wall" on the suspicion that he was a "security risk," was awarded the Fermi medal and was to have received it from Kennedy's hands. It was growing increasingly impossible to see the whole of international politics in terms of a cold war between the "free world" and Communist "slavery." The fears of the mid-1950's, to which American cold-war policy had been a response, were proving increasingly illusory. Nasser had not opened a bridge for Communism into Africa. Southeast Asia had not fallen like a "row of dominoes" to Communist domination and, whatever the outcome might prove to be, the metaphor seemed increasingly inapplicable. Much of the "free world" appeared to be growing increasingly unfree in the old terms of liberal constitutionalism; but much of the "unfree" world appeared to be exerting a capacity for organization, change and growth that was beyond control by American military or economic aid or even by the Peace Corps or its Point Four predecessor. As the original fears tended to diminish through the ten years, the practical difficulties of policy became not less, but only greater. At the end of 1963 the United States had been learning, in Castro's Cuba, in Ngo Dinh Diem's South Vietnam, as it had already begun to learn from Syngman Rhee's South Korea, that everything was far more complicated than the simplicities of cold-war strategy had suggested.

A working international politics could simply not be organized around the two poles of Communism and democracy. It was apparent that over great areas of the globe much time would have to pass before anything at all closely resembling Western representative democracy could evolve from the patterns of populistic dictatorship that were becoming more and more the norm in international politics. In the new international system the Western powers had to adjust to and make use of them; the Russian and Chinese power centers, in trying to use them, also had to adjust to them. Khrushchev, yielding to nationalist pressures from which even Communism has never been free, admitted that there were "different roads to socialism." The West was being forced to admit on its part that there were different roads to "freedom" and that they might as often go by way of military-bureaucratic dictatorship as by way of the majority vote and a representative legislature. But if it was no longer possible to frame the whole of international politics in the crass terms of "Communism" against "democracy," the rigid bipolarization that had formed around these terms could not be maintained. Politically, economically, culturally and even scientifically the iron curtain was much less impenetrable by 1964 than it had been ten years before; and if the phrase "cold war" was less often heard, it was because it was no longer an adequate or useful description of the actual processes of international politics.

All this change was visible in the ten years or so between the development of the hydrogen or thermonuclear weapons and the signing of the test-ban treaty.[2] The period is at least long enough to justify an extrapolation from trends that appear to be at least as clearly marked as those which from the early 1930's led more and more steadily toward World War II.

It is not, I think, at all unreasonable to predict today that the nuclear stalemate will continue indefinitely. The so-called nth-power problem, which ten years before seemed the most dangerous aspect of the nuclear arms race, has in fact been developing toward nuclear stability. Only in France and China is there today any serious effort to enter the "nuclear club"; virtually all other nations have

[2] By tragic accident, it is also the period delimited by the death of Stalin in March, 1953, and the assassination of Kennedy in November, 1963. The first event removed a major obstacle to world development. The effects of the second cannot be fully foreseen, but it appears to have reinforced rather than reversed the new tendencies with which Kennedy's name is associated.

accepted the test-ban treaty. French nuclear development has given no indication that it can or will produce an independent military threat with an independent effect in international politics. Largely symbolic, as has been said, it appears to be directed more toward establishing French power positions within the Western group than toward bringing military force directly to bear upon an international power balance that France cannot independently affect.

In the fall of 1964 the Chinese achieved a nuclear explosion, but it will be many years before their material and industrial resources will permit them to build this success into a completed weapons system (including carriers, directional and target systems, warning and protective devices and reserves) in any way comparable to the two giant systems controlled by the Soviet Union and the United States. Even with a modest nuclear arsenal, the Chinese would still be in much the position of the French. A small Chinese nuclear "capability" would be under all the political restraints imposed by their basic alliance system and would have more relevance to the power balances within the Communist empire than to those in the world.

"Accident," whether political or technological, is of course always possible in a world filled with such staggering amounts of such dangerous explosive. But barring accident, there is nothing pointing today toward an ineluctable thermonuclear exchange, and one is justified in projecting this situation indefinitely. As it continues, what will be the effects on the world political system? It is granted that the power struggle, international and national, will never cease. It follows that if major war is excluded, alternative methods for conducting it must develop. Again, the trend has been continuous over the past decade. As has been argued earlier, the whole course of Cuban history since Fidel Castro emerged from Oriente supplies a case history in the conduct of the power struggle, certainly not without violence, but without major war, even though an explosive complex of local, social, class, national and international power issues is involved. Whether or not the outcome as it has stood so far has been "just" is a matter of passionate dispute and is perhaps impossible of resolution. One can say that on balance it has been at least less unjust, and far more workable within accepted frameworks of international politics, than anything that could have been achieved through the vast destruction of a thermonuclear war.

Any review of the tangled history of Indochina from the Japanese defeat in 1945 to the overthrow of the Ngo Dinh Diem regime in 1963 and the intensification of guerilla war thereafter must lead to a similar conclusion. Neither Soviet nor Chinese Communism on the one hand nor Western democracy on the other ever succeeded in "taking over" the Indochinese states or finally determining their destiny. The basic issues in Southeast Asia were of a kind in fact irrelevant to cold-war strategy and tactics. In the early postwar years, when the Communist leader Ho Chi-minh organized a nationalistic revolution against the French, it occurred to some that the West might do well to accept Ho, an apparently capable leader of local nationalism, as its ally in the reorganization of the world rather than force him into the role of agent of Soviet and Chinese power. Such a policy might have been a rational one at the time; it was also an obviously impossible one because it would have run so deeply counter to the whole psychology and strategy of the cold war. So long as international politics was conceived of exclusively as a battle between democratic "freedom" and Communist "slavery," rational political maneuver was excluded. It is rather striking that by 1964 new tendencies were looking toward the organization of the power struggle in Southeast Asia around the real power factors available rather than merely continuing to fight on ideological lines of little relevance to the area.

President De Gaulle was adumbrating the policy of neutralizing all four of the Indochinese states under what would amount to acceptance of Ho Chi-minh's leadership throughout the area and had initiated it by the recognition of Peking. If this would mean ultimately a "Communist victory" in Indochina, it would not necessarily mean a Chinese victory. It would, rather, detach Indochina from the Chinese Communist empire; and would utilize the fact that the area is ethnically, linguistically and economically distinct from China and looks back upon a long and unhappy tradition of Chinese conquest to create a more stable balance of forces in Southeast Asian power struggles. It would be substituting the actual power factors available there for the unreal fantasies of cold-war strategy.

Whatever may be the course of events in Indochina, solutions of this general kind must be increasingly accepted, so long as the nuclear arsenals rule out a major war and it becomes increasingly apparent that even conventional armies are inapplicable in less than major war situations. The conflict situations that will continue to arise in the less stable areas of the world will in general be of two kinds. On the one hand there will be those—as in Berlin, in the Formosan dispute and perhaps in some others—in which resort even to conventional war involves so immediate a risk of major or general war as to exclude it. On the other hand there will be those—of which the whole Indochina complex is a good example—in which the risk of "escalation" is slight or nonexistent but in which the resort to conventional war can accomplish none of the desired results. The major reason why the United States did not intervene militarily to "save" China from the Communists in the late 1940's was not fear of a major war with the Soviet Union, but the sheer impossibility of controlling the Chinese problem by a military effort, even on an enormous scale. The same situation obtained in the case of Indochina when the French defenses were collapsing in 1954. If the French army, even with large American military assistance, could not "save" that situation, it was most improbable that an American army could do so, even if it were raised to the forbidding levels that General Matthew Ridgway, then Chief of Staff, warned would be necessary even for the attempt. The American failure to employ armed invasion against the Castro revolution in Cuba was due much less to fears of Soviet intervention and of general war than to the patent fact that nothing could be gained by a full-dress American invasion—though America possessed overwhelming conventional military power—except the probable creation of a costly chaos. Again the principle had to be accepted that foreign war was no answer to the Cuban problem (as under the very different international conditions of half a century earlier it had been, more or less); in the last analysis only the Cubans could "save" Cuba. American policy was forced to the lamentable expedient of the

Bay of Pigs invasion. That it proved a fiasco does not alter
the fact that it was about the only even theoretically practicable remaining device through which to apply armed
force to a situation of this kind. And this kind of situation
will increasingly govern in the power relations of the great
military states both with each other and with the lesser
powers. Some will be more responsive to violent solutions
and more productive of violence than was the Cuban situation. But organized war, prepared and conducted by
major forces of the great armed powers, or even of the few
lesser ones that can be considered (such as Israel or Sweden) as seriously armed to meet foreign war, will become
an increasingly unlikely possibility.

What this situation must imply is that the military
establishments will progressively decline into forces policing, through their defensive roles, a more or less established world order, while international politics advances
to the generally nonviolent regulation and adjustment of
the power struggles that will continue to take place in it.
The threat of war, as it becomes increasingly less "credible" and less usable, is bound to become less and less
prominent in international affairs, while the question of
whether the enormous costs and even more enormous
perils of the supermilitarized system cannot be dispensed
with is bound to become more urgent. A general and complete disarmament already seems to most authorities to be
necessary; it will come increasingly to seem possible and
practicable. Again, it is a matter of extrapolation from
presently observable trends.

Today general and complete disarmament is irremedi-
ably bogged in the old dilemma of disarmament conferences—that by lending maximum political importance

to the weapons systems they are trying to abolish, they automatically halt any progress toward their abolition. I think it quite impossible today to draft a general disarmament treaty so exactly balancing all the military factors—force levels, controls, inspections and so on—that it will be generally acceptable either to the few military great powers or to the many smaller ones. Nor is there any escape from the dilemma in the often heard argument that since it is "international tensions" that lead to the creation of armaments, advance must lie through the reduction of the tensions, whereupon the reduction of armaments will follow. This argument presents two difficulties: for one thing, it is very largely the armaments that produce the current tensions; for another, the elimination of "tension"—in the sense of conflict of will or even of interest in the international system—is impossible. The realization is already beginning to emerge that, whether regarded as cause or as effect, the great armaments are increasingly *irrelevant* to international power politics. It is impossible today to draft a generally acceptable disarmament treaty; but in a few years' time it will be possible at least to draft a constitution for a demilitarized world to which the great weapons systems will be irrelevant, upon which a disarmament treaty might therefore be founded.

The authors of the American Constitution, after all, first produced a workable design for their "more perfect union." Only with this general design in hand did they proceed to the specific clauses establishing the mutual disarmament required by the general design—the clauses forbidding the states to make war, bringing their armed forces (the militia) under the control of the central government and so on. Similarly, disarmament conferences will increasingly be forced to begin with the constitutional problem of a demilitarized world, rather than leaving this as a decorative afterthought to be appended to their nice balances of force levels and inspection systems. Studies such as the very modest one conducted in 1963 by the Peace Research Institute (on behalf of the Arms Control and Disarmament Agency) into the "political control of an international police force under general disarmament"[3] will more and more provide the foundations for demilitarization, supplanting in this respect the present technological investigations into such matters as the detectability of underground nuclear explosions. The testban treaty has given us our first small inkling of the truth: it is only as such technical issues as detectability or energy release or similar comparative military factors become irrelevant in international politics that advance toward demilitarization will become possible.

A few years hence people will be talking much more about demilitarization than about disarmament and will be seeing demilitarization as a constitutional problem rather than as the technical problem now apparently subsumed under the heading of disarmament. There are already, of course, many proposed constitutions for a peaceable world, from the Covenant of the League of Nations or the Charter of the United Nations to Grenville Clark and Louis B. Sohn's *World Peace Through World Law*. All, I think, suffer from the fact that they start from the assumption that organized international war is a factor inherent in international social organization and confine

[3] Arthur Waskow, "Quis Custodiet?" with accompanying papers (Washington, Peace Research Institute, 1963).

themselves to attempts at suppressing it or at least miti-
gating its incidence. The developing draft constitution of
a demilitarized world will differ from these; it will have to
start from the assumption, not merely that major wars can
be suppressed, but that the war system itself is actually
passing into desuetude and can be abolished. Since organized war will in fact be growing increasingly unlikely
and increasingly peripheral to the normal conduct of international politics, these tentative constitution makers will
be compelled to face frankly the possibility of its total
disappearance. They will have to ask themselves (as no
one, I think, has as yet really done) what new intercon-
nections, feedbacks and servomechanisms this trend is
bringing into the total system of international politics,
and how they would continue to operate if carried to the
logical conclusion of general demilitarization. From such
questions it is bound soon to emerge that the problem of
war is not really one of partially diluting or chaining up
the war system; it is the much more creative one of how to
make positive use of the possibilities opened up by a demilitarized world.

In a way, this process is the one used by the authors of
the American Constitution. One requisite of their "more
perfect union" was the mutual disarmament of the states.
But their system was not founded upon state disarmament, which came more as a consequence of the new
federal system than as the basis on which it was established. There was no precise apportionment of military
power among the states; inspection systems were not set
up to insure, for example, that New York would not be
surpassed by Pennsylvania's militia or that Virginia's regi-
ments would have a precisely balancing equality with

those of Massachusetts. The Civil War may suggest that the solutions were imperfect; it does not alter the fact that this was the way in which solutions had to be sought then, as it still is now.

It is plain that the accomplishment of the unusually able men who made up the leadership of the Philadelphia Convention cannot be repeated today. They were dealing with a generally homogenous community of about four million souls, sharing long and common traditions of law, politics and military organization. The global problem of today involves a total population almost a thousand times as great, with no common language and with a wide disparity of cultural and political traditions. Even if the world had at its command brains as able as those of Madison, Hamilton, Adams and Washington, they could not in a single summer's session produce a constitution for a demilitarized globe approximating the soundness of the constitution for a mutually demilitarized America produced at Philadelphia in 1787. But the new constitutional work, if it proceeds less rapidly, will have to proceed along the same lines as the old. The organization of the power struggle comes first; control over the various instrumentalities, military or otherwise, of power can be attended to once the basic organization is understood and agreed on.

As attention turns in this direction, it will be seen that the underlying objective is the creation of a world policed, in place of the present world, periodically torn to rags by its own military establishments. The essential requirements for a world in general controlled by police rather than military actions must soon become clear. It cannot be the function of an international (or supranational) organization to resolve the world's power struggles; the most it can expect to accomplish is to see that they are as far as possible constrained to nonviolent means. In this world system as a whole the coercive or police power requisite for this task will overwhelmingly be supplied by the national governments and their national police forces. Some power problems will remain, however, and these can be dealt with only on the international level. As the nuclear stalemate continues, it will be seen that they are much less extreme and much less intractable than they had appeared to be in the system based upon major organized war. But to police such problems—to insure, that is, that the international power struggle is continued with a minimum of violence—will call for the same essential elements as are required to maintain a comparatively nonviolent "order" within a nation or any lesser community. These are: at least a minimum body of police-enforceable law generally accepted and agreed to by all; a judicial system capable of interpreting and applying this law, within the areas to which it is relevant, in specific cases; and an over-all coercive power capable of seeing that the regulations are generally observed and the judicial determinations are accepted.

The minimum of law necessary, not to resolve international power struggles, but to restrain them to substantially nonviolent means, is not in fact very complex. It need go little beyond the fundamental principle that armed aggression by any state upon another's territory is illegal and that any attempt (after disarmament has become general) to revive the armaments capable of effecting such aggression is criminal. This much law is enforceable by a police; there is universal agreement upon the first part of it already, and as organized war tends, for the reasons discussed above, to become more and more clearly superfluous, agreement upon the second should become easier. Supranational governmental institutions strictly confined to administering this much of world law, and provided with coercive or police forces rigidly limited in their authority to uphold it, should then become feasible.

One can picture a global conference of the nations being summoned within not too many years from today. Its object would be general demilitarization; but in its approach and its methods it would be unlike any disarmament conference so far held. It would begin, not with the technical balancing acts that are the customary preoccupations of such gatherings, but with the design of a global system, or constitution, that would be workable under a state of demilitarization. Even in this it would not conceive its task (as international conferences have so often done) as that of creating a system to "enforce peace" or to "keep the peace"; its object would be a system capable only of enforcing that minimum of global law necessary to make peace—in the restricted sense of the absence of major organized warfare—possible.

Such a convocation would not regard itself as a legislature, or even as a "constituent assembly" of the kind that has loomed so large in French and other modern histories. Its purpose would not be to make law, but rather to discern and declare those elements of law, order and organization already available to the world for the working circuitry of a demilitarized system. It would have to be broadly representative in character, but the precise weighting of the voting rights would be as unimportant as they were in the Philadelphia Convention, because the aim, as was true of that convention, would be not to record the triumph of the majority over minority views but to state fundamentals on which all participants could and would substantially agree. Out of such a gathering there would—and quite probably will, in the not too distant future—emerge a working diagram of a world "policed."

The diagram will be submitted for general ratification. To succeed, it must obviously receive the unanimous acceptance of all the great military states and of as many of the lesser ones as may seem necessary to avoid the subsequent destruction of the system. The pressures for universal acceptance will be very powerful: the desire to escape the appalling threat of the great weaponry; the fact that the diagram will make better provision for the security and survival of all major interests involved than the weapons can do; and the fact that it will represent, not a blueprint for a drastically revised world system, but rather no more than a statement or codification of the actual mechanism visibly at work in international politics. Stated in only slightly different terms, these were the pressures that secured the ratification of the American Constitution. The perils of rejecting the "more perfect union" of 1787 were much less extreme than those of rejecting a demilitarized world system; yet, because the Philadelphia draft had been prepared essentially in the way here suggested, its rejection was hardly possible.[4]

4 It is, of course, idle to ask what would have happened if some of the closer votes in the big states had gone the other way; but the general promptness of the ratification indicates that there was really no workable alternative and that the country would in any event have had to come to something very close to the Philadelphia draft. The two "hold-out" states—North Carolina and Rhode Island—which did not return their ratifications until after the new government was in opera-

With an agreed diagram or program for a demilitarized world thus firmly in hand, disarmament itself will have a solid base on which to stand. It can and will proceed thereafter as rapidly as the economic and internal political difficulties involved will permit. The military difficulties will have become irrelevant, as they were to the American states once they had agreed in the Constitution not to make war on each other and to leave the ultimate regulation of their armed forces to the Congress. They were so little relevant, in fact, that Congress thereafter largely neglected its responsibility for the regulation of the "militia," which decayed in a general disinterest in all military factors until the Civil War.

The parallel, of course, is merely suggestive. The Constitution established its thirteen federated states as a community that would be policed rather than subjected to the useless arbitrations of war. This is not merely a modern interpretation; the *Federalist* papers frequently argue the necessity of union in order to avert wars among the states, leaving all internal power struggles to the police power. The projected global constitution, or diagram, will have to accept the necessary requirements of a policed community. Doubtless the first of them is that the authority of the policeman, so long as he is acting within his authority, is absolute. No man can be left free to decide for himself whether he will or will not obey a police order. The order may be challenged afterward on the ground that it was wrongfully given, but the order itself must be obeyed. In a world policed there must not only be a cer-

---

tion, may find their counterparts among some of the small nations; if so, their experience is reassuring, for they also had no real alternative open to them save to give their assent in the end.

tain minimum of police-enforceable international law, but there must also be a supranational authority of some kind to direct the enforcement. The nations, having agreed in their own self-interest to be bound by certain minimum regulations (the most important of which is disarmament to their own police-force levels), must accept an authority to administer these regulations whose decisions will be beyond veto by any one nation or group of nations. This course seems unavoidable, not only to insure that the regulations are observed, but also to give confidence to all members of the global community that the rules are being, and will continue to be, observed by all others. And it will become possible in the measure that the sanction of this supranational authority is restricted to administering and enforcing only those laws and rules that have been agreed to by all to be indispensable to the safety and viability of the global community.

The authority would, presumably, be composed and appointed in much the same way as the United Nations Security Council, but the requirement of great-power unanimity would have to be dispensed with. The authority would have to be capable of action where action became necessary. It may be asked what possibility there is that the great powers would ever acquiesce in such an action. The present unanimity rule is not merely (as so many now seem to imagine) a Russian invention preserved only in order that the Soviet Union may abuse it. It is a reflection, rather, of a fundamental fact of international politics and perhaps of all political action—that order under law can advance only where there is common consent. Since law is essentially a restriction upon freedom of assent or dissent, this circumstance represents

a dilemma that has never yielded to philosophical resolution; it is, indeed, the dilemma Calhoun unsuccessfully
attacked in the gathering crisis before the Civil War with
his doctrine of the "concurrent majority." But it yields
every day to practical necessity. There are many veto-free
international authorities operating today in special and
minor areas where it is recognized that action is more
essential for the good of all concerned than the precise
balance of power that the action may represent. It is true
that in such minor authorities each participating nation
normally retains the right of secession if the decisions go
against it. But the decisions are binding until the secession takes place. And there are rarely any secessions.
The old military rule that "a bad decision is better than
no decision at all" is understood to apply, and even
sovereign states will accept unpalatable decisions for the
sake of getting a decision.

The states will do so the more readily as the decisions
are technical and administrative rather than political.
Politics concerns the organization of power—the power
struggle as such—while administration and technique
concern simply its application. The supranational and
veto-free global authority will become a possibility as its
authority is restricted to technical and administrative
rather than political problems. Neither the Soviet Union
nor the United States nor any other sovereign national organization will accept a supranational and veto-free authority empowered to decide issues on which the rise or
fall of national power will depend. All will much more
readily accept a supranational authority empowered only
to see that such issues are decided by nonmilitary and
in general nonviolent means. In an American industrial

quarrel both management and unions will bitterly resist any effort by the central government to decide their power struggle, while both will readily and even gratefully accept all the legal and police measures that ensure its conduct by nonviolent means. That the nations, sitting under the unimaginable terror of thermonuclear destruction, will not accept this much seems improbable.

Assuming that the draft convention for a demilitarized world has progressed thus far, a good deal else will follow. The veto-free supranational authority must be restricted to decisions that will not themselves alter the basic power relationships between the member states, great or small. It must, at the same time, be provided with the coercive force necessary to discharge its responsibilities within the restricted area of suppressing violence. It will have two functions: one to declare and, as necessary, to amend the minimum of law that by general consent is seen to be necessary; the other to govern and direct the police force necessary to insure its observance. The institutional arrangements have been adumbrated already in the United Nations. The declaratory and legislative functions will be vested in a committee like the Security Council, which will appoint and control the actions of an administrative officer—playing a role like that of the U.N. Secretary General—who will direct the international police. The acts of this director, like those of any other administrative officer in a great organization, will not be subject to veto unless and until he oversteps the limits of his authority. There will have to be a judiciary system capable of passing upon the issues that will undoubtedly be raised here, as well as a good many other issues, such as what constitutes "rearmament," what may be regarded as "preparations for aggressive war" or what acts of the supranational authority may overstep the limits of its authority and may tend to "load" the power struggle rather than to secure its nonviolent prosecution.

The Security Council of the United Nations has been paralyzed because the way in which it was set up and empowered makes it, inevitably, the arena for the power struggle among the great states. Majority votes in such a body never will and never can be accepted as determinative in a fundamental struggle for power. But a body detached from the power issues, concerned not with the question of whether the United States or the Soviet Union or any other nation is to "dominate the world" but only with the elimination of organized war as a means of determining such issues, need not suffer a similar paralysis. The coercive force at its command need not, and cannot, be an army conquering the world. In a world that has agreed to face up to the real problems of a demilitarized society its role would be little more than that of the traffic policeman or the investigating agency. It would have to see that some rules were kept and that some kinds of conspiracy against world order were suppressed. To fulfill these tasks in a world already agreed upon general disarmament it would not have to be equipped with thermonuclear bombs or maintain a great army. Its job would be a police job; and the question of who was to "dominate the world"—to make its laws, to determine its power relationships, to affect its cultural course— could be left to nonmilitary instruments.

The probable continuance in such a situation of local violence, guerilla war, subversion; the possible misuse of national police forces against neighbor states; or the possibility of collapse in any of the presently organized great states—all these admittedly present problems to a demilitarized world order for which the solution is not immediately obvious. All that can be said is that by the end of 1964 a world effectively demilitarized at the moment by the nuclear stalemate appeared to be dealing with them rather satisfactorily. The projected supranational authority would have to be endowed with some legislative and judicial powers in order to be able to amend the accepted law as the development of the world community required. Better principles for dealing with such a problem as the Congo will doubtless be developed and announced. It is as useless to go into the terms in which they might be expressed as it would have been for the authors of the American Constitution to go into the terms of all the laws that might be generated by the system they conceived. The only point to be stressed here is that demilitarization does open the possibility of a rational global constitution—of a generally self-consistent and viable means of running world politics without threatening disaster to any of the great power interests involved. It constitutes no more than the way in which the world is actually being run today. When this rather simple fact generally sinks home, demilitarization will become, not only possible, but even inevitable.

The notion that the total abolition of organized international war was becoming a political possibility was advanced by this author some years ago; that it met with a complete incredulity is hardly necessary to say. The plainly required answer was to develop a demonstration that a warless world was practicable and possible; this demonstration was apparently persuasive to many minds, but was eviscerated by a question that became something of a platitude in the discussions at the Center for the Study of Democratic Institutions. "You have produced a Utopia that is logical, attractive and self-consistent. No doubt it would work. But how do we get from here to there?" This chapter is my attempt at an answer. I have tried to show how it is quite possible (and in my own mind quite probable) that the transition from "here" to "there" will take place. I have avoided the introduction of emotional, moral or psychological factors —these are, after all, the constants in all socio-political equations down through the ages and have little effect upon the solutions arrived at from time to time. I have tried to concentrate on the variables of political relationships and to derive from them equations soluble in the terms of a world generally disarmed and demilitarized. I have tried only to project trends—of history, of thought, of power organization, of growing law and order—already clearly visible. As these continue—and in the absence of a huge military catastrophe they must continue —I believe we shall find ourselves "there" much sooner than now seems possible to most people.

PROPHECY

THROUGHOUT THIS BOOK THERE HAS BEEN AN EAR-
nest effort to avoid Utopianism in either spirit or
method. The Utopian first imagines his ideal society or system and then searches back from it to establish
what connections he can with the actualities of the dis-
tressful present. Here the consistent attempt has been to
reverse this approach; to use only known data and observable present trends in order to search forward into
a future that, while making no claims to perfection, at
least looks as though it might be possible. But even so,
one is virtually forced into a kind of Utopianism at the
end. When the projection has been carried as far as it
reasonably can go, the resultant model of the demilitarized world order leaves too many gaps, too many
unanswered questions. How, in such a system, will this
or that specific problem be met? Just how will the international power struggle proceed? In the absence of the
organized war system and its powerful threats, what will
be the working techniques of international relations? How
will a general relapse into war be averted? Or what possibilities will open for greater progress toward general

freedom and justice in the world community?

All these questions have been discussed already, but in necessarily general terms that many find vague and unsatisfactory. Yet, since the future is unforeseeable, more precise answers must rely upon the imagination. One can resort only to the inventions—inherently undemonstrable —of the Utopian or, if one prefers, the science-fiction writer. In a sense, this concluding chapter is science fiction, and as such is no less open to the assaults of the skeptical. It has no other claim to validity than the extent to which it is inherently plausible. It has no ramparts of scholarly fact behind which to defend itself from those who do not wish, or cannot bring themselves, to believe it. It makes no appeal to the new mathematical techniques (or pseudo-techniques) of socio-military analysis—operations research, games theory, informational theory, systems theory and so on—to give it a meretricious authority. It does, however, have one answer to skepticism that the Utopian cannot usually command: what is your alternative? And it is a fairly crushing answer when it is backed by all the awful authority of the fifty-megaton bomb. The actual, physical existence of weapons with a destructive energy release, not of one ton or even of ten tons (the World War II maximum) of high explosive, but of fifty *million* tons or even more is a fact. In the arsenals of the major powers there is now a stock of actual, existing weapons capable, if not of obliterating the human race, at any rate of reducing its survivors to "unmen." With this fact the world society must deal in one way or another; and those who will not or cannot believe that it will deal with this fact more or less in the way here imagined are under a deadly serious obligation

—personal, moral and also intensely practical—to say how they think it will or can be dealt with. Skepticism is usually salutary; but in this context skepticism alone is more than immoral, it is practically disastrous. Here is an area in which one may be as skeptical as one likes, but in which one *must* back the skepticism with something better.

Successful fiction must always proceed from certain assumptions, mutually agreed between author and reader. The assumptions here adopted were, generally, stated in the preceding chapter. It is assumed that in the not too distant future the conditions and considerations making possible a demilitarized world society will have begun to emerge. There will have been no thermonuclear interchange and no major war will have occurred; there will have been no revolutionary changes within any of the presently stable great-power systems and no serious internal wars in any—the United States, Western Europe, the Soviet Union, China, India will still constitute the major famework of the international order. They will look much as they do now, and the world order built around them will not differ drastically from what we today see before us. In some respects it will have recorded considerable improvement; but in others it will have raised new difficulties and perils.

The time is, let us say, 1980.[1] The problems of West Berlin and the German frontiers have been settled, at least in that basic sense that is the only way in which in-

[1] Or any other date one may prefer. One simply needs a temporal base line. The year 1980 is sufficiently plausible; it rounds off a decade and provides an interesting symmetry. Today the Berlin blockade of 1948 lies sixteen years in the past, while 1980 lies sixteen years in the future.

ternational issues ever are settled. Diplomatic arguments may still be going on over occupation troops, rights of access and even more significant questions of trade or currency, but the steam has gone out of them—for the simple reason that everyone has realized that Germany is not worth a Soviet-Western war. The German question has become irrelevant to the international power problem. To accept the situation substantially as it had existed in 1964 is still disagreeable to many in East Germany, in West Germany, in the Soviet Union and the United States, but the time has gone by in which it is possible for anyone to risk a general war in their behalf, and the constellations of real power in the world no longer revolve around the regulation of convoys on the autobahn. The German question has been settled, as truly as was the question of Alsace-Lorraine through the forty years after 1871; and short of another world cataclysm arising out of different causes, no one is expecting its revival.

The Formosan question has been settled in much the same way. There has been no formal treaty, and the Chinese in Peking still keep the issue alive for political and propagandist purposes, much as the Allied powers after 1918 kept the issue of the defaulted Russian Czarist bonds alive long after it was apparent to everyone that it was not an issue of the kind around which great international power struggles could crystallize into war. Should another global war ever arise, Formosa might take on pressing strategic importance, but it will not itself provide an exciting "cause" for one, and a third world war is in any event excluded from international politics. Indeed, since the passing of the old dictator, Chiang Kai-shek, the Chinese have themselves been working toward a reunion of the "two Chinas." It is not a development on which Washington has looked with enthusiasm, but since it is proceeding by nonviolent means, Washington has no way (and no real wish) to prevent it.

Indochina has been brought together into a confederation under the leadership of Ho Chi-minh's Communist successors in North Vietnam. This union has been brought about with Chinese aid and support; but, once accomplished, it has tended to free Indochina from the domination of Peking. Indochina is not a satellite of Peking; it has, rather, followed the pattern of Tito's Yugoslavia or of Nasser's United Arab Republic, which made much use of Moscow's support in establishing itself but never became a Soviet satellite or even, in terms, Communist. India has continued as a still poverty-stricken but stable and successful as well as independent national community; Indonesia has suffered more internal troubles but has likewise maintained her independence and seems a viable form of socio-political organization. Among all these medium and major power centers—embracing, between them, a considerable majority of the inhabitants of the planet—conflicts of interest or policy continue to arise, but they are seen to be of a kind, on the one hand susceptible to resolution by negotiation or diplomacy, and on the other hand incurable by resort to war. It has already become apparent that in all this great context organized war is not only forbidden by the nuclear arsenals but has also quite lost its meaning as a "continuation of policy by other means." The "other" means cannot continue policy, or politics; once resorted to, they can only destroy all policy. But with the "other" means for the time being excluded, it is becoming increasingly apparent that politics or policy itself is serving very well as a regulator of the relations of the great armed and more or less stabilized power centers.

Elsewhere, however, international politics is less simple. The Middle East, North Africa and most of sub-Saharan Africa are seen to have assumed a greater measure of stability than they had appeared to promise back in 1965. Throughout all these areas the "new" governments (already fifteen or twenty years old and a number representing revivals from a great antiquity) generally operate under democratic constitutional forms but are in fact populist dictatorships. They are governed, typically, by very small and largely foreign-educated elites, battling fiercely to maintain their own local power and prestige, but who have, at the same time, a genuine interest in raising the cultural and power levels of their primitive peoples—many still living in nomadic or tribal cultures, many more representing the almost equally primitive slum dwellers in the ancient commerical or more modern industrial urban complexes. Nationalism, a great if dangerous tool, has provided these leaders with the main source of their power, but it is not a very helpful ideology for peoples short of education, short of capital, short of trained bureaucrats, short of technicians and of accepted legal institutions. Under the circumstances the military *coup d'état* and the palace revolution have been endemic, as they were for so long in Latin America.

Historians, indeed, have been taking an increasing interest in the parallels (no less than the great differences) between the development of Latin America after the collapse of the Spanish colonial empire at the beginning of the nineteenth century and the development of Africa after the collapse of European colonial empires from 1945 on. There were at least enough similarities in the two developments to suggest that the same underlying social and historical process was at work in both. Both Africa and Latin America were, as colonialism ended, large, fairly populous areas, fertile in natural resources and badly underdeveloped by comparison with the societies of the northern temperate zone. In Latin America there was a large indigenous Indian and imported slave population, exploited and governed by small Iberian and Creole elites. In Africa, history had moved more slowly and perhaps more majestically, but there was still the indigenous Negro mass, mingled with importations from Eurasia that had been coming in since antiquity, all in general ruled by small elite groups stemming from a foreign culture. The parallel, of course, cannot be pushed too far. But if the native Creole elites who in general took power in Latin America were representatives of an alien culture, so in considerable measure were the native but Western-trained African leaders who took command after 1945. The Bolívars and San Martíns rose in the name of liberty to reject the dominance of Spain, from which they were descended; the Ben Bellas and Nkrumahs rose in the name of liberty to reject the dominance of the Western culture of which they were exemplars.

By 1980 African politics has come to look very much like Latin American politics after 1808. For a variety of reasons there have been no great intra-African wars comparable to those (the Paraguayan War of 1865, for example) that did so much damage to the Western Hemisphere system. At the same time Africa, as was true of Latin America through the nineteenth and early

twentieth centuries, has triggered no great wars among
the major military powers. The new African leadership,
slim as may be its base among the peoples it represents,
has on the whole been doing very well. There has been
too much military revolt and internal stress, as there had
been throughout the previous century and a half in Latin
America; but no African state has mounted formally organized war upon another (just as no Latin American
state had done so since the Chaco War of the 1930's—
a half-century earlier), although they have not infrequently provided bases, weapons and logistic support
for guerilla or revolutionary wars waged in neighboring
territories. The long and bloody guerilla war in Angola
remains as an example. The Portuguese empire in Angola was finally overthrown in much the same way as
was the French empire in Algeria in the 1960's—by a
bitter partisan warfare sustained from without, with the
Congo and Ghana playing the roles of Tunis and Mo-
rocco in the North African conflict, but in an international political context that rendered great-power intervention and great-power war as impracticable as it had
been in Algeria. Africa on the whole has been successfully carving out her own destiny, and the great military
powers have seen no interests of their own so vitally involved in the process as to bring them to the risk of a
thermonuclear war.

To the average newspaper reader in 1980 the world
seems about as safe and stable as it seemed to the average
newspaper reader in, say, 1912. Yet there is ample reason for alarm. Perhaps the most immediate is the problem of South Africa. Since the end of Portuguese rule
in Angola the issue of race relations in the Union (and

Southern Rhodesia) has been looming as the one "irre-pressible" and seemingly insoluble conflict. Since the mid-1960's thoughtful men had been predicting that there was no final answer for it save a Negro insurrection that could not stop short of the destruction of white supremacy throughout the southern end of Africa if it did not, indeed, lead to the bloody extermination of the white population. It is apparent that the sub-Saharan African states, driven by African nationalism, are already doing all in their power to foment this struggle. If it comes to a bloody outbreak on any great scale, they will supply bases, support and light weapons and might easily in the process entangle the great military powers in issues in which the direct national interests of the great powers themselves are not engaged.

Elsewhere in the underdeveloped world, especially in Latin America, it is evident that the basic problems of social revolution have received no good answer. Wherever a small and wealthy power elite continues to control a great mass of poverty-stricken, uneducated, unhealthy and exploited people, the seeds of violent revolt and civil and guerilla war are present. Some states, including those both of the dictatorial and democratic type as well as more subtle mixtures of the two, are showing increasing promise of ultimately achieving evolutionary and largely nonviolent answers to situations of this kind. For others there seems no possible solution short of the total destruction of the existing power structure and its reconstitution along new lines. This process may entail a greater or lesser degree of actual violence (when it occurred in Cuba in the early 1960's, there was comparatively little bloodshed), but it cannot happen with "justice" under the legal system enshrining the old power structure. Force and violence are implicit in situations of this kind. Such situations are not so much themselves "causes" of revolution—for societies in which a wealthy few have unjustly and grossly exploited the many have often endured over centuries—as they are invitations to the violent and opportunities for those of revolutionary and egotistic ambition. Modern revolutionaries are essentially manipulators. As such they are trebly armed— by the new "expectations" of the poverty-stricken peoples to whom they offer their leadership; by the power of modern communication and propaganda facilities, more effective both in the suppression of truth and the propagation of error than the authors of the First Amendment ever dreamed could be possible; and by the contradictions inherent in all contemporary sociopolitical ethical systems, which makes it a simple matter (with the aid of the raucous loud-speakers) to turn any system against itself.[2] The modern revolutionary leaders (and to some extent, perhaps, it was always true) are manipulators of inherently unstable and explosive situations, at worst simply in the interest of their own power

[2] The ramifications here are almost endless. It is often said that the Indian elite turned the British Raj out of India by utilizing its own Victorian ethical system against it. Throughout Latin America there is a deep-rooted belief that the ills of the continent flow uniquely from the exploitations of United States capitalism. Such a belief could not have arisen from an examination of the economic ethics of Latin American systems; it could only be generated out of the conflicting ethical principles North Americans have tried to apply to their politico-economic operations. In his assault on American sugar and mining interests in Cuba, Castro has found perhaps his greatest ally in North American doubts and criticisms of the ethics of these operations. While democracy may suffer more than totalitarianism from its ethical inconsistencies, the problem is not unknown behind the iron curtain, as Peking turns the Leninist ethic against a Moscow whose purposes it no longer serves.

and glory, at best in the interest of some vision of national prosperity and power, but more commonly, no doubt, in some mixture of both motives. Such revolutionaries and the movements they generate have never been easily dealt with in the international system. By 1980 they are becoming serious.

So long as the revolutionary operated within his own national system, he was not a cause of too great alarm. There have been many violent and sometimes extremely destructive revolutions in this or that area of the world which the international political system as such took calmly. With the increasing integration of the world system, unfortunately, the local revolution became less and less local. Increasingly the local leaders were driven to seek outside support, outside bases and outside weapons supplies; they could get them only from the great military powers, who would supply or withhold them only in accordance with great-power interests. The revolutionary, primarily intent only on destroying an internal power structure, was thus soon involving the whole international power structure in his hopes and ambitions. The international order of the 1960's had only just managed to swallow the Castro revolution in Cuba without disaster; as it began to be propagated throughout the more vulnerable areas of Latin America in the 1970's, flourishing always on Soviet support and on the basic contradictions in Western politico-economic ethics (which recognized that much in the South American economy was wrong and unjust but that any drastic and violent revision would also be wrong and probably even more unjust in the end), it was creating dangers for which the statesmen, the soldiers and the political philosophers of the time could not find any good answers. By 1980 students are looking into the broad problem of social revolution in a new and far more sophisticated way than they had examined it in the past; they are approaching it, rather, in the way that sociologists of the early 1960's had begun to approach problems of industrial warfare and collective bargaining—as a process to be understood, rather than as a war to be adjudged for its "merits." Their analysis is instructive; unfortunately, they have not carried it too far as yet.

But if by 1980 the racial problem in South Africa and the more general problem of social revolution in the underdeveloped areas are both threatening, the one most threatening problem of all—the one that fills every lesser international issue with an appalling peril—is the problem of the superweaponry. Since Hiroshima, now thirty-five years in the past, no nuclear weapon has been fired "in anger" anywhere. Even the nuclear arms race has, since the test-ban treaty of 1963, tended to level off on a stabilized plateau of horror. Even the regimented scientist-technicians are not frantically looking for new "breakthroughs"—such as multimegaton missiles launched from orbiting satellites or superperfect antimissile defensive systems—partly because the technology has become too complex (and too unreliable) to be carried further, but mainly because the effort has been coming to seem increasingly pointless. The "nuclear club" has only five members: the American and Soviet giants, Britain and France with their much smaller establishments, and China, which has successfully developed nuclear weapons of her own but as yet has hardly more than a token arsenal. Disarmament, on the other hand, has made no significant progress. For economic reasons the major military powers have somewhat further reduced their conventional military establishments, but the great weapons remain—standing always on sleepless alert, mobilized always for instant action in their missile silos, Polaris tubes and long-range bombers. The international atmosphere of 1980 has already been compared with that of the generally confident, manageable and generally unsuspecting years before 1914; but in 1980 no thoughtful man can forget how that optimistic world was suddenly destroyed by its own "deterrent" weapons systems, its overgrown defensive armies, its massive armor and artillery, its irreversible mobilization tables. The nuclear deterrent system has worked better than that which the soldiers and statesmen of the early twentieth century had tried to put together with their vast conscript armies; but the price of failure has risen exponentially. The "balance of terror" has grown so complex and so delicate that the risks of mere technological accident —the malfunction of a detection or control circuit or of a psychopath introduced unwittingly into the command system—are becoming insupportable. But there are much more frightening risks than these: the risks of political or diplomatic "accident," like the vast accident of 1914, in which fear and miscalculation of motive and of potentials combined to produce the disaster that no one wanted and from which none really profited.

Superficially, the course of international politics may seem rather more serene than usual, but there are the latent forces in all the peoples—the forces of hatred, of suspicion, of thirst for personal power, of nationalist ambition, always standing ready to convert even a minor contretemps into a major catastrophe. The international order had without much difficulty withstood the Congo crisis; in the Cuban missile crisis of 1962 it had perhaps come somewhat closer to the brink; the final liquidation of Portuguese rule in Angola in the early 1970's had been an even "closer call," with Soviet and Western policies often at variance, with the Chinese shipping small arms to one faction in competition with Soviet support for another, and with the impracticability of U.N. police intervention on the pattern of those in Palestine and in the Congo because the only legitimate government in the area—the Portuguese regime—refused to ask for it. For some years the situation remained not only ugly but dangerous, always capable of fanning the flames of nationalistic reaction to the explosion point.

But in the end, as in the case of the Congolese bloodshed and the Algerian civil war, it led to no great-power war because none of the great powers felt that its whole fate and future were committed to the outcome in Angola. Actually, the West was more embarrassed by the continued supremacy of the white Portuguese regime in Angola than it was committed to its defense (the same had been true in the case of the Belgian-backed regime in Katanga in the early 1960's), and no really serious great-power issue was involved. The great-power systems —China, Russia, Western Europe and the United States —were prepared to fish for advantage in the Angolese power struggle, but the outcome was not of vital or critical importance to any of them; and as the Portuguese collapse became inevitable, they were willing enough to support a U.N. police operation (on the Congo model) that would help to limit the carnage and bring the independent African Republic of Angola into being. It was noted with interest that the Russians this time met their financial commitments in support of the U.N. neutral police force, while it was the Chinese (now full members of the U.N. and occupying a permanent seat on the Security Council) who refused.

The Angola crisis was successfully surmounted, but South Africa, to say nothing of other very perilous problems, remained, while the whole international order still danced recklessly upon the fuse caps of fifty-million-ton bombs. There was no room, in this appalling situation, for complacent relapse upon the conclusion that since the thermonuclear weapons had kept the peace for some thirty-five years, they would always continue to do so. The old, conventional military systems had, after all, kept the peace in Europe for some forty years when they suddenly blew up in 1914. During the 1970's a great deal of very serious thought had been given to the possibility of a demilitarized world and to the constitutional structure it would have to assume. The question was debated long and seriously in the U.N. session of 1979, with the result that an Assembly resolution was adopted, and assented to unanimously by the Security Council, setting up a commission to sit during 1980 and prepare a draft constitution for a demilitarized world.[3] It has to be kept small, in order that it can act and decide; it has to be roughly representative, at the same time, of all the conflicting interests of billions of human beings and of the six-score national governments under which they are organized. The specifications are met by provid-

[3] This is, of course, the "global conference of the nations" referred to on page 232.

ing that it is to be composed of two or three representatives from each of the governments sitting at the time as members of the Security Council. Since China has by this time replaced Taiwan as a permanent member, and since the nonpermanent members are still being rotated by custom in such a way as to keep a general balance of regions, races and cultures, this provision gives an adequately representative character to the drafting commission while keeping it small enough for accomplishment. The delegates will necessarily be official representatives of the appointing governments, though the enabling act emphasizes the necessity of nominating only men of the broadest possible outlook and education. The commission's decisions on procedural matters will be by majority vote of the participating states; but the commission is instructed in the enabling act that its final, substantive report must be unanimously agreed to. The object is not to wage a political battle, but to discover the maximum area of general consensus. It soon develops that this is considerable—the basic issues involved have, after all, been under intensive study and discussion for years—and by the end of 1980 the commission brings in its draft constitution for a demilitarized world.

The draft is predicated upon the continued existence of the present independent national sovereignties, among which almost all of the three to four billion human beings alive in 1980 are apportioned. It provides for the establishment above them of a modest system of supranational, or genuinely "world," government. This plan is not advanced in any sense as a final or ideal system of human socio-political organization; it is not even designed to meet all those vast issues of freedom and justice with which society must continue, no doubt forever, to wrestle; its simple object is to state the minimum arrangements that must be substantially accepted by all —by all peoples and groups as well as by all existing national governments—if the general disarmament and demilitarization of international politics is to be realized. In effect, the report says to all peoples, to all governments and to all leaders: "If you want a demilitarized international order, this is the least that you must accept. Hopefully, it will prove only a foundation upon which much greater advances toward reason, justice and freedom can be erected. But it is the indispensable foundation. If the world as a total society cannot accept this much, it will be compelled to return all issues of peace, of freedom and of justice to the erratic and now certainly disastrous arbitrations of organized international war."

The report is in three parts. The first describes the international laws, or normative rules, that must be enacted and accepted by all as the basic and essential contract. The second describes the initial institutional arrangements necessary to see that these rules are made effective and are generally observed. The third describes the institutional arrangements necessary to deal thereafter with the continuing problems of power in a society from which organized war and its massive armaments have been eliminated.

The first part is perhaps the simplest. The essential laws are seen to be few, and some of these have long standing in world acceptance. They will prohibit resort to war as an instrument of national policy and armed aggression by any state upon the territory of another. They will guarantee every nation-state the territorial limits it occupies in 1980, except as such limits may thereafter be altered by arbitrational, negotiatory or other nonmilitary means. They will require that general and complete disarmament to police-force level be achieved within a reasonable term of years; and that on its attainment no rearmament, whether by governments or private groups or individuals, be permitted and that no state expand its national police forces or the weaponry they carry beyond the limits defined by general treaty engagement.

For the administration and enforcement of these rules, the report recommends the creation of a supranational authority. It will be composed and elected in the same way as the U.N. Security Council (with the proviso that no individual may serve on both); its powers will be clearly and precisely defined by the Security Council, to which in this sense it will be responsible, but within the limits of these powers it will operate free of the great-power unanimity rule, or veto. To this degree it will be supranational. Its decisions will be beyond veto by any government or state; they will, however, be subject to challenge before the World Court on the ground that they have exceeded their constitutional authority, while the authority itself will be subject to revision, on the advice of the Assembly, by the Security Council operating under the unanimity rule. The report considers at some length the question, which it is unnecessary to go into here, of strengthening the statute of the Court to enable it better to assume the responsibility involved.

The primary initial function of the new Authority will be to secure the observance of the general treaty of disarmament and to see that the prohibition against armed territorial aggression is obeyed. For this task it will re-

quire its own global police force; and it will be empowered to recruit, train, equip and provide for the command
of such a force, under agreed limitations as to its size
and armament. While the report does not attempt to go
into details on this point, it stresses certain principles
that must be observed. This police force must have an
independent existence—it cannot, for example, be formed
ad hoc out of contingents merely earmarked from the various national police forces or militias. The Authority will
recruit as widely as possible from the different peoples;
and although for linguistic or cultural reasons it may find
it desirable to draw different formations en bloc from different regions, such action will be at its own discretion.
The Authority must have its own independent sources of
revenue, specifically allotted to it and subject to collection
by its own agents. (A number of ways in which this might
be done—as, for example, through a small tax on international trade—had been much debated in the years before
1980.) The Authority will, presumably, set up an executive under a single responsible head—a kind of global
police commissioner, fulfilling the role adumbrated in the
early 1960's by the Secretary General of the United Nations.

Finally, the report particularly stresses the principle
that the global police force will be a small one. On the
assumption that the nations have, in their own interests,
agreed to a general demilitarization, little action will be
required to enforce it. Some of the remaining national
police and "militia" forces will, of course, be very large;
but to organize a supranational police (or army) capable
of doing battle with them will be unnecessary as well as
self-defeating. The global police will be in two parts:

one, an investigatory, intelligence and reportorial agency, whose main function will be, not to *prevent* the clandestine retention or rebuilding of military organizations and weaponry, but to reassure the global community that such actions are not taking place; the other, a uniformed force necessary to intervene in difficult local situations of chaos and bloodshed. The two will correspond roughly in function and operation to the detective divisions and the uniformed police found in all ordinary municipal police establishments. As organs of international law and order, the one will provide a supranational replacement for the vast, dangerous and generally misleading "intelligence communities" now maintained by all major and most minor powers; the other will provide a supranational replacement for the vast, dangerous and now ultimately destructive military establishments.

Given the initial agreement that general disarmament is in the interests of all, this much, the report argues, is sufficient to provide the conditions of security for national organizations and respect for national rights necessary to permit the actual process of disarmament to begin. It will protect that process from casual or irresponsible recalcitrance; and, so protected, the process itself will be self-reinforcing, moving more rapidly and easily as it advances. The report points out that if any of the major military powers, or any faction that may seize control of its government, decides to overthrow the whole agreement and revert to war, neither the Authority nor its modest police force can prevent it. At most it can create, in the first place, the conditions under which any such reversion will be extremely unlikely and provide, in the second place, for prompt alerting of the world to what

is going on and enabling the remaining powers to prepare the retributory steps that must be anticipated by
the violator. The report rejects any close parallel between the disarmament of the American states under
the Constitution of 1789 and global disarmament—
it notes how vastly different are the conditions—but it
does point out how easily the American states accepted
their mutual disarmament and suggests that if there had
existed not simply a federal (or "interstate") government,
but a limited "suprastate" authority capable of understanding the approaching danger of sectional war and of
warning all sides against the consequences it would entail, the rearmament and war of 1861 might have been
averted.

The second section of the report has shown that general disarmament is quite possible if it is generally desired. The third section faces the more difficult problem
of what had once been lightly called a "lasting peace"
—that is, of a continuing system of working international
politics under general disarmament and demilitarization.
The report observes that in the absence of any major international war for the previous thirty-five years, international politics has proceeded in anything but a static
fashion. The end of colonialism, the incorporation of
the innumerable new states into the international system,
the rise of China as an independent great power, the
problems of Sino-Soviet power relationships no less than
the problems of the power relationships within the Western alliance, have all been managed without a great war.
All these processes are the basic stuff of international
politics, far more important to the history of the human
race than the outcome of even the bloodiest battles.

The change has proceeded without great battles primarily because of the great weapons systems, far too formidable to be used in war or politics. The commission
opens the third section of its report with the simple statement that what is proposed is nothing more (nor less)
than the substitution of disarmament for armament as the
basic guarantee for the safety and security of all nation-
state organizations. It points out that the purely technical effects will be about the same. The armaments have
averted war among the great military powers because
the means for it are impracticable; disarmament will
achieve the same result because the means will no longer
exist. With the great power centers reduced to police
forces armed only with police weapons, they will be
physically unable to mount a military threat against any
save immediately contiguous territories—that is, not
without long preparation unconcealable from the supranational police authority—and there are few if any bound-
aries where motives for military aggression exist. With
disarmament, the great power centers will be just as
incapable as they now are in practice of invading, destroying, partitioning or subverting each other. Each of
the great national or regional systems will enjoy all the
actual security it now possesses, while being released
from the terrible insecurity suspended over it by the
weaponry.

The report goes on to point out that with the elimination of threatening armaments, international politics—
the organization of power and of the power struggle on
the international level—will be freed of its greatest burden. Overwhelmingly in modern times, international politics has turned, not on conflicts of material interest—

conflicts over markets, raw materials, control of communications or land as a resource in itself—but primarily on strategic issues. Almost exclusively, the object has been the obtaining or the retention of strategic, which is to say military, positions of strength or advantage. Alliance systems have always in modern times been promoted or maintained, not in the first instance to improve the economic or social functioning of the member states, but to improve their military posture. Territories have changed hands, not because of the intrinsic value of their productivity, but because of their strategic value as positions of defense or offense in war—because they supply "strategic frontiers" or "strategic materials," or perhaps only "prestige" values with military but no other utility. Commanding positions at the nodes of world communications—such as Suez, Gibraltar, Panama—are of relevance only in times of general war. Short of a great global conflict, it makes little difference which national flag may fly over them. In times of war monopoly control over materials, communications, military manpower or other social values can be of utmost importance; but in times of nonwar monopoly control can never be worth more to the possessor than the value the total society is prepared to give to it.

This idea, the report observes, is a rather difficult one to establish; and in order to do so it makes a brief historical excursus into the Egyptian sequestration of the Suez Canal in the late 1950's. This action, it was said at the time, would give Abdel Nasser, the Egyptian premier, supreme control in the world struggle. He would have the power to strangle Israel, to strangle Western Europe by controlling its oil supply—drawn mainly from

Iraq and Iran through the canal—and to strangle the great volume of world trade of all kinds that passes from the Western to the Eastern Hemisphere through the canal. The report observes that none of these expectations materialized. The canal was of value to Egypt only as it had been of value to the Suez bondholders—as a major artery of world trade, for the use of which the world would pay tolls. Egypt could, perhaps, make some minor political uses of her control over the canal; but she had to maintain it as a great international highway available to all if it was to be of any use to her. The change of ownership has made a minimal difference in the operation of the canal itself. It is interesting that not a few of the purely technical personnel—the pilots and engineers who actually take the ships through, maintain the structure and the navigational aids and operate the facility—were as ready to work for the Egyptian government as they had been to work for the bondholders.

The canal continued to perform its vital function. The way in which the pieces of paper representing its "ownership" were redistributed was immaterial—because the world was not at war. In a world that had deprived itself of all means of waging international war, a problem like that presented by Suez would be settled in essentially the same way. The technology of an interconnected world system, the report notes, is already outrunning the military considerations in which it has always been involved but which are growing increasingly meaningless to its actual functioning. If the nations, by agreeing to a general and complete disarmament, signify their belief that there is not to be another great war, most of the substantive material of contemporary international politics becomes irrelevant—just as dynastic problems became irrelevant when it was realized that the personal fortunes of the monarchical families had in fact very little connection with the welfare of the peoples concerned.

The report uses an even more apposite illustration by observing that in the major democratic systems, such as the United States or Britain or West Germany, the two-party *battle* does not in itself greatly affect the shaping of long-term national policies. These emerge gradually from economic, social or ideological forces to which the rival parties are about equally sensitive. The party struggle for votes and office is of the utmost utility as a device for maintaining orderly, responsible and responsive government, but as an instrument of decision it is not of great relevance. The same situation, the report argues, has obtained for most wars and certainly for the major military threats that for a generation have forced all important global decisions back upon the technicians of diplomacy, science and economics. Once freed of the strategic burden, the politics of international administration will continue to reach decisions in much the same way as national administrations reach decisions in any of the great stable states, whether democratic or totalitarian. And the decisions will respond in a similar way to the basic economic and social forces that are shaping an ever more closely integrated global society. It has long been agreed, the report observes, that the problems of Berlin and the two Germanies cannot be resolved by a major war. With the removal of the threats of major war themselves, international politics will find it far easier, rather than more difficult, to reach a resolution of the real power factors involved.

The commission's report includes numerous appendices dealing specifically with each of the important international power issues visible upon the horizons of 1981 and showing how a demilitarized international political system can be expected to deal with them. Each has been prepared by an expert subcommission, composed in the same way as the main commission; with each, the object has been, not to draft a treaty definitively resolving the political issues involved, but to analyze the available social and political factors permitting of resolutions. This work is too detailed to allow of summary here; but it becomes the center of prolonged discussions in the United Nations, in the several national administrations and in the great propaganda machines —whether democratic or totalitarian—that under either system link the peoples with international public affairs. Under the force of these analyses it becomes reasonably apparent before long that under demilitarization the great power centers can take care of themselves and of their direct relationships with each other just as well as they have been doing for a generation under the military stalemate. They will retain their economic and productive power; their national police forces will enable them to control their own immigration, trade and tariff policies as before, but freedom from the strategic imperatives of the past will enable them to bring these policies into far better accord with the requirements of the global economic system. The strategic boycotts, which quite foolishly and ineffectively distorted global economic relations in the middle 1960's, will have lost their significance with demilitarization, which will permit the underlying economic and social factors on which global welfare actually rests to assert themselves more clearly and accurately.

The beginnings of this trend were, after all, observable as far back as the Soviet and Chinese "wheat deals" with the capitalistic West in 1963; the process has since advanced so far that the commission's analysts are able to make an overwhelming case for the fact that between the major and stable power centers there remain no issues (other than the purely strategic ones) in which war would be either a necessary or even a useful mode of decision. Excluding the strategic, or military, factor, they are already in a stable power balance; and without the military factor the organization of international power must shift, if it does, in accordance with their relative economic strength, the success, justice and flexibility of their own internal power organizations, the appeal (and the workability) of their own ideologies or myth systems. So long as the major national power systems remain reassured, by demilitarization, of their own security and self-confidence, such power issues as may arise between them in the international field will be manageable on the level of global administration rather than of global government.

The appendices dealing with some of the problems that looked most dangerous in the early 1960's—the problem of Germany, for example, or that of Palestine —point out that such a shift has already occurred; the problems have been reduced to the levels of administration by the governments immediately concerned and require no more world government than that necessary to insure that the means of major military violence are not revived.

Beyond the direct relationships of the great power centers the analysis becomes, unfortunately, more complex. The studies of such problems as those of race relations in South Africa, of social revolution in Latin America or of continuing nationalistic chauvinism in Southeast Asia differ, of course, in many details, but they reveal certain factors more or less common to all. The governments concerned are usually weak and often corrupt; they have insufficient control over their own national police forces, or the police forces themselves (and the individuals who can seize command of them) are the actually dominant element in the government; social conditions are usually unstable, and revolution, waged with varying degrees of bloodshed and sequestration, is always a peril. The national police forces themselves are much greater threats to neighboring states than are those of the Soviet Union, for example, vis-à-vis the United States. International relations in such situations have not for a long time been characterized by organized international warfare, including military invasion, "victory" and annexation or subjugation. They have instead been defined by the indirect warfare of propaganda, of subversion, of the support of one faction within a turbulent state against another, by the provision of safe bases and police weapons, even volunteer fighting men, to support the internal turmoil.

At times such situations have primarily involved only the smaller states immediately concerned, and the fabric of international life has been able to absorb the shocks with comparative ease. At other times the power interests of the great military states have come dangerously into play. With direct war between the major power centers no longer practicable, they have tended to wage their struggle for power and prestige vicariously through the disorders of the smaller communities. Sometimes they have directly fomented and then supported a local civil war in their own power interests (a number of footnote references here include the Chinese fomentation and support of Communism in Indochina in the 1950's and early 1960's); more often they have intervened to "take over" and support a local movement that had arisen more or less spontaneously in the first place. (To this point the Soviet Union's "capture" of the Castro revolution in Cuba affords an example.) Whatever the circumstances, the presence of the great military power in the background has been one of the most dangerous and disturbing aspects of all situations of this kind. How can, or will, a demilitarized world deal with them?

One of the most widely scrutinized and debated of the analytical appendices is that concerning Brazil. By 1981 Brazil is approaching a state of chaos. One of the principal of the "middle states" in land area, population and productivity, she is reaching a condition of financial, political and social collapse. A bloody guerilla war, promoted and in some degree weaponed by Castro's Cuba, is paralyzing her northern areas; "left-wing" strikes, mob violences and civil disobediences, taking North American capital investment as the great enemy and the great evil, have disrupted life even in the more populous and better-educated areas. The United States has been as active as the tangled Brazilian politics will permit; the Soviet Union, on the other hand, has taken no direct action though consistently supporting Fidel Castro (who, though now aging greatly, is still the effective dictator of Cuba) diplomatically and economically and failing to oppose any obstacles to his Brazilian policy.

The appendix on the Brazilian problem begins by observing that the militarized world system has been unable to prevent the present situation from arising. Nor will a continuance of the great armaments in any way assist toward its resolution or alter outcomes in Brazil that will probably have to be accepted anyway, as they would be by a demilitarized world system. Since 1945, organized war, whether an intra-American or global one, has been inapplicable to the Brazilian question and has certainly held out no promise to any of the parties principally involved in it. If, through a general act of disarmament, organized war is not only technically but politically excluded from the situation, what will be the actual forces, or factors, through which the situation will work itself out? Much careful study in recent years of the actual processes of violent revolution and guerilla war has shown that there is, in general, but one stable outcome for such situations: the emergence of a competent administrative bureaucracy, strong in popular acceptance, which can run the country with some degree of efficiency, with a minimum of violence and a maximum of social return for all those living within it. The analysis observes that, initially at least, the ideological label borne by the bureaucracy makes less difference than is often supposed to the people of the country concerned. Whether it operates as a Communist dictatorship, a military dictatorship or under the command of a small dictatorial elite using more democratic forms, it works initially in much the same way, so far as the mass of the people are concerned, assuming that it works at all. The labels do make a difference to those struggling within the disrupted country for the prize of power and to outside nations trying to influence events in favor of their own prestige and power positions and military strength.

In Brazil the principal parties concerned are the major power systems—the United States, the Soviet Union, Western Europe and China—and the Brazilian people. The report notes the extent to which the actual, material interests of the great power systems in this situation coincide not only with each other but with the best interests of the Brazilian people. It is to the best interest of each that there should be a strong, stable, modern and productive internal system in Brazil. Trained by considerable experience, the Western democracies are as ready as the Soviet Union to admit that this result must imply the dethronement (if not necessarily the total destruction) of the small moneyed power elite that has proved incapable of providing the nation with the coherent institutions and popularly supported leadership it demands. After all, Western democracy has for a long time encountered no difficulty in supporting dictatorial and antidemocratic regimes, so long as they gave evidences of stability and did not carry a Communist label; it is ready to back any strong leader now who does not champion Communism. Brazil is, in fact, being victimized, not by foreign aggression or exploitation, but by the competition of the great power systems for control of the revolutionary processes that are admitted by all to be unavoidable.

The report asks quite seriously what this competition for control of an irreversible revolution really amounts to. Even in a world still dominated by armaments, Brazil, owing to her geographical position and the very modest scale of her own military development, has no great strategic significance. Success in the great-power competition for control of the Brazilian revolution will carry with it prestige and power factors that may be of importance in the future development of international politics but that will in any event be nonmilitary in character. Under a state of general disarmament (down to, but not below, police-force level) the situation would not be very different and the outcome would be about what it now promises to be. Under a situation of general disarmament—a situation that would leave large amounts of police weapons, of rival propagandas, of plays for power and prestige as the elements of international politics—the global system may be expected to deal with the problem of Brazil about as it is now doing. But, the report observes, there is a question of whether it might not deal with it a great deal better.

The basic parallelism of the interests involved in Brazil raises the question of whether it is really to anyone's interest to make that troubled country the arena for a power struggle from which no one—especially not the Brazilian people—can really benefit. The great Communist countries, no less than the great Western democracies, have, after all, learned much from the experiences of the past fifteen years. In the bloody aftermath of the Belgian grant of independence to the Congo in the early 1960's—a situation similar to that which has now arisen —the Soviet Union refused to support any international intervention which did not promote a Communist or pro-Communist regime to power. At the same time, it did not seek positively to prevent or nullify the U.N. intervention, with the effect of leaving the Congo to the ablest center of order and power available. Now, in the 1980's, the Soviet Union's interests in world order are much greater, its practical, political interests in distant revolution are much less, than they were then. Even in the Congo, the Soviet Union, while failing to support rational solutions, did much less to obstruct them than it might have done (or than its Chinese colleagues at the time wished it to do). Its attitudes toward world politics have advanced considerably since then; and there is a real political possibility that it will be willing to combine with the West (through the machinery of the United Nations) to support as well as to permit a rational solution, based upon international acceptance and support of what appears to be the strongest and most efficient power source within Brazil, regardless of the label.

The report points to two possibilities here. Such situations as that in Brazil can remain, under a demilitarized as under the existing militarized world, as major arenas of the international power struggle, which will continue to be waged—as it has always been waged in some part and has now been waged exclusively for a generation—through indirect aggression, infiltration, propaganda, the supply of small weapons, bases and funds by outside powers. Alternatively, this particular kind of violent conflict can be ruled out of international politics as not worth the candle in the end (one thinks of the way in which poison gas was, by tacit consent, ruled out of World War II), and those peoples which have not yet attained a viable domestic politics, and a viable international position vis-à-vis the global system, can be left to work out their internal power struggles among themselves and by their own efforts.

The appendix report on Brazil merely adverts to this situation, as do many of the others; the main commission report discusses its implications at some length. The argument is that general disarmament (to police-force level) is equally attainable and equally likely to endure, whether the international power struggle continues to be waged through interventions in local revolutionary situations or whether this form of activity is to be excluded from the processes of international politics. This, the commission observes, is a basic constitutional question, on which it is not authorized to make a recommendation. But it feels that it can say, with both knowledge and conviction, that *if* the problems of local revolution are to be removed from international politics (as indeed they often were during the last great revolutionary age at the end of the eighteenth and beginning of the nineteenth centuries) there will have to be certain additions to the proposed constitutional law of the global system. Besides agreement on the divestment of weaponry and on the military inviolability of established frontiers, there will also have to be agreement on the illegality of the export of arms, especially police arms, across any frontiers; on the illegality of the maintenance by any nation of bases on its own territory in support of armed forces on the territory of another state; and some agreed limitation on the extent to which any nation (or its individual nationals) could finance insurrection in a neighbor.

Provisions of this kind, the commission concludes, will be adequate to prevent local revolution from becoming a football of international politics. They will be enforced (and must be enforceable) by the international police. If the consensus is to accept such prohibitions, the powers of the supranational authority controlling and commanding the police must be extended. An international police capable of insuring, mainly by the police methods of investigation and report, that disarmament was being maintained and that the national police forces were not being expanded beyond their agreed limitations in numbers and weaponry would probably be adequate to insure the suppression of the traffic in police weapons and perhaps in financial subventions to rival factions. A supranational (and therefore veto-free) police authority could, in the current Brazilian case, do more effectively what the *ad hoc* U.N. forces and the Organization of American States are trying to do— which is to say to isolate the problem, prevent the importation of arms and volunteers from Cuba (as well as from China, whose statesmen had also seen possibilities in this distant field) and thus keep Brazil "stewing in its own juice." To do this much, however, is inevitably, though unfortunately, to involve the supranational authority in those essentially *political* issues from which its authority requires it to remain aloof. Just to "hold the ring" must give the advantage to the political faction that at the moment commands the greater muscle. If the supranational police tries to go farther, to "keep the peace" and suppress disorder and bloodshed within the distracted community, it must become even more deeply entangled in politics—merely to exclude bloodshed and violence is to keep the peace for those in positions of power as against those who have raised a violent challenge against the existing power structure. "Order" is itself a political much more than a military or a police phenomenon; the authority that keeps the order is the authority that establishes itself in political command. The very reasons why the current U.N. and O.A.S. police operations are proving ineffective in Brazil would operate equally to undermine a supranational police authority unless it were endowed with political responsibilities going beyond those of merely maintaining general disarmament.

The demilitarized world, the report argues, can function equally well whether it continues to operate, as the stalemate world is now doing, with a considerable degree of local chaos, revolution and indirect international competitive violence, or whether it empowers the supranational authority to make certain further rules to control in international political relations—to define those degrees of chaos that demand the intervention of an international police, to intervene with its own police forces in such situations without fear of the veto and to make such political decisions in the area as are unavoidable if the police intervention is to succeed. This, the report declares, is the central question raised by the possibility of demilitarization. It is a very large question indeed, and the report grants that it is one to which no answer can be returned save by a general consensus of the world community. Posed with this clarity, it immediately becomes the focus of the intense study and discussion that thereupon ensues.

The Brazilian case does not seem to present insuperable difficulties, and in fact in the course of 1981 the United States and the Soviet Union, with the assistance, not only of Britain and the Western European powers, but also of the Chinese, have achieved agreement upon the isolation and neutralization of the Brazilian chaos. The model for this agreement goes back to the neutralization of Laos in the late 1950's and to the similar but far more successful neutralizations afterward achieved in Indochina as a whole. All the contracting parties are bound to refrain from the export of arms, funds or volunteers to the area and to refrain from supporting the export of arms or volunteers by others. They agree to recognize and support what appears to be the most effective faction in the country—a fairly extreme but non-Communist left-wing faction led by a man rather closely resembling the younger Fidel Castro, but who has consistently rejected any obligation or subservience to the Cuban dictator. They agree to support, to the extent of helping to pay for, a modest U.N. armed force in the country, which by its presence is to discourage further bloodshed while refraining so far as possible from entanglement in the internal political struggle. This last task is obviously not going to be always easy, but that it proves not wholly impossible is due to the underlying great-power agreement on neutralization. It had been possible to achieve a reasonable degree of stability in the Congo in the early 1960's because the great powers in the end at least tacitly accepted the principle that it was more important to have stable and competent government there than it was to put on the government one's own label.

Not only the Western foreign offices but those of the

great Communist powers as well have acquired a much
better understanding than was common in the mid-
1960's of the real and complicated forces at work in
revolutionary situations of this kind and of the resources
available to international politics for meeting them. And
while this Brazilian agreement has not been negotiated
through the machinery of the U.N. Security Council, its
successful achievement provides a powerful argument for
the practicability of generalizing and institutionalizing
the principles on which it is based through a veto-free
supranational police authority. Even if it is given the
somewhat enlarged powers of local intervention suggested by the report, the great states can live with it and
most of the lesser ones should vastly profit by it in
face of most of the actual problems visible in the world
community. But there is one problem—that presented
by the approaching racial crisis in South Africa—which
raises doubts. The government and white community
in South Africa are bitterly rejecting the creation of any
supranational authority with even the most limited of
police powers inside its territory; the neighboring African states are just as bitterly rejecting any suggestion that
they be bound by enforceable laws to withhold arms
and support from African revolutionaries within the
South African Union. The extent to which great-power
and world opinion may be willing or able to go in trying
to bring this appalling situation within the control of a
supranational police authority is, at the opening of
1982, being passionately argued and is unclear at best.

Meanwhile, after receipt of the report and its appendices, the U.N. General Assembly has continued the
commission both as an advisory body and as one specifi-

cally charged with preparing for the proposed general
acts of disarmament and demilitarization. In the face of
the African dilemma, the commission, in its reports and
comments, reverts to what has been, perhaps, its central
argument throughout. The outcome in Africa, it insists,
will not be and cannot be determined by the question
of whether the world disarms to police-force level or not.
The great weapons systems simply cannot and will not
be employed in an area whose destiny is bound to turn
in any event upon the police weapons and police arrangements that now exist and that will remain in a generally
disarmed world. It is for the nations in congress assembled to determine how far they do or do not wish to
limit the violence and bloodshed implicit in the African
problem, but this decision, in whichever way it may go,
will not affect the inutility of the great weapons systems
themselves or the desirability of their complete abolition.
Despite the darkening aspect of the African problem,
the commission proceeds to propose and to prepare two
great world conferences, in each of which all sovereign
states will be represented by delegates chosen in accordance with the internal institutions of each. These conferences are conceived as bearing somewhat the same relation to all the prior work done by the commission and
others as the San Francisco Conference of 1945 bore to
the preliminaries at Dumbarton Oaks and in many diplomatic and public debates elsewhere.

One conference is to be convened in Moscow and is to
draft a working constitution for a demilitarized world.
The other is to be convened in Washington and is to draft
a working, technical schedule for a program of general
disarmament. Each is explicitly instructed by the conven-

ing authority (the General Assembly and the Security Council of the United Nations) that it is to proceed on the assumption that the other will be successful. The Moscow political conference will draw the constitution of a disarmed world, regardless of the technical details of the disarmament process. The Washington techno-logical conference will lay down the details of disarma-ment on the assumption that this is a desired and politi-cally possible development. The Washington conference will have to deal with some difficult questions, including the allowed size and armaments of the national police forces, the time scales over which the several national economies can absorb the inescapable shocks of dis-mantlement and reconversion and the extent to which the supranational police must be authorized to intervene in national affairs in order to validate the observance of the general agreement. But it will not have to waste much time on problems of inspection and verification, since it is assumed that an adequate constitution for a demili-tarized world, which all major power centers will sub-stantially desire as well as accept, is being worked out in Moscow.

The Moscow conference will also have to deal with difficult questions—the most basic of all being the ques-tion of how far the demilitarized world wishes to accept a continuation of local revolutionary bloodshed and dis-order or of the extent to which it may decide to bring such events within the confine of nonviolent world order. But in adumbrating such decisions, it will not be under the overwhelming drawback of conflicting national mili-tary strategies, since it will be entitled to assume that the Washington conference will produce a working sched-

ule of demilitarization. Through the rather chilly southern winter and unusually torrid northern summer of
1982 the two conferences labor on to good effect; and
the firm outlines of a working constitution, both political
and military, for a demilitarized or policed world are
clearly being developed.

The plan is not in time, unfortunately, to avert the
South African catastrophe—the final, irrepressible African revolt against Apartheid, accompanied by massacres
and other savageries beyond anything previously seen in
Africa. No one on any side of the racial issues involved
had ever really believed that the situation could arrive
at these vast destructions of the productive capital prop-
erty on which the community had to live, at the brutal
murders of whole communities, both white and Negro,
at exterminations, expropriations, starvations and collapse. Over the past two centuries or so, men had
rarely foreseen the full costs and consequences of any
resort to armed violence or organized war; in this case
neither the white nor the Negro leaders in South Africa
had any prevision of the horrors that are reported in the
newspapers side by side with the accounts of the two
conferences on demilitarization. Yet, somewhat unexpectedly, the tragedy in South Africa serves to promote
rather than to obstruct the movement toward the abolition of war.

It is of course obvious from the beginning that none of
the principal contemporary weapons of warfare is of the
slightest use or applicability in the South African situation. Nothing can be gained by anyone through adding
thermonuclear and biological destruction to the excessive
destruction already being effected in South Africa by more

old-fashioned methods; while whatever conflicting political interests the great powers may have in the South African disaster cannot be advanced by a suicidal thermonuclear war in the Northern Hemisphere. The one possible solution for the South African tragedy is a massive outside intervention by "conventional" or police forces to arrest the bloodshed, to find the strongest center of local power and to support it by asserting command over the situation. But precisely this solution is rendered more or less impossible by the great-power war system. In the long run it will make little difference to the secure and stable states —either the great democracies or the great Communist states—whether South Africa is stabilized under a left-wing African leader or a reactionary descendant of the Boers; indeed, many if not most people in the West are already convinced that the only lasting solution in South Africa must entail an African government. But in a still hyperarmed, explosive international system the terms of the settlement are far less important than the question of who presides over it. Effective international action in South Africa has been unobtainable basically because, while the Communist and Western worlds may be in considerable agreement over the essentials of what action should be taken, they are bitterly opposed over the question of who should take it and who should acquire the prestige and political power implicit in the action. Under the fearsome shadow of the great armaments this question is insoluble; and it follows that the whole international war system—the system of a militarized international politics—has no contribution to make to the tragedy in South Africa.

Toward the end of 1982 it begins to appear that a

resolution in South Africa is going to come anyway, without a great international war and without benefit of the war system. A strong African leadership has emerged, so clearly asserting command that the great powers have agreed to supply it with a U.N. police force to assist in the restoration of order. Very little justice is discernible in the extent to which the whites have been murdered and expropriated—or in the savageries committed upon the Negroes for that matter, sometimes in the political interests of their own leaders—but some such outcome has probably been inevitable from the beginning. It could not, in any event, have been averted by a great war and seems not to have been materially influenced or deflected by the colossal military threats. While the demilitarized world politics being adumbrated in the Washington and Moscow conferences will hardly deal differently with such another situation (if one ever arises) as that in South Africa, it will at least permit the international political system to deal with it more promptly, at much less cost in blood and destruction, than has been possible under the war system. The South African catastrophe becomes the most powerful argument for the two treaties that early in 1983 are laid before a solemn conclave of all the nations of the world by the Moscow and Washington conferences.

The first treaty embodies a working constitution for a world from which organized war has been excluded, primarily through the reduction of all armed forces everywhere to police systems. It establishes the supranational police authority as previously described; it provides it with precise powers, carefully restricted but extending (after the South African experience) to limited powers of intervention in situations of extreme local chaos; it strengthens the global judicial machinery for interpreting and applying the global constitution, though reasserting the legal sovereignty of the nation-state; it assigns certain tax revenues to the Authority and empowers its agents to collect them in national territories; in support of the Authority's responsibilities in securing and maintaining disarmament, it gives its agents certain limited powers to investigate the actions of individuals as well as of governments and defines certain international crimes in this area for which it may bring individuals to trial before their own national courts.

It is anticipated that once the nations are fully committed to general disarmament, their own courts will be as anxious as any others to enforce its provisions. But realizing that extraordinary situations may arise, the Authority is given a reserve right to appeal the acquittal of an individual in the national courts to the World Court. Nothing in the nature of a criminal charge may or can be brought against a government. The World Court will have jurisdiction in cases of conflict between a government and the supranational Authority over the interpretation of its powers, as well as normal jurisdiction in cases of conflict between governments.

This constitution for the demilitarized world, clearly laid down in the first treaty, supplies the foundation upon which it has at last been possible to erect the second treaty, providing precisely for an actual program of general and complete disarmament. It begins (rather than ends) with a careful definition of the armed forces—the national and international police—that will remain upon the conclusion of the disarmament process. They will be limited as to organization, weapons and "infrastructure"

as well as in numbers. Organized and armed reserve formations will not, as a rule, be allowed; while the manufacture anywhere of any weapons, carriers, armed ships
or airplanes exceeding the allowed weapons types will be
absolutely prohibited. The disarmament conference has
worked out the allowed force levels for the national police
establishments primarily on each nation's own estimate of
its requirements; except in a few special cases, comparison
with neighboring police forces has not entered into the
calculation. The allowed size of the international police
has been established similarly on an estimate of its probable needs. All the limitations are to be initially laid down
as permitted maximums, not required minimums, and
all are subject to revision in accordance with changing
conditions. In the case of any of the national forces, any
upward revision will be at the discretion of the Authority;
but for any material enlargement of the size or power of
the international police force the Authority will have to
secure authorization from the Security Council operating
under the great-power unanimity rule.

With the end result thus clearly defined, the disarmament treaty lays down a detailed program for its attainment by definite stages within a definite term of years.
In developing this schedule, much more attention has
been given to the economic difficulties that divestment
and demobilization may bring to the different national
economic systems than to a precise equalization of the
military power to be retained at any given stage. Since
the general act itself is recording a universal conviction
that military power has become superfluous, inapplicable
and useless as an instrument of international politics, it is
unnecessary to go to great lengths to make certain that

it will be laid aside in exactly equal proportion. Exact balancing of military power has never been practicable at best, as many past efforts to achieve disarmament on this principle have shown; and as long as the belief remains that one's nation may at sometime wish to or be compelled to resort to war, the competition in armaments—even in the negative form of competing to see that one does not disarm any more speedily than anyone else—cannot be ended. Now, however, the constitution of a demilitarized world has removed the belief or any ground for it, and all that is necessary is to provide a rough general correspondence in the divestment process. Once disarmament is initiated, it must proceed by its own logic or internal momentum, and whether or not the divestment of battalions, bombs or missile submarines is in every case exactly proportional is more or less immaterial. What is important is to insure that the process itself is not interrupted or reversed. If at any stage one of the great nations (or its government) decides, in face of all the thought, analysis, discussion and experience that has gone into this question over the past dozen years, that it stands to gain by stealing a march in a military sense over the others, it cannot be directly prevented. What can be done is to make it absolutely clear to such a government that it cannot enjoy the best of two worlds. It cannot hope to achieve the advantages of a militarily powerful state in an otherwise disarmed world (as in some measure Adolf Hitler's Germany tried to do). Any attempt to "cheat" on the disarmament agreement means the end of the disarmament process, the failure of the demilitarized constitution and a revival for the cheating state as well as for the rest of all the perils of militarism from which the world society is in the process of emancipating itself. The act of disarmament need not provide for exactly parallel reductions so long as the level of armaments everywhere sinks at about the same rate, so that if any state does decide to interrupt the process by holding out significant elements of military power, the rest will not be helpless to respond in kind.

The disarmament schedules are detailed and exact. They begin with the complete dismantlement of the nuclear weapons industry and the conversion of 75 per cent of existing weapon stocks into nuclear fuel for industrial purposes. They continue with the reduction of conventional forces and weapons to the agreed police-force levels and the conversion of all munitions industries to nonmilitary or purely police production; and they throw open the operations of military staffs and of all secret intelligence agencies to examination by the supranational authority. The final phase, which is not to be reached for a decade under the schedule, involves the destruction of the remaining stocks of nuclear weapons and of all forms of carrier, whether based on land, sea or air.

The one treaty provides a working constitution for a demilitarized world system; the other provides a workable schedule for attaining it. Both are submitted for signature to the great congress of all nations in 1983, with the proviso that they will go into full force and effect when ratified by a majority of the then existing nation-states, each acting in accordance with its own constitutional provisions. Since the treaties have been primarily the work of the great states and their lesser allies and associates, no difficulty is expected or experienced in receiving their ratifications; actually, ratifications from an overwhelming majority of all states have been received by the end of 1983, and on January 1, 1984, the demilitarized world system is proclaimed in effect at the headquarters of the United Nations. There have been a few instances of bitter resistance to ratification in some of the smaller states; but it is apparent that whether they ratify or not cannot be a matter of much practical effect. They do not possess nuclear or other arms industries of the kind that have now been made illegal. Their armed forces, in numbers and equipment, are below the levels allowed them under the police schedules, and they are not in fact engaged in the "export of revolution" to an extent requiring the intervention of the supranational authority. Some of these states will withhold formal ratification for years, but their reluctance means little to the successful "circuitry" of the demilitarized international order; and in the end, in the normal course of internal change and development, all are to give their assent to the fact of a warless, though by no means a bloodless or nonviolent, world.

Beyond this point it is difficult to push prognostication —or science fiction. Human affairs are too infinitely complicated and various to permit of reasonable preview of the ways in which they will in fact develop. All that has been argued here is that the nations are reaching the point at which they will accept the present organization of power in international politics as a working norm, preferable to anything any longer attainable by war. Power on the international stage has been successfully assembled in three or four great and stable centers, each fundamentally invulnerable to the others. They will of course continue to compete, for competition seems inseparable from any power organization, but they will compete by nonmilitary means—by their economic strength, their true ideological appeals, their positive ability to serve international or global goals rather than their negative ability to destroy any kind of rational international action from which they do not perceive any gain to themselves. The gains from international cooperation—from "coexistence" in a nonmilitary rivalry—are becoming more obvious with every passing year; the losses to everyone entailed by a military struggle for power are becoming more appalling. Here are all the elements of a working, nonmilitary world system, which it is necessary only to assemble; we need only to hook up the available circuitry, put together the parts, make the connections that are crying out to be made, in order to create an international system from which the great armaments and their overpowering military threats have been eliminated. One cannot, of course, predict in any detail just how the new system will work; one can, I believe, say with some confidence that it will be workable and that, while it will leave much violence and bloodshed in the world, it will operate free from the immemorial scourge of massive and organized war.

Some final issues remain. This projected world of post-1984 has been founded upon a presumed stability and permanence of the major power centers. Does it imply an end to revolution everywhere except in some of the smaller and less well-organized states? If not, how will the demilitarized world deal with violent revolution, "overthrow" and chaos in one of the major centers—in the Soviet Union, for example, or in the United States? Neither question, it seems to me, is well put. It is not that the adoption of a demilitarized world politics will put an end to revolution in the great states; it is, rather, that the effective end of the revolutionary era has made and is making possible a politics without war. The processes of political and social invention, like those of the physical sciences and engineering, have made enormous strides in the past two centuries; and they have been excluding disasters like the French Revolution as they have been excluding disasters like the Napoleonic Wars. England has not known violent revolution since the seventeenth century (though there has been, of course, plenty of violence in her internal affairs since then); the conditions that made possible the American Revolution have never recurred even remotely in our own experience; while a repetition in Western Europe of anything at all closely resembling the French Revolution seems about as impossible as anything in the future can be. The Russian Revolution, when it came, resembled its predecessor in France only superficially, and the possibility that the conditions out of which it arose could be reproduced in a demilitarized system is even less than the presently very remote possibility that they could be reproduced in the militarized world of today. Those who like to frighten themselves with visions of the "overthrow" of the American constitutional system "by force and violence" are frightening themselves with imaginings of an event for which there is absolutely no precedent in recorded history.

It consequently seems pointless to ask how a demilitarized world will deal with a case of "violent overthrow" of the American government, or of the Soviet or Chinese government either. These great power systems will obviously continue to undergo internal change, as they have been doing since their revolutionary origins. The changes will in retrospect seem as "revolutionary" as do those that have overtaken the American system since 1789; but it is no longer probable that they will necessitate resort to bloodshed and the barricades. The problem of "revolution" seems about as irrelevant to the constitution of a demilitarized world as it does to the "constitution" of the stable small powers of Scandinavia.

Violent revolution, no less than the organized war system, is after all a cultural phenomenon. If there is any final validity in those theories of war that relate it to the underlying psychological mechanisms in man—to his instincts of fear, aggression, dominance and subjection, his propensities to murder and to flight—then the prognosis of this concluding chapter must be laid aside. Our instinctive equipment is subject to little change and at best to only imperfect control. But the controls that are established over it are a function of the culture. The basic instinctual apparatus may be invariable under all cultural systems, but it is the culture that determines how it is expressed or suppressed. If organized war is regarded, as it has been throughout this book, as essentially a political and cultural phenomenon, then the way lies open to its abolition—and to the abolition of the revolutionary forms of violence arising from and associated with it—by a global culture that has long been moving in that direction. In most of the vital relationships of most of the three billion persons now alive, organized war and organized violence have become "dysfunctional." They reflect culture patterns no longer serviceable in themselves and tending to dwindle from world affairs. It is the prediction of this book that they will dwindle toward extinction, to be replaced by developing culture patterns, developing social and political inventions already upon our horizons.

No one can know whether or not this prediction will

be falsified by the history of the future. But those who contend that it must be falsified—that it is foolish, or Utopian, or impractical, or contrary to the facts of human nature—must produce some more realistic or persuasive prediction of their own. So far as I am able to analyze the war problem, it seems to me that the future must rather closely follow along the lines here indicated, or else end in a general catastrophe of civilization. Those who believe that catastrophe is the only possible outcome are unquestionably entitled to their belief, but they should state it frankly. Those who believe that there is some middle road (through perpetual deterrence or "arms control" for example) are equally entitled to their view but are under an even more imperative obligation to say just what they conceive this middle road to be, just where they expect it to lead and just how they anticipate that it will achieve the destination. And those (of whom there may be many) who feel that all this speculation represents a very pallid approach to the problem of war, that far more drastic remedies and more radical solutions are called for, must, I think, fairly face up to the question of where in the cultural patterns of our times they are to find the dynamics, the energy sources, that will support their proposals. The plans and the proposals are easily made. The Covenant of the League of Nations was a rational plan for the elimination of war. It was not the plan that was defective; the fault was in the absence of the cultural and political dynamics that could bring it into operation. In this book I have tried to present a social and cultural dynamic that could lead to the desired result. Whether it will or not no one can know. I can however state my own private and personal belief that this is the most probable way in which events are likely to develop. I have made no effort to provide myself or my children with bomb shelters—partly, no doubt, because of the overwhelming moral horror implied by the whole idea; but more immediately because of a pragmatic conviction that such artifacts will never be needed or wanted, and certainly will never be used, in the great and creative world that lies before us.

INDEX

WALTER MILLIS

Walter Millis was born in Atlanta, Georgia, in 1899 and was graduated from Yale University in 1920. A staff member of the Fund for the Republic and Director of the Fund's study of demilitarization since 1954, Mr. Millis was, for thirty years before that, an editorial staff writer for the New York *Herald Tribune*. During World War II he was a columnist for the Office of War Information. He is the author of *The Martial Spirit, Road to War, Why Europe Fights, This is Pearl!* and *Arms and Men*. Mr. Millis wrote *Arms and the State* with Harvey C. Mansfield and Harold Stein, and *The Abolition of War* with James Real. He also edited *The Forrestal Diaries*. Mr. Millis is married to Eugenia Sheppard, Women's Feature Editor of the New York *Herald Tribune*. They make their home in Glen Head, New York.

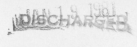